THE SUPPER
BOOK

Peter Burnett is the author of two novels,
The Machine Doctor and *Odium*

THE SUPPER BOOK

An inventory of the liquid and solid foodstuffs ingurgitated by me during the course of one year.

Eaten, written and illustrated by
Peter Burnett

LEAMINGTON BOOKS

First published 2008
Leamington Books

British Library Cataloguing-In-Publication Data.
A catalogue record for this book is available from the British Library.

ISBN 10: 0-9554885-0-8
ISBN 13: 978-0-9554885-0-4

Typesetting: Gerry Hillman
Jacket Images: www.singlefish.biz
Cover Layout: Flesh ltd
Printer: Cromwell Press, Trowbridge, Wilts.

**For Todd McEwen,
who provided.**

The Marinated Man

Acknowledgements

For both sustenance and solitude, I would like to thank the director, the admissions committee and the staff at the Hawthornden Castle International Retreat for Writers, Scotland, without whom there would be no *Supper Book*. Special thanks are due to the Castle's administrator Daniel Farrell, who cooked many of my meals during my four week stay.

It's necessary to mention that *The Supper Book* was inspired by Georges Perec's "Attempt at an Inventory of the Liquid and Solid Foodstuffs Ingurgitated by Me in the Course of the Year Nineteen Hundred and Seventy Four" (Georges Perec *Species of Spaces and Other Pieces*, Penguin 1997).

For the thousandth time – let's eat!

Pete Brown

Peter Burnett has suppered for his art.

Tadg Farrington

Whatever it is – it makes the dead stand up and walk!

Zombie Flesh Eaters

We are what we all abhor, and Cannibals, devourers not onely of men, but of our selves; and that not in an allegory, but a positive truth: for all this mass of flesh which we behold, came in at our mouths; this frame we look upon, hath been upon our trenchers; in brief, we have devour'd ourselves.

Sir Thomas Browne (1643)

Cooks burn your books, and vail your empty drains,
Put off your feigned aprons and view the strains,
Of this new piece whose author doth display,
The bravest foods, and shew the nearest way,
T'inform the lowest diner how they may dress,
And make of the meanest veg, the highest mess.

Will Rabisha (1661)

9

CONTENTS AND BILL OF FARE

INTRODUCTION

The Supper Book is an annotated list of everything that I ate and drank over the period of one year. The lists are grouped both generally and specifically as per my own interests and by venue. The food and drink is glossed, especially when I have realised the incredible natures of the many concoctions I have purchased or been served. Everything in this book one way or another contributed to the invention of myself. "You are what you eat" is the most common maxim that describes this process.

Today, what we desire on our plates is variety – as if eating the same foods every day would be to deny the richness around us. [1] Our eating is motivated by a love of superfluity that causes us to engage in ceaseless experiment. At the same time we bind ourselves to eating styles which reinforce the idea of food as an expendable commodity.

The Supper Book is provided with notes in which are included information as to the wonderful adventures we have through food. Among these particulars are the advertising strap-lines which promoted my food's properties on its packaging. I have tried to demonstrate the natures and virtues of my foods and collected notices of the history and culture of many of the meals that I found worthwhile to comment upon. The book also details manners of eating and drinking, includes a list of the cafés, restaurants, bars and private homes visited and offers history, legends, opinion, quotations and anecdotes in account of these dishes.

I am guilty of trying to understand food, or at least trying to rescue some significance from it. I am most of all gratefully indebted to all those who fed me, because in doing so they also fed this book, and spared me the work of my own hands.

*

---

[1]   I counted the variations of nourishment fed to our cats. Including water and the herbs they browse in the garden, the cats enjoy only seventeen different foods. Their *Supper Book* would be significantly shorter than mine.

The idea of this list has always had its attractions for me, but it has frightened me as much as it has intrigued me. The list frightens me because I can see it stretching to thousands of pages in which every pea, grain and potato crisp would need to be counted and glossed. To produce an accurate list of my diet, each glass and cupful would need to be measured and in fact, every minute of every day could be spent with scales, measuring jugs and notebooks.

In order to control what was beginning to smack of disordered eating (and thinking), I have tried to restrict myself to 300 pages and kept the list as flexible as possible, simply mixing much of it up. In most cases I've done my best to share the very minimum of my experience by quoting food packaging and as often as is convenient, recorded where the food has come from. I've refrained from calculating the entire volume of my diet for the year, largely because of hidden anxieties concerning the amount.

After all is listed and eaten, I'm left with the same bizarre conclusion – that nobody is exactly sure of how much they're consuming and what it's made up of. I similarly believe that we have very little understanding of the strength of our bodies, given that they not only deal with these varied concoctions, but actually thrive on them and grow. Further along in this book I have taken a page to ask myself the question "Am I still alive?" – which seems to me to be the most apt query when I think honestly about what I'm eating.

For me, writing the book has been a deep pleasure – a duty on some days and a hysterical joke on others. Gnaw at the corners of the book and try not to choke, or wolf it down in one sitting. Maybe there'll be something in here to give you pause for thought, or maybe something that'll make you laugh – either way I'll be delighted.

PB, Edinburgh , 2007.

GRAZING THROUGHOUT THE DAY

We've known all our lives that eating more frequent small meals is better than eating two or three larger meals a day. [2] Hence grazing means eating when the mood strikes you, often in small amounts and with much poking through refrigerators, cupboards and shops, sometimes ending up with foods that don't necessarily combine well together. Say what you like about "square meals" but they're usually balanced in their content. Grazing is dangerous as it often directs us towards foods that are convenient but have little or no nutritional value.

I grazed more than I dined, as the following list will demonstrate:

1 *Tunnock's* milk chocolate mallow biscuit known as *"The Teacake"* [3]

Half a *Co-op* plain quiche with baked tomatoes and salad leaves

250ml *Copella* apple juice [4]

2 prawn crackers eaten in the "Cookie Monster Style" [5]

1 bowl of *Simply Organic* Mediterranean tomato soup – *"Good food for life"*

---

[2] By *unhealthy* food we tend to mean food that raises cholesterol and body weight. By *healthy* food we tend to mean food that keeps glucose levels in balance and results in the stomach feeling full. The stomach must never be considered while eating and drinking because it is unpleasant to think of our food as subject to heuristic churning amid digestive fluids.

[3] This mallow biscuit is known as "The Teacake" although the word *teacake* does not appear on the wrapping.

[4] If the ingrediennts of this drink are "apple 100%", then why does the producer also state that ascorbic acid has been added?

[5] How to eat in the Cookie Monster Style: Using your fists, press the food against your mouth. Ignore food that does not enter your mouth but concentrate on saying the word "COOKIE!" as gruffly as possible. Keep pressing the food into your face and repeat the word "COOKIE!" until your hands are empty (see figure 62, page 276).

3 x *Yaoh* Organic Raw Food Hemp Bars – date and walnut with brazil nut and extra hemp – *"Rich in essential fatty acids – no added sugar"* / *"Uncooked to preserve full nutritional status"*

6 (= 65g) *Nabisco* Oreo biscuits produced by United Biscuits Iberia – *"La galletta màs vendida del mundo"* [6]

1 bowl of crème fraiche and sprouted pinto beans [7]

1 330ml "Choco-Plus" flavour *Drink Fit* milk drink

1 500 ml bottle of *Perrier* water

1 330ml can of orange flavoured *Fanta* "Light" [8]

1 500ml plastic bottle of *Fanta* *"orange soft drink"* [9]

1 500ml plastic bottle of *Fanta* "Fruit Twist" flavour soft drink

---

[6]   Oh wait! That's right. We don't do Oreos in the United Kingdom. Strike that whole "tasting an American classic" line because the British rarely purchase them. The executives at Nabisco have not worked hard enough in selling these biscuits to our country. It seems odd that America's biggest seller should be unknown on these shores.

[7]   Soak the beans overnight and leave in a ventilated jar to sprout, rinsing every eight to twelve hours. Drain your sprouts well, swishing them about to remove the seed hulls and stop any rot – and in three to five days they'll be ready. Pintos are rarely prolific sprouters, so expect a crop of about half of your original batch.

[8]   Was Fanta invented by the Nazis? In the 1930s, Fanta and Coca-Cola were the same drink, labelled differently for Nazis and Allies. Fanta's inventor Max Keith was a businessman and not a Nazi – and due to supply shortages in 1930s Germany, he made Coca-Cola orange flavour to ensure consistent sales. Trade claims to eschew (or be above?) politics, and what we forget today regarding Nazi Germany is the decade of support and acquiescence from business and political leaders prior to WWII. Fanta is a great case-study in Capital's silent complicity.

[9]   Import problems in Germany in 1941 meant that cheese by-products and apple fibre from cider production made their way into the Fanta.

A quarter tomato

4 crispy coated chocolates

2 garlic and coriander nans, 260g the pair [10]

3 garlic and cheese hors d'oevre

2 x 50g portions of *Dairylea* Dunkers – "*Original Sticks Flavour*" [11]

1 50g *Eat Natural* macadamia and fruit bar sold as part of the "*It Makes me Feel Good*" promotion.

1 truffle from *The Masterpiece Bakery*, Edinburgh

3 x 11g sachets of ketchup

3 slices of garlic bread

1 slice of mushroom pizza

1 slice of candyfloss [12]

1 150g *Co-op* layered yoghurt with honey

1 small glass of mandarin juice

---

[10]   Human nature being what it is, the diet seldom pursues an even course. The quarter tomato and the 4 crispy-coated chocolates kept me going while I waited for the nans to warm in the oven.

[11]   With the original flavour of sticks? Hardly.

[12]   Rachael was exceptional. Not only was she able to dine on candyfloss while others boarded on crisps, but she was able to offer me a share in the form of a slice.

1 33cl can of *Spring* brand strawberry and banana drink (labelled "*Nectar*") [13]

1 fudge flavoured *Wall's* Cornetto

1 piece of lime flavoured Edinburgh rock [14]

3 slices of millionaire's shortbread from the *Ford Bakery*, Prestonpans

2 x 200g *Dragonfly* organic Beanies [15]

1 small plate of roasted squash

1 *Ashbury* hazelnut brownie flavoured truffle

1 canapé biscuit with whipped cheese and walnut

2 date biscuits – the origin of which was Inverness

2 slices of my Mum's ginger cake and butter

1 *Onken* Lemonlite Biopot yoghurt – "*Made with bio cultures*"

---

[13] This canned drink came with the slogan: "all natural" – but words like *natural* have virtually lost all meaning. Due to the facts of food's production and distribution, it is never natural and always unfamiliar. In such a culture, nobody is either properly 'at home' (á la Mrs Beeton) or properly abroad (in the manner of Elizabeth David.) Are all things made by man to be considered natural? Because they lack trace elements found in natural forms, some people consider natural chemicals made in factories as synthetic – vitamins being a prime example.

[14] Edinburgh Rock. What is it? "Friable, fluted sticks of pastel shades and pastel flavours." (Lady Violet Bonham-Carter) The original Edinburgh rock is made by the firm founded by Alexander Ferguson ('Sweetie Sandie'), born in 1798 in Doune. Ferguson brewed sweet and bubbling liquids in the parental outhouses, to the scorn of his father, a joiner and skeely craftsman. Sandy however left home and learned the trade of sweetie maker in Glasgow before setting up by himself in Edinburgh, whence his famous creation.

[15] Packaging lines include: "New appleheart shape" / "Keeps you going! OK?" / "2 savoury soya bean & rice burgers with fresh vegetables" / "Wake up to Dragonfly Beany Time". Beanies come with one of the busiest food packets ever seen.

2 *Jacob's* Lincoln [16] biscuits

1 roast pepper and 1 roast vine tomato with mascarpone and grated Parmesan cheese

1 50g *Hempower* fruit and nut bar with 9% hemp seeds – *"Gives Power"* [17]

1 plate of *Epicure "Organic"* penne pasta [18] with roast pepper, vine tomato, Parmesan and mascarpone

2 fajitas with lettuce, *Jordan Valley* baba ganoush and 1 roast tomato in mascarpone with Parmesan and one yellow pepper

3 porridge biscuits. These are also known as "fudge biscuits" and are made with Golden Syrup and porridge oats. (Figure 01)

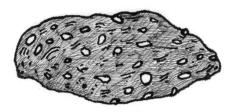

FIGURE 01. A porridge biscuit, as made by Mrs K. Burnett

---

[16] One pleasure of the Lincoln biscuit lies in the arrangement of full stops on the top, either in concentric circles or in a tightly packed pattern like the ends of stacked pipes. But what are the full stops for? Perhaps the full stops give the Lincoln superior traction and non-slip grip? Perhaps they are intended to invoke Olde Worlde cobblestones? Maybe they are a reminder to stop eating them.

[17] Leonardo da Vinci did not approve of hemp bread, which he described in the *Codex Romanoff* as a "dangerous dish indeed".

[18] The Futurists, who delighted in attacking tradition, saw the Italian love of pasta as an ideal target for their broadsides. The poet Marinetti used his manifesto *La Cucina Futurista* (Futurist Cooking) in 1932, to lambast pasta as "the absurd Italian gastronomic religion", calling for its annihilation.

2 glasses of freshly squeezed grapefruit mixed with freshly squeezed orange

1 *Green and Black's* butter biscuit covered in dark chocolate

1 500ml bottle of *Dr Pepper* [19]

1 330ml can *Dr Pepper* [20]

1 25g *Lyme Regis Foods* Grizzly Bar − "*Blackcurrant and apple chewy fruit and cereal bar*" / "*No preservatives, No artificial colourings*"

1 31g *Quaker* Dipps biscuit [21]

1 *Chicago Pizza Company* individual four-cheese pizza with salad of my own devising

1 litre of *Danone Volvic* Natural Mineral Water from Volcanoes in France − "*Authorised by the French Ministry of Health*" / "*Enables Volvic to fill you with volcanicity*"

4 x *Danone* Activia with red cherry, "*With Bifidus Digestivium®*" / "*Made with fructose and sweeteners*" / "*Produced on a line handling almond, hazelnut, walnut, wheat*"

4 x *Danone* Activia with prune fruit layer and *Bifidus Digestivium* ® / "*Danone Activia, it's actively good for you*"

---

[19]   The strap line on Dr Pepper questions the drinker: "What's the worst that could happen?" The drink prompting an instantaneous laxative effect, I expect.

[20]   Elsewhere on the Dr Pepper can is printed a most generous claim: "Solves all your problems". So I'm happy now.

[21]   The Quaker pack-quotes: "Caramel with Real Milk Chocolate" / "Made with Real Quaker oats". As is common in marketing these days, we are dealt a fair amount of evidence concerning the REALITY of this food!

So many claims – so little evidence, so much information – such great ignorance, so much printed matter – such heavy landfill. Look at the label on your *Volvic* bottle (p26) – and you'll see that even the French Ministry of Health is invoked in case you don't feel that what you're consuming will improve you in some way.

Some of the above could be said to constitute *meals* – although most of what's listed in *The Supper Book* falls into the category of *snacks*. [16] There is no law restraining the desire for snacks and no authority able to stem our random repast. I am guilty of the modern habit of informal eating. That is: my formal eating is often ignored, and I do not so much take *main meals* as graze throughout the day.

The random repast of an average day might look something like this:

8AM	–	Water, Biscuit
9AM	–	Banana
10AM	–	Coffee, Scone
11AM	–	Breakfast Cereal, Tea
12 noon	–	Biscuit
1PM	–	Biscuit, Coffee
2PM	–	Sandwich, Tea, Water
3PM	–	Fruit or Fruit Bar
4PM	–	Tea, Biscuit
5PM	–	Water
6PM	–	Crisps, Beer
7PM	–	Water
8PM	–	Vegetables, Cheese, Pasta
9PM	–	Beer
10PM	–	Beer, Water, Chocolate
11PM	–	Water

---

[22] If BEER be a snack.

Food & Drink Away from Home (A to E)

Restaurants / Cafés / Bars / Stands / Hotels
Pubs / Functions

What shall we do for food when society breaks down? We shall eat out as they did in the days of the French Revolution. Had I been left to myself, I don't know if I would have had the strength to leave the house and eat, but as it is so few of us eat out alone. I struck up many friendships over meals and cemented more. I consequently became disillusioned with my own cookery, which remained hidden within its own merits, the final stage being to invite people round for dinner. People did not come round for dinner, for fear that they would end up in *The Supper Book*. [23]

Eating out is about more than just food and drink. The range of connotation in the phrase "eating out" defies easy description but could loosely be said to contain food that someone else made for me that I, or someone else, paid for.

What follows is a list of what I ate and where I ate it. There were salads, shiny with dressing and fragrant with herbs; pizza, robust and full of earthly charm; coffee, quagmires of it waiting in every café in the city. There is always a fair amount of eating out – one cannot help it.

Restaurants didn't originate in 18th century France as many think. It's known that a restaurant culture developed in Sung Dynasty China (960 – 1279 CE) and that the travellers in Chaucer's *Canterbury Tales* enjoyed a jolly meal at an inn in late 14th century England. What properly defines a restaurant is a menu and we don't know if Chaucer's pilgrims were provided with one. One can serve food, but without a choice of dishes one is not running a restaurant. Although it's often said that the first "restaurant" appeared in Paris in 1765, it can't be overlooked

---

[23] AN INCONCLUISVE NOTE: Here in East Tennessee we use the word SUPPER to denote the last meal of the day. I've noticed that in other places DINNER is used – mostly in the North – to decsribe the very same meal. What are the origins of these words, and where and how are they used? Pinning down the uses of the terms SUPPER and DINNER is not possible by class, region or historical preference. Every general statement regarding when SUPPER is taken will be contradicted by individuals or families who follow different customs.

that other social ambitions needed to be integrated before the concept of eating out could be properly developed.

Now one can eat one's way around the world in our major cities, and restaurant dining is a simultaneous mark of our success as both producers and consumers.

Here is where I ate and drank:

The Ability Centre, Livingstone – 1 cup of tea and milk / 2 cups of water

Al Quds Restaurant, Bethlehem – 1 felafel in pitta with salad

Alegro Café, Ronda – 1 cup of milky coffee

Andrew Edmunds, Soho – 1 asparagus served with lemon butter and Parmesan / 1 penne pasta with courgette, peas, pousse spinach, tomato, feta and garlic and chilli oil / 2 slices of bread and butter / 1 glass of Hildon spring water / 1 large espresso

Anguepied, Edinburgh – 1 cup of black coffee

Antipasti, Glasgow – 1 Diet Coke and 1 crostina [24]

Applecross Inn, Applecross – 1 macaroni cheese [25] and salad / 4 slices of garlic bap

Babelon Café, Edinburgh – 1 hot chocolate / 1 Diet Coke / 1 black coffee

The Balmoral Hotel, Edinburgh – 1 cup of black coffee / 1 piece of shortbread

---

[24] I didn't know what a *crostina* was but it is like a *bruschetta*. It is possible however to offend cookery-conscious Italians by calling this comparison. *Bruschetti* are always thicker than *crostini*, and retain their outer bread crust. Differences are dear in cuisine and are guarded preciously.

[25] "You come as opportunely as cheese on macaroni." George Eliot, *Romola*.

The Bangalore, Edinburgh – (six visits) 17 papad with mango chutney, lime pickle, pink sauce and red onions / many crumbs of papad / 2 bombay chana massala / 2 chana dopiaza / 1 potato korma [26] / 1 chana madras / 1 spoon of pilau rice / 9 chapati / one and a half nan bread

Bar Alfredo, San Pedro, Alcántara – 2 glasses of house red / 1 glass of sparkling water / 5 asparagus and mayonnaise / 1 *rosada a plancha* [27] / 1 aniseed liqueur

Bar Roma, Edinburgh – 50ml *Surgiva* water with "*added carbondioxide*" (sic) / 3 slices of avocado / 1 bruschetta / 3 slices of garlic bread with a shaving of Parmesan

The Barony, Edinburgh – 1 glass of sparkling spring water and ice / 1 chip from Richard Cherns' plate & the batter from Richard Cherns' fish

Bennets Bar, Edinburgh – 1 ginger beer

Berrington's, Edinburgh – 1 scrambled egg on toast

Bethlehem Hotel, Bethlehem – 1 cup of black tea

Betty Addison's Retirement Party – One party plate consisting of goat's cheese salad / hummus / salt and vinegar kettle chips / 1 plate of salad potatoes / 4 mini cheese and chive spread sandwiches

"Bill's Do" at the Beach Ballroom, Aberdeen – 1 red pepper stuffed with saffron rice / 1 portion of pasta salad / 1 portion of celery salad / 1 portion of potato & chive salad / 1 serving of fruit salad / 2 Diet Cokes / 1 black coffee

---

[26] This was not what I ordered! What I tried to order was a *chickpea* korma, stressing that I did not want *chicken* korma. This confused the chef, who created the nightmare meal that is *potato korma*. My eating of this korma was punctuated by imperceptible halts during which I decided that due to hunger I should attempt to clear at least half of the plate.

[27] Cartesian horrors: René Descartes forwarded the notion that non-human animals are automata incapable of suffering and therefore goo (sic) for you to eat. At Port-Royal, 17th century Cartesians sliced and maimed living creatures with great gusto, "laughing at any compassion for them and calling their screams the noise of breaking machinery."

Black Medicine, [28] **Edinburgh** – 1 decaffeinated black coffee / 1 rocky road bar

Blue Moon Café, Edinburgh – 2 cups of tea, 1 with milk and 1 without

Bombay Spice, Bonnyrigg – 4 papad and chutney / 1 chana dansak / 1 sultana nan / 1 saag paneer

Bonaparte's, Glasgow – 1 hot chocolate

Books and Beans, Aberdeen – 3 glasses of *SPA* mineral water

Borders Bookshop Coffee Shop, Glasgow [29] – 3 black coffees / 1 and a half chocolate fudge brownies / a half caramel shortbread

The Bow Bar, Edinburgh – 1 Diet Coke / 4 *Schweppes* ginger beers and ice

BUPA, Murrayfield – 2 *Bronte* chocolate chip cookies / 2 *Bronte* "Golden Crunch" biscuits

Burger King, Kings Cross, London – 1 regular Diet Coke

Café East, [30] **Edinburgh** – (four visits) 4 papad and chutney, lime pickle, and red onion / 2 salad portions / 6 quarters of nan / 2 chapati / 1 cup shaped

---

[28] When people eat communally they're able to see each other's mouths opening while their own are in action at the same time. Despite the positive social possibilities of so many people sharing such a small space, the cutlery and teeth in Black Medicine were to me expressive only of the idea of *attack*.

[29] Bookshops now come with cafeterias! Are the connections logical? Does the link between books, coffee and cakes yield a weird meaning concerning our feelings on consumption? Would it be appropriate if Gap, Comet and Virgin Megastore opened cafés on their premises? I fear that books are too boring by themselves these days and need to be supplemented with coffee and biscuits to make them tenable. Clearly we're doomed as bookstores now encourage mastication and lounging.

[30] The Café East in Edinburgh was the home of the MEAL DEAL. During 2004, a curry, a nan bread, poppadoms, rice, a salad and a beer (!) were offered at Café East for the staggeringly generous price of £5. This was a popular offer and all Edinburgh flocked. Each evening of the week citizens dined like heroes, brilliant and rich.

portion of Pilau rice / 1 spoonful of Pilau rice / 1 chana kabuli / 1 chana dopiaza with fresh coriander and tomato / 1 hot chana dish on request / 1 chana vindaloo / 4 spoons of tarka dhal / 2 peppermints

Café Provencal, Edinburgh – 2 cups of coffee / 1 croissant and butter / 1 slice of cake with vanilla icing / 3 camomile teas / 1 bowl of carrot and coriander soup / 2 olive oil croutons

Café Rouge, Edinburgh – 1 black coffee / 1 portion of French Fries with salt, ketchup and mixed salad [31]

Café Royal (Downstairs), Edinburgh – 1 and half glasses of fresh orange / 1 Swiss cheese sandwich [32] with salad

Café Royal (Upstairs), Edinburgh – 2 glasses of lemonade and ice

Café Society, Aberdeen – 1 penne primavera with Parmesan and pepper / 2 slices of bread / 1 *Deeside* Natural Mineral Water (from the Pannanich Wells, Ballater – that's what it said) / 1 black coffee / 1 *Matthew Algie* brand caramelised Lotus biscuit

Caffe Luccano, Edinburgh – 1 cup of lemon and ginger tea

Caledonian Hilton, Edinburgh – A snack buffet at the *"Getting the Best from Your Advisers"* seminar gave me: 4 mini cheese paste sandwiches [33] / 2 baby

---

[31] This feeding was my birthday treat to myself.

[32] John Montagu (1718-1792). The French disagree with the English claim to have invented the sandwich saying that medieval workers would take meat or fish between two slices of bread, for work or travel. Mr Tadg Farrington tells me that the 4th Earl of Sandwich bribed voters by means of a coin embedded in the bread. The favoured story of origin concerning the sandwich concerns a game of cards and a hungry aristocrat seeking to invent fast food. Aetiology, as we shall see throughout *The Supper Book*, is perpetually spurious.

[33] But consider this! "I have been thinking of taking a piece of bread and placing it between two pieces of meat. But what should I call such a dish?" Leonardo da Vinci, in the *Codex Romanoff*. People are so tenacious. Why would they prefer an unfounded legend concerning the origin of the sandwich when Da Vinci has beaten them to it?

egg flans / 1 profiterole with white chocolate / 1 mini fruit flan / 2 glasses of Strathmore slightly sparking spring water

Cameo Cinema, Edinburgh – 1 small carton of salted popcorn

The Cask and Barrel, Edinburgh – 1 cheese and onion toastie [34]

City Arts Centre, Edinburgh – 1 black coffee / 2 cups of cooler water

Coffee etc ..., Edinburgh – 1 black coffee / 1 felafel & hummus wrap

The Cookie Company, Waverley Station, Edinburgh – 500ml cup of Diet Coke

County Hotel, North Berwick – 1 veggie-burger with salad and fries, plus ketchup and brown sauce / 1 ginger beer

Crêpe à Croissant, [35] **Edinburgh** – 1 toasted bagel and cream cheese / 1 black coffee with sugar

Anton Dalu, (baptism of) – 2 sugared almonds / 1 glass of Sprite / 1 glass of *Chardon* non-alcoholic sparkling pear drink / 1 slice of sponge, caramel, almond, marzipan and cream cake [36]

Demartino, London, W1 – 1 black coffee

Dollars Restaurant, [37] **Bethlehem** – one serving of cheese on toast (Figure 02)

---

[34] Distressed by a sudden estrangement from the pleasures of my student years, I decided to order a "toastie" in a public house.

[35] The name Crêpe à Croissant means nothing less than "Croissant Crêpe". The name of this establishment translates as gibberish, with no actual meaning.

[36] Quite possibly the richest single thing I have ever eaten.

[37] Comedy translations of foreign menus. Offered on the menu at Dollars restaurant in Bethlehem were the following meals – "Fele Meat with Mushroom Churn" / "Beef Steak Rose Beef with Potatoes" / and "Costalita Sheep Limp".

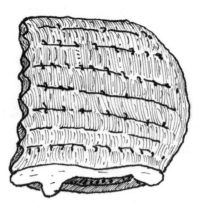

FIGURE 02 – Cheese on toast is still available in Occupied Palestine

Doughnut Company, Edinburgh – 2 cups of tea with milk in a poly cup with 1 fresh doughnut dunked in sugar.

Dunbar Indian Tandoori, Dunbar – 1 saag matar paneer passanda / selections shared from puri, roti, nana, paratha [38] / 1 portion of basmati rice

Easter Road Stadium, Edinburgh [39] – 1 coffee with cold milk

Edinburgh Airport – 1 black coffee / 1 Danish pastry [40]

Eliott's, Gibraltar – 1 Emmenthal sandwich on brown bread with salad and plain crisps on the side

---

[38] In Karachi one can find as many as 100 varieties of paratha. The main difference between roti and paratha is that roti is made with flour and water whereas paratha usually incorporates ghee or oil. The dough is rolled out and brushed with oil, folded, and cooked on a buttered griddle. The heat makes the layers of dough puff up slightly, resulting in a more flaky texture.

[39] Leeds United won the football match. Stadium food never fails to support the fans through footballing disappointment, due to its rigid dependability.

[40] Coffee has become an important supplement to travel and is available in plastic, ground, instant and percolated form at all stops on your weary journey to the grave.

COOKERY

Joseph Conrad's wife, Jessie, published two books on cooking. The Great Man provided the preface for the first of these in 1923 and after praising her frugal skill in their early, lodging house days, concluded that "*of all books, only those on cookery are morally above suspicion. Their aim is to increase the happiness of mankind, to add to the cheerfulness of nations.*" Conrad adds as a negative proof that the ferocity of the Native Americans was caused by their wives' lack of culinary skill. "*The Seven Nations around the Great Lake and the Horse tribes of the plains were but one vast prey to Raging Dyspepsia.*"

It is assumed that cooking is an ancient art, begun when man left a piece of meat too close to the fire and discovered that once burned, it tasted better and was easier to eat. Cooks as seperate craftsmen were later to arrive and according to both the *Iliad* and *Odyssey*, the host, no matter how elevated or important, prepared a dinner party himself with the help of friends.

The modern cookbook is written to satisfy our social hopes as much as our domestic diets. Before Mrs Beeton published her cookbook at the age of 24 (she died in child-bed a few years later) cooking manuals were designed for professional use only. In Mrs Beeton's *Household Management*, every recipe is accompanied by a price tag and the tone is couthy – food being treated as the primary instrument of survival. Later in the 20th century, Elizabeth David set a new fashion and introduced the now-popular concept of *food from other places*.

Subsequent to Elizabeth David, food left the planet altogether and became a sphere of choice and experiment – a leisure concern no less. Most crucially, the foods of Italy, France and India are now seen in Britain as more sophisticated than that of home, a trend which shows no signs of reversing.

In *The Supper Book*, what follows the plate and cutlery symbol (🍽) are my recipes from that year of our supper, when I tried to write down everything I had eaten. I have not included directions for these recipes, for fear that readers may attempt to emulate them. In many cases there were in fact no directions at all, and the ingredients were merely mixed and heated to taste.

Asparagus Tips and Hollandaise

Hollandaise sauce was made from lemon juice, butter and egg,
and tasted of lemon meringue pie.

The asparagus was served with Parmesan from *Sainsbury's* and a side dish
of steamed broccoli. A genuine Hollandaise sauce proved impossible for me
to prepare.

Barely A Meal

1 carrot / 1 vine tomato / 7 cloves of garlic / half an onion /
half a red pepper
all roasted in oil, mixed with ground coriander and ground pepper. [41]

The above was warmed to create something from the fringes of gastrologie.
This made 1 serving only, tidy and Ambrosian in its quality.

---

[41] I was drunk when I cooked the recipe I have called BARELY A MEAL, and I
hacked at the onion and garlic with a fierce blade. *More than a case of why bother?* I thought
as I approached another victim. Anger was not the only feeling admitted via the Trojan
Horse of drink. I also felt shame, being unable to imagine what I was going to do with the
cut vegetables of grocery. *I can collect the many bits and pieces that pass as food*, I thought, *and I
must now adapt them to make a meal.*

Broch [42] Soup

In this soup were: 2 leeks / 16 cloves of garlic / 1 very large onion /
half a neep [43] / 1 very large potato indeed / 3 carrots / 8 sprigs of parsley /
1 and a half litres of *Knorr* vegetable stock

This recipe produced 6 bowls of soup, which I ate over three days. The basis
for this soup was learned by watching my grandmother. [44]

Catchy Little Meal

1 onion / 3 cloves of garlic / olive oil / 1 420g tin of *Safeway* Mixed Beans in
spicy sauce (*"in variable proportions"*)

This was served with crème fraiche, fresh coriander and a portion of boiled
basmati rice.

Some rescued rice and coriander from the bottom of my cupboard and
the bizarre addition of some tasteless tinned beans, combined to form the
proverbial dog's dinner.

---

[42] Pronounced as in "loch". *The Broch* is the domestic name for the Scots town of
Fraserburgh, the origin of this great soup.

[43] Swedish turnips are properly known as *neeps*. Scotland is celebrated for its neeps,
which in its semi-barbaric past were often eaten raw before dinner, as turnips are in Russia
to the present day. Little is spoken these days of the flatulent properties of this esculent,
because now too many products give us gas.

[44] Osmosis describes the passage of a solvent through a semi-permeable barrier, until
both solvents on each side of the barrier have the same concentration.

CROISSANTS

Croissants are funny. When these flaky bread rolls were first sighted in the United Kingdom, English speakers refused the correct French pronunciation, and called them "croiss-ayrants", or "qwassants". In Aberdeen I have even heard them called "crescent buns."

For once, something culinary is not French and the *croissant*, traditionally found paving the streets of Gaul, is in fact illustrative of the emblem on the Ottoman flag, and originated in Budapest during the Turkish siege of 1686.

Over the period of one year I ate my apportioned lot of croissant as follows:

7 croissants and *Lurpak* spreadable butter

3 and half croissants from the *Tesco* "Quality" range – two and a half of them with berry & cherry conserve

3 croissants unadorned

3 *Sainsbury's* croissants and butter

2 croissants and goats' cheese with fresh tomato

1 croissant and *Flora* spread

1 croissant and unknown butter

1 *Spar* croissant with butter and jam

SOME TASTY FLAPJACKS

For once we are not being lied to. Devon – with its wooded river valleys and rugged coasts, evoking great thick dollops of the choicest cream – and Vale, the literary word for a valley, connoting old world simplicity and rustic charm. Devonvale flapjacks and cereal bars are really made in East Devon – and also in a vale, that of the River Otter, in a charming market town called Ottery St Mary. It is a rare marketing victory.

5 *Cadbury* make-them-yourself chocolate chunk flapjacks

4 145g *RJ Foods Ltd.* cherry & sultana jumbo flapjacks

2 90g *The Handmade Flapjack Company* cherry & coconut flapjacks

2 95g *Devonvale Bakery* [45] apple strudel flapjacks

2 95g *Devonvale Bakery* cherry Bakewell [46] flapjacks

1 95g *Devonvale Bakery* maple and walnut flapjack

1 95g *Devonvale Bakery* maple toffee flapjack

1 95g *Devonvale Bakery* Black Forest gateau flapjack

1 95g *Devonvale Bakery* strawberry multigrain bar

1 95g *Devonvale Bakery* strawberries and cream flapjack

---

[45] In Edinburgh, residents are always within range of the well-placed produce of the Devonvale Bakery. The pack quote is: "Delicious oatey bar, wheat and whey free."

[46] Bakewell is the name of a small town in Derbyshire. It joins with Eccles, Dundee, Bath and Lamington in the cakes-that-are-also-places stakes. Consider Madeira, Genoa, and Mecca Cakes (*pains de la Mecque*). Naming cakes after places is a particular science in itself (it is called *libumappology*) and in Europe, since the earliest times, every locale has produced cakes, breads and pastries for which it is noted.

1 *The Handmade Flapjack Company* fruit flapjack

1 75g *Cookie Coach Company "guilt free"* original flapjack

1 *RealFoods* [47] wholesome fruit and nut flapjack

1 *O'Brien's* fruit flapjack

1 90g *Mighty Oat* oat flavour flapjack

1 90g strawberry pieces flapjack

1 110g *Ma* ♥ *Baker* brand [48] Smoothie Bar – cherry flavour *"A deliciously moist cereal bar made with real cherries and a yoghurt topping"*

1 100g *Ma* ♥ *Baker* banana flapjack bar, *"A deliciously moist flapjack made with real bananas"*

1 100g *Ma* ♥ *Baker* cherry flapjack

1 plain syrup flapjack

1 *RJ Foods* toffee flapjack

1 65g *Snickers* flapjack

1 toffee apple flavour flapjack

---

[47] RealFoods is a health food store, marketed with the following slogans: "Alternative lifestyle shops" / "Organic vegetarian, vegan, special diet supplements organic fruit & veg". Now. Are ill health and poor diet so ubiquitous that merely eating well is considered to be an *alternative lifestyle?* The ploy is this: the moment one steps over the threshold, one joins the RANKS of the CRANKS.

[48] These Ma ♥ Baker foods were more than just edible and tugged at a long neglected heart-string. Of course, a mother baking is one of the most basic gastronomic images of all times. In food we are people of history, despairing of our advances like wounded nostalgics.

Chicken Style Supper

Buy a 175g packet of *Quorn*[49] Chicken Style Pieces. On this packet is the desperate entreaty: *"Create your favourite recipes with this delicious Quorn ingredient."*

And that is exactly what I did, adding to it: 1 orange pepper / 2 carrots / 1 tablespoon of Italian hot sauce / the juice of one orange / 1 onion / 8 cloves of garlic.

This made 2 bowls of Chicken Style Supper, eaten over 2 nights.

Brothel Broth

300g broth mix shall be soaked overnight and cleaned (*Great Scot* brand broth mix contains barley, yellow split peas, marrowfat peas, green split peas, and red split lentils)

Quote: "I want Christian broth!" *Weir of Hermiston*, R.L. Stevenson

Also: 2 leeks / half a turnip / 1 very large onion indeed / 2 large potatoes / 3 carrots / 1 bulb garlic = 16 cloves / 20 chives / olive oil / lots of parsley, in hurriedly snatched handfuls / 1 litre of vegetable stock.

Noo see, sirs, hoo the ladle stauns o' itsel in this potch. Yer Broth's mooth-waterin an pairt o the yearly rhythm o things. It's ferr warrim and gars us sing fir mair! This recipe made 5 bowls of soup which I ate over 4 days.

---

[49] QUORN was born of a moment of Malthusian angst in the 1960s when nutritionists predicted that population growth would mean global food shortages. Food scientists searched the planet for new food sources until amazingly, an organism was found occurring naturally in the soil in a field in Marlow, Buckinghamshire. This gave the subsequently named Marlow Foods the opportunity to develop a completely new food ingredient - and *mycoprotein* (the substance of Quorn) was born. A slowing down of world population growth combined with improved food production techniques meant that the expected world food shortage never materialised – at least not as expected.

FIGURE 03 – The supermarket chain Lidl sell a great range of good-value juices.

GRAZING AND BROWSING

As if we are not slaves enough to the photographic fantasies on food packaging, some companies believe that their name should also participate in the great sell. Hence companies with silly but suggestive names such as HEALTHYCO, VITAFIT and INNOCENT vie to press their produce into our diets. Heck, it worked for me.

1 *Cuisine de France* apple Danish pastry

A handful of roasted seeds [50]

1 205g tin of *Morrisons* macaroni cheese [51]

1 *500ml* plastic bottle of *Volvic* spring water

1 litre of *Vitafit* Multivitamin Fruchtsaft [52]

1 litre carton of *SOLEVITA* red grape juice (Figure 03)

2 bowls of mum's lentil and carrot soup with parsley

1 portion of jam and pastry pie with cream

---

[50] Farmers can be treated as criminals for saving seed. This is a brilliant theft of biodiversity. The Intellectual Property Rights clauses of the general agreements on tariffs and trade are where the collective innovation of millions of farmers around the world are now being earmarked as the intellectual property of the corporations – whose faceless attributes stretch the imagination beyond human experience – and endurance.

[51] The earliest existing reference to *macaroni* dates to 1279. It appears in an Italian notary's list of items left by the deceased Ponzio Bastone. What kind of man leaves *pasta* in his will? Or could this "macaroni" be a coded term for something more valuable?

[52] German drink with German strap lines: "Angereichert mit wichtigen" – "Vitaminet und 1 provitamin".

200g of *Stockan and Gardens* Original Orkney Oatcakes – *"Thick"* [53]

1 415g tin of *Baxters* – *"Vegetarian Soup"* range – tomato and orange flavour [54]

1 litre of *Co-op* pure apple juice from concentrate

1 250ml carton of *Innocent* ® pure fruit smoothie with cranberries and raspberry [55]

1 *Mattessons* (*"MMM…"* and *"Since 1846"*) classic cheese & onion sandwich [56]

1 50g *Healthyco* simply nuts mixed nut bar – *"Naturally delicious"*

1 37g *Tracker* bar, roasted nut flavour – *"Chewy oats, nuts, cornflakes and crisped rice bar."*

1.5 litres of *Solevita* 12 fruit Multivitamin Light Nectar – *"55% MIN"*

2 litres of *Solevita* apple drink – *"fresh and fruity taste"*

---

[53] The British English Microsoft ™ spellchecker does not recognise the word *oatcake* but offers as its correction *octave* – as in *octaves and cheese*. A second Microsoft option offers the word *octane*. Cf: "High Oatcake Petrol"

[54] "This uniquely tasting soup is an appealing combination of tomatoes and zesty oranges with a hint of basil. Delicious served chilled with Crème Fraiche." Audrey Baxter. Baxters have gone from strength to strength in the ambient wet soup market while Campbell Soup Company have had to catch up with an image hijacked by Andy Warhol.

[55] In fact, the company named Innocent listed this product was made with: two and a half pressed apples, half a mashed banana, 6 crushed raspberries, half an orange and 62 crushed cranberries. They are a food reckoner's dream.

[56] *Classic* is another much used word. A "classic" should be a ubiquitous and unique symbol of a time gone by – even if the product in question just plain sucked. Sometimes everything about a product is a cliché, even the clichés.

1 litre of *Parmalat* brand "*Santal*" – 100% Mela (apple juice)

1 small piece of soap that I mistook for food and ate. It was trapped beneath my fingernail. [57]

3 litres of *Vitafit* Multi-Vitamin drink

1 donut shaped wafer with chocolate and coconut topping

26 ginger snaps

3 brown bread, Brie and chutney sandwiches

1 leek and potato cheese croustade with nutmeg and 3 big lettuce helpings

1 *Crocodile Snacks* Giant Banana Fudge Muffin – "*A banana flavour muffin containing fudge pieces*"

1 bag of butter flavour *ACT II* microwave popcorn – "*America's No. 1 popcorn*"

1 117g *Popz* ready salted flavour premium microwave popcorn

30ml of *Diet Pepsi* – "*Less than 1 calorie*" – "*Low calorie flavoured soft drink with sweeteners*"

1 avocado and feta sandwich on brown bread

1 and half Sconethornden [58] (Figure 04)

---

[57] A good year! This was probably the worst thing I ate.

[58] A welcoming scone served at Hawthornden Castle, is known as a Sconethornden.

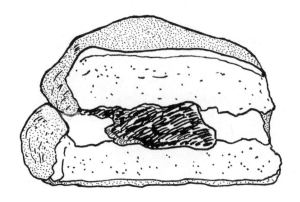

FIGURE 04 – A half scone prepared at Hawthornden Castle, Laswade.

2 slices of *Leerdammer* cheese, dipped in cheese and chive dip

200g of *Co-op* digestive biscuits

1 *Skinnies* cheese sandwich [59] – *"Low on fat full on flavour"*

4 glasses of water with *Belvoir* brand passion fruit cordial

106ml tub of *Ben & Jerry's* Chunky Monkey ice cream – *"Banana Flavoured Ice Cream with Chocolatey Chunks & Walnut"* / *"Spoon Inside"* [60]

106ml tub of *Ben and Jerry's* Honey I'm Home ice cream – *"Honey Vanilla Ice Cream with Chocolatey Covered Honey Candies"*

---

[59] "There is no respectable reason for wishing not to be fat." Evelyn Waugh. Few today would agree with Waugh and many of us dedicate our lives to dieting. Food companies are in an awkward fix. They are catering for increasing appetites but have adopted (without being asked) the job of keeping us thin.

[60] Ben and Jerry are real people! At least I have come to believe they're real people. Some foods are marketed by fictional characters such as the cake-crazy Edwardian gentleman, Mr Kipling – and of course Ronald MacDonald, the very nice clown. These characters lend an uncertain touch of humanity to the food in question.

1 slice of apple flan and whipped cream

Half a walnut & caramel muffin

Quarter of a Danish pastry

1 bowl of strawberries, sugar and fromage frais

1 slice of focaccia bread and feta salad; a quarter of cheese pickle sandwich; a quarter of an unknown vegetable paté sandwich; half a cheese, chive and tomato sandwich; half a salad and cheese savoury sandwich; half a cheese and tomato sandwich; a quarter of a chickpea sandwich … all of these from a lunchtime office buffet [61]

1 sauerkraut sandwich on brown bread

4 large *Co-op* pancakes

1 toasted slice of baguette with Brie, herbs and chutney

1 tub of strawberry *Frucht Quark* (Figure 05)

4 oatcakes and Port Salut cheese

4 oatcakes and Port Salut cheese and butter

---

[61] When was the first ever buffet? When will we see the return of buffet cars? Which of the great meals of history have actually been buffets? And when does a buffet become a smorgasbord? The buffet is the natural home of foods that are imported and yet not indigenised. This way people can try handy amounts of foods that they may like only a little, or foods that they wish to try a small amount of – perhaps on an experimental basis. Some foods come into their own under buffet arrangements – such as *tongue*, which should, where it is available, never be obligatory. An ancient etymological myth states that the word *beefeater* is a corruption of the French *buffetier*, a server at a buffet. Servers are absent from buffets these days, to allow the gluttionous demon in us the chance to enjoy what we call "All You Can Eat", which by necessity needs to be an unsupervised affair.

FIGURE 05 – A tub of Frucht Quark

5 double chocolate chip cookies of unknown origin [62]

3 slices of tomato quiche with mashed potato

4 oatcakes with butter and cheddar

1 plate of fruit crumble with apple, redcurrant and pear

---

[62] And why should one eat in the Cookie Monster style? Human beings have neither claws nor fangs. They do not eat by pressing their mouth into their food but instead raise their food to their mouth, which is the organ of speech and therefore the organ of reason. The mouth is the centre of the face and it is in the face that the human person is most immediately encountered in the form of looks, glances and words. Cookie Monster Style is a way of acknowledging this conundrum.

On dull days in the city, when one can't see the sun or even feel its warmth, the population tire of looking for the right meal and graze their way from task to task. On each city block there's a variety of options, each as colourful as the next. Diversion calls from every biscuit tin and bakery, every supermarket and stall.

You would imagine me to be sick when combining all of this food – but remarkably, I never feel the slightest twitch of complaint from the same stomach that eats prawn crackers, lentil soup, chocolate chip cookies and tomato quiche.

THE MILL OF SNACKING

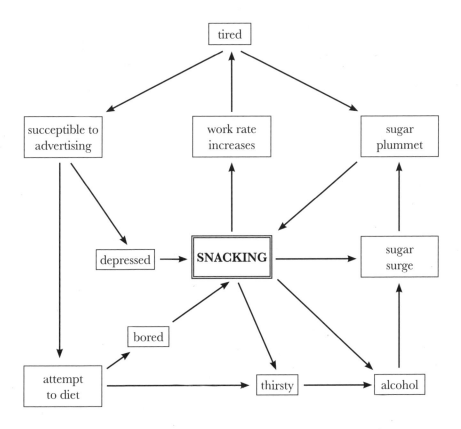

CHIP SHOPPING

As plankton to the whales of the sea, so chips to Scotland. As tea to China so chips to Scotland. As oranges to the healthy Floridian skin, then so chips to the complexions of Scotland.

Fish and Chip shops were once so common in Scotland that any other type of street food would have been heresy. There are still over 90 fish and chip shops in Edinburgh, proving that any lurking health concerns are outweighed by the passion for fried potatoes and meat.

A chip is not a French Fry. Chips are larger than French Fries, although French Fries contain a larger amount of fat. French Fries are sometimes cooked twice and are in essence classier than chips, the quality of which can be variable. Finally, chips are not as crispy as French Fries, and tend to come with a solid potato centre, as opposed to the fluffy heart of the ideal French Fry.

Chips and fries have recently been involved in politics. On March 11, 2003, the cafeteria menus in the United States House of Representatives office buildings changed the name of French Fries to *Freedom Fries* in a symbolic rebuke of France's opposition to the United States' war on Iraq. *French Toast* was also changed to *Freedom Toast*, and French wine was poured into gutters in disgust.

Why the chiding did not extend to non-foodstuffs, I do not know. French kissing, French polish, French windows and the French Horn remained unmolested. In such moments of blood-rushing xenophobia however, some other French named foods were overlooked – French dressing I believe being one.

In response to this strange admonishing, the French embassy issued a statement to the press with the rather childish retort that French Fries were Belgian. [63]

---

[63] I am not alone in finding the name changes spiteful. If America had given its name to anything at all then we could treat them to the same lesson. OUF! American Ginger Ale could become *Jihad Ginger Ale*; Kraft American Cheese could become *Kraft Manifest Destiny Cheese*; and Americano Coffee could become *Overseas Operations Hot Drink*. BOUF! State by state the options are even more enticing! Baked Alaska could become *Chile Declassificastion Project with Ice Cream*; Kentucky Fried Chicken could become *Native American Menu-Snatch*; California Salad could become *Rumsfeld on Toast*; New York Steak could become *Roasted Senate Inquiry*; Chicken Maryland could become *Chicken Slave States*; Maine Lobster could become *Homeland Lobster*; Mississippi Mud Pie could become *Chocolate Intelligence Shake-up*; and Boston Clam Chowder could become *Bay of Pigs Mash*.

Returning to the subject of good-old-fashioned Scots chips, it appears that I visited chip-houses on average once every fourteen and a half days and over twelve months came away with:

The Concorde, Lothian Road, Edinburgh – (12 visits) 3 white pudding suppers / 3 veggie-burger [64] suppers / 2 onion ring suppers / 3 bags of chips / 1 large bag of chips

The Castle Rock Chip Shop, Edinburgh – 1 white pudding supper

Nerio's Fish and Chip Bar, Oban – 1 white pudding supper

South China Inn, Edinburgh – 1 white pudding supper and tomato sauce / 4 mini vegetable spring rolls and chips

The Ashvale, Aberdeen – 1 corn on the cob supper [65]

The North Berwick Fry, North Berwick – 1 plate of chips

Globetrotter, Edinburgh – 2 bags of chips

The Aqua Marina, Edinburgh – 1 bag of chips

The Rose Street Chippy, Edinburgh – 1 bag of chips

The Babylon, Edinburgh – 1 bag of chips

All of the above chip suppers and chip portions were served with salt and vinegar. [66]

---

[64] The defenders of chip shops remind us that efforts are made to minimise animal suffering by including non-meat delicacies such as the veggie-burger, an item of the most variable quality and composition. Many vegetarians such as myself are in denial as to the animal content of the white pudding supper.

[65] Trumped only by the PINEAPPLE RING SUPPER, the CORN ON THE COB SUPPER is the second-most exotic chip supper available in Scotland.

[66] I shared the long, pre-dawn walk to work with a colleague who had recently moved

The Supper System

I've often been asked about the Supper System by those curious as to what goes on in fish and chip shops. Should you enter one of these establishments, you will be expected to choose either chips by themselves, or a delicacy from the hot cabinet which is to be served as part of a SUPPER.

If you wish one of the delicacies with chips (let us say, the King Rib), all that is required is that you say "King Rib Supper" (nobody says *please*).

In the case of fish it is common nowadays to receive two smaller fish as opposed to one large fish. The European Union lays down minimum sizes for fish which may *not* be caught (35cm for cod, 30cm for haddock), but sadly baby cod don't realise that they're not supposed to follow mummy into the net.

Here are Frequently Asked Questions about the Scots fish and chip shop Supper System:

Does *Single Fish* have chips?
No.

Is *Fish and Chips* a "Fish Supper"?
Yes, it is.

What is a *Fish Tea*?
Fish tea is battered fish, chips, peas, bread and butter, and a pot of tea.

Can I buy two single fishes?
Yes, but beware. You may receive four fish and no chips. This is different from a single fish with no chips, which may not be available. (In Dublin a fish supper is called a "one-and-one" which only adds to the confusion.)

---

to Edinburgh. Our rumbling stomachs led us inevitably to talk about food and she began to spit with horror at the concoction known as SAUCE that Edinburgh chip shops serve. Not local to Edinburgh I was able to sympathise with her, and she seemed more horrified yet when I told her that the city's favourite condiment is actually a mixture of brown sauce and water.

Four fish?

Yes. If Single Fish is two fish, then you'll receive four fish in asking for two fish.

So "Single Fish" is different from an actual single fish.

It can be. You have to be clear about how many fish you want.

What if I don't want two fish?

If single fish means two fish, you must take two fish in ordering either a fish supper, or a single fish.

But I really didn't want two fish.

You won't find establishments willing to compromise on this rule. Eat up. It'll make you big and strong.

I expect that fish and chip shop [67] staff are aware of these pitfalls and are ready to help the less sure customers?

Yes. Fish and chip shop owners are aware of the confusion caused by the Supper System. It serves them well.

---

[67] "Why does Sea World have a seafood restaurant? I'm halfway through my fish burger and I realize, oh my God... I could be eating a slow learner." Lyndon B. Johnson, 36th president of the United States.

AVOCADOS

The avocado looks simple and delicious with its leathery green skin and its plump pear shape. Strangely, the name *avocado* comes from the 17th century Spanish, *aguacate*, [68] a loanword from the Nahuatl, and meaning testicle, alluding to the form of the fruit.

The flower of the avocado has both female and male organs, but they don't function at the same time. For an avocado to fruit an insect must transfer pollen from a different flower to the stigma of a first-opening flower. Sperm from the pollen grow under the petals to fertilize the female egg, which then grows into the mature fruit.

I have searched for facts concerning the avocado that have nothing to do with sex but it is with sore disappointment that I admit that there are none. It seems that this great swinger of the fruit world, with its pendulous cone shaped form, could contend with all the mighty rajasic foods of yogic sexual practice.

My personal total of *aguacate*, was:

12 *Sainsbury's "Taste the Difference"* [69] "*ripe & ready*" Hass avocados, [70] eaten plain

3 avocados, eaten plain

2 avocados with fresh lemon juice

---

[68] The Nahuatl for testicle is *ahuacatl*.

[69] I am so bored with low quality. I want to pay more for the fine foods I deserve. The Sainsbury's TASTE THE DIFFERENCE range is equivalent to the Tesco THE BEST range (now known as Tesco FINEST) and other premium brands. Waitrose is the UK supermarket that is the exception – it doesn't have a premium brand but instead markets itself as the premium brand of supermarkets. Quality is a commodity that is not easy to measure. I will say this however. Premium brand products such as the above, typically cost 75% more than the standard brand equivalents. Higher prices do not guarantee better tasting food – but we continue to consume according to want, not need, and the brand is both a badge of identity and a means of personal fulfilment.

[70] And Sainsbury's say: "These soft, buttery, avocados are fully ripe to ensure they have a deliciously rich and nutty flavour." At the receiving end of this great wisdom, I remained emotionless, bemused as ever with the important commentaries.

THE THEORY OF EVOLUTION

It is one of the astonishing things about the marketing of foods that products are forced to evolve as the market expands. The easiest way for this to happen is for existing forms to mutate, such as:

1 *Kellogg's* Crunchy Nut Bar [71] *"Cereal bar made with golden flakes of corn, rice, wheat and hazelnuts, with a honey flavour, dipped in a smooth milky layer."*

1 strawberry flavour *Weetabix* ® Chunkyfruit Bar – *"Cereal Bar Packed with REAL FRUIT pieces"*

When they first appeared among us in the 1980s, food bars were marketed for athletes and survivalists. When these intriguing foil wrapped "food vehicles" came to the attention of the rest of us, we decided that our hectic lives made athletes and survivalists of us all, and that we were all special enough to deserve our meals in bar form. We liked that food bars were uniform, powerful and technological, and like laptop computers and mobile phones, they seemed to contain a great amount of clever functions in a small and mysterious space.

I have never seen anyone eat a food bar and then sit back with a satisfied expression, as one may after a meal. Yet a bar exists for every occasion, including as a breakfast replacement, healthy snack or simply as a sweet treat. This is because successful bars share several basic common properties. A food bar should be made using a smart new scientific development. It should target the needs of a specific consumer, by age, social class, condition and gender. Finally it should be sweet, because if a bar doesn't taste a certain way, it won't be purchased again. This brings me to the single weirdest thing about this fast-evolving food – the fact that two unlikely diet-mates, cereal and sweets, have combined. To make matters worse, food bars must be moulded using new proteins, binders, sweeteners, fortifiers and texturisers – everything in short that allows manufacturers to squeeze their ingredients into the fascinating and modern *bar* form.

---

[71] A breakfast cereal, roughly speaking, becomes a snack bar. We must not try and fathom these changes, but be prepared to decide as to whether we will participate or not.

YOGURT or YOGHURT

Few food stuffs have benefitted more from the advent of plastic than yoghurt – not even milk which has long been delivered in a paper-plastic combination. Plastic weighs less than glass and is cheaper to produce. The only thing that comes close to a compostable plastic yoghurt pot is made from a by-product of genetically engineered corn, but the only bio-degradable alternative is a container made from sugar cane or sugar beets, which melts if it comes into contact with heat. This ordinarily shouldn't happen, but what if your mobile phone sat next to your yoghurt in your bag, and rang so much it overheated and you ended up with yoghurt on your dossiers? That would be the end.

2 x 125g *Mamie Nova* yaorts aux fruits framboise *"au lait entier"*

2 x 125g *Mamie Nova* yaorts aux fruits cerise *"au lait entier"*

1 125g *Mamie Nova* yaort aux fruits ananas *"au lait entier"*

1 125g *Mamie Nova* yaort aux fruits peche *"au lait entier"*

1 125g *Mamie Nova* yaort aux fruits abricot *"au lait entier"*

1 125g *Danone "Shape"* lemon yoghurt *"Greek Style"*

5 x 125g *Ski* strawberry yoghurts from the *Ski* variety selection

4 x 125g *Ski* peach yoghurts from the *Ski* variety selection

2 x 125g *Ski* raspberry yoghurts from the *Ski* variety selection

2 x 125g *Ski* black cherry yoghurts from the *Ski* variety selection

2 x 125g *Alpro Soya* low fat vanilla soy yoghurts – *"Your health is your wealth. Invest wisely for the future."*

BREAD

Were all the varieties of bread known to one person then this person would be as holy as the proverbial sage who had mastered all the names of God. In Scotland alone, the range of bread is baffling, from Cappie, Hawick and Bakin-Lotch, to Snoddie, Sod, and Soutar's Clod. Although more bread than ever is produced in factories and not bakeries, it is done so with a loss in terms of variety, and perhaps also quality.

It may be that bread will continue to suffer its gradual extinction. Modern living has not been kind to households which previously saw bread making as a daily event. Now bread making is industrial, both locally and nationally, and the art has died with the domestic hearth. Consider the native warmth evoked in *Marmion*, when Sir Walter Scott describes the kitchen of an inn in the Lammermoors in the early sixteenth century:

The chimney arch projected wide,
Above around it, and beside,
Were tools for housewives' hands;

Alas, for bread is dead. [72] Those of us who have made bread ourselves know this only too well. Bread and butter still go together, but butter is also firmly in the grip of the manufacturers. As a young boy, I ate homemade churn butter, an experience I am unlikely to return to. I recall the churn butter as being rich and quite smelly, probably why it is now illegal.

I have tried to limit what has been included in this list of breads and have mentioned elsewhere many of the bread-related foods (eg sandwiches and pittas) that were devoured during my daily graze.

---

[72] When the staff of life is dead, think of Democritus who, sensing his 109 year-old body slipping into death, asked his sister to place a hot bread on his face. It's said that the aroma of this bread kept Democritus alive for three days. And even if this is expected to stand as an example of the philosopher's powers, it really captures the powerful emotions and sensations we feel when fresh bread is near.

The list otherwise looks a little something like this – let's start with the toast: [73]

Toast

14 slices of toasted brown bread and butter

12 slices of rye toast and butter

11 slices of brown toast with butter and Jan Stewart's marmalade

7 slices of brown toast with butter and marmalade

4 slices of white toast with butter and blackcurrant jelly

3 slices of brown toast and cranberry jelly

3 slices of brown toast with *Flora* and marmalade

2 slices of brown toast and marmalade

2 slices of brown toast and *Lurpak Spreadable*

2 slices of white toast and butter

2 slices of brown toast with butter and golden syrup

---

[73] I have tended to favour the 125g pack of salted *Scottish Pride* Pure Scottish Butter and *Lurpak Spreadable* Slightly Salted – "*Since 1901*". Butter is in fact spread indiscriminately throughout this book. *The Supper Book* contains no estimate of how much butter I consumed, nor can it even think of a decent way to measure this. I have conducted weighing experiments as follows:

WEIGHT OF A SLICE	38g
WEIGHT OF A BUTTERED SLICE	43g
TOTAL SLICES	137.5
=	**687.5g of butter**

2 slices of white toast and blackcurrant jelly

2 slices of white toast with butter and blackberry jam

2 slices of white toast with *Flora* and Jan Stewart's marmalade

2 slices of toast with cream cheese and strawberry jam

1 slice of brown toast spread with more blackcurrant jam than the toast could handle

1 slice of brown toast with butter and runny honey

1 slice of brown toast with blackcurrant jelly and butter

1 slice of brown toast with *Lurpak Spreadable* [74] and strawberry jam

1 slice of brown toast with *Lurpak Spreadable* and cherry jam

2 crusts of brown toast

1 crust of white toast

1 bite of toast and butter

Baguettes and Nudgers [75]

6 x 25g slices of garlic baguette

5 mini baguettes

---

[74] Once there was BUTTER and then there was MARGARINE. Now there is just SPREAD – middle-aged spread.

[75] The word *nudger* is used as an alternative for a mini-baguette.

3 nudgers with spread [76]

One and a half nudgers without spread

1 baguette roll

1 slice of baguette and butter

1 baguette [77] with butter

Half a baguette [78] with butter and strawberry jam

1 *Safeway* half baguette – *"part baked white baguette"*

1 half of a garlic bread – made as is traditional in these parts, with a baguette.

4 pieces of baguette – One with watery red chutney dip and Gouda and spicy bean pate. Another piece was eaten with Gouda and watery red chutney. Another piece was dipped in watery red chutney. The final slice was covered with spicy been pate, Gouda, and was dipped in watery red chutney.

---

[76] A MINI-BAGUETTE and a NUDGER? It is a question of size. A nudger is more snub-nosed than a mini-baguette, and will be smaller, maybe even whiter, perhaps even made by Scottish people.

[77] My table manners are appalling but I took a tape measure nonetheless and measured this baguette which turned out to be 76cm – nearly 30 inches – long.

[78] There's something esculent on the streets of Paris. The French government have now legally codified a specific type of baguette, the *baguette de tradition*, made using precise pre-modern methods. This was thanks to historian Steven Kaplan and his work on the history of French bread. Kaplan called upon the French to reject the modern baguette, which he denounced as a "tastless, odourless monstrosity". The key to decent baguettes, Kaplan argued, is the 18th century practice of allowing the yeast to develop overnight, which results in a baguette with a cream-colored interior, rather than the familiar white. The French have enthusiastically adopted Kaplan's recommendations and he has been twice knighted by their grateful government.

Rolls, Muffins, Baps and Crumpets

6 x *Kingsmill* "perfect" pancakes

6 x *Sainsbury's* Scotch pancakes [79] – 3 with butter and syrup, 2 with butter and blackcurrant jam, and 1 with butter and raspberry jam

4 rolls nude

4 *Kingsmill* muffins – 2 with spreadable butter and marmalade, 1 with spreadable butter and honey, 1 with butter

1 *Kingsmill* crumpet and butter

2 large sesame baps with butter and marmalade

1 ciabatta roll, heated from frozen and sprinkled with ground black pepper

2 brown rolls with *Flora* spread

2 sesame rolls of *Cuisine de France*, one with lettuce, ketchup and mayo

1 plain muffin

1 white floury roll and butter [80]

---

[79] The Scots now ignore their own word for the pancake – *bannock* (cf. Gaelic *bannach* and Celtic *bannuc*). Many Scots are so confused they also now ignore the word *pancake* and favour the ridiculous misnomer *crumpet*.

[80] Bland uniformity of presentation, content and aesthetic, is not the preserve of roll and butter. Roll and butter stands for the most delightful simplicity, whereas blandness is the characteristic of so-called fast food, no matter how well wrapped it may be.

1 roll and jam

1 white roll

Other Breads Du Monde

6 slices of *Warburton's* Premium brown medium sliced bread with *Lurpak Spreadable* butter (because "butter skites and winna spread" as Charles Murray noted in his poem "Winter")

11 wholemeal pitta bread

6 white pitta of *Bart* ® foods [81]

5 slices of ciabatta [82]

3 slices of ciabatta and butter

4 slices of *Rossisky* Russian [83] inspired rye bread [84]

3 slices of toasted sunflower seed bread with butter and honey

---

[81] Bart foods ("The art of good food") make pitta that is "Ideal for picnics and packed meals." If stuck for ideas, the public are told that they may reasonably "Serve with dips or split into pockets and add fillings of your choice."

[82] Globalisation has made available food from other places and even other times. We call these foods *foreign* to differentiate them from our own domestic ways. The ciabatta is still very common around here, but is not yet near being adopted as one of our own.

[83] Poor Russia and blessed bread! In November 1936 a directive was passed in many provinces which prohibited the sale of flour. In those days people still made their own bread, and were henceforth pushed into industrialisation, obliged to buy bread from state centres and factories – if it was available. *Merde* to that form of socialism!

[84] This "inspired" rye bread was according to its producers, "Based on a sourdough from historic Kostroma on the Volga river."

2 slices of the homemade bread and *Gold* spread

1 segment of buttered, toasted pitta

1 corner of buttered tea bread

1 chunk of rustic bread [85]

1 *Sainsbury's* crusty white bread baton

2 slices of seeded loaf and butter

1 slice of sunflower toast with butter and peanut butter

1 slice of rye and spelt bread and butter [86]

300g *Demeter* Essene bread – *"Biodynamic more than organic"*

2 chapati

3 slices of Essene bread toasted with Philadelphia cheese [87]

1 bite of toasted pitta with cheese, ketchup and mayonnaise

---

[85] A baker who became fed up with seeing his sales slip as customers followed the low-carb craze has written a book for the Da Vinci bandwagon, based on the Golden Ratio. Stephen Lanzalotta has drawn up *The Da Vinci Diet Code* and signed a publishing deal with Warner Books.

[86] SPELT – the past participle of *to spell* – and an ancestor of modern wheat.

[87] David escaped across the River Jordan fed with the "cheese of the kine" (2 Samuel 17:29). He is also said to have presented ten cheeses to the captain of the army drawn up to do battle with Saul (1 Samuel 17:18). The best Biblical quote regarding cheese is spoken by the hard-pressed Job to his bullying creator. "Have you not poured me out like milk and curdled me like cheese?" he asks, referring to the creation of his own, slighlty off-smelling soul.

Bagels

11 *Sainsbury's* bagels "with everything" [88]

5 cinnamon and raisin bagels

2 *Tesco* plain bagels

1 *Safeway* blueberry bagel

1 *Safeway* plain bagel

Half a plain bagel [89]

Incidental Bread Consumption

The heel of a *Hovis* Farmhouse Loaf with *Lurpak Spreadable* butter

1 slice of wet rye bread and peanut butter (I had to rinse my mouth out with Ribena after this slice of bread, it so dried my jaw)

2 slices of fried bread

---

[88] "Everything" is, in this case, sesame, poppy seed and onion.

[89] The other half was stale! Just like the half that I ate was stale!

Loaf Case Study

It was essential in looking at all of this bread that I tried to capture the fate of one particular loaf. For this I chose a Warburton's Wholemeal Sliced Loaf, which weighed 400g and came with the slogans – *"Deliciously Soft Wholemeal Bread"* and *"Family Bakery Since 1876."* This loaf was sliced and wrapped, and unnoticeably tasty as most bread is. Being factory produced, this bread did not come with a rich crust, although loaves in this format are massively convenient for toast and sandwiches.

I wouldn't have called this loaf "deliciously soft", but the description is at least legal, given the subjectivity which is permitted in these matters. Bread might be the oldest and most important solid in our diet, and so perhaps it should be taken a little more seriously in light of this. Time is marching on in every field, including the baking industry, and already electronic devices are being developed that can bake a loaf by means of high-frequency heat in three minutes – a purely economic measure, given the average loaf baking time of forty five minutes in most factories.

The 16 slices of this loaf were used as follows –

4 slices eaten with butter and rhubarb, ginger and mint jam from The Plough, in Potten End

4 slices eaten with blackcurrant and apple jam from The Plough, in Potten End

5 slices with butter and golden syrup

3 slices without butter, or anything.

TAPWATER

What flows from the tap is that which the Lord God created on the first day, before He created light, and far in advance of His scheme to create humanity and its mysterious struggle with fast food. [90] The tap is a sign of plenty but in our wasteful times it is also an increasing source of worry. My prediction for the future is a generation of gourmet waters.

The Scottish people, believing in the properties of their Highland streams, drink more tap water than their neighbours. It is unthinkable that Scottish water could ever be polluted but it could be happening despite its glorious image.

There are too many factors impacting on tap water quality. Pollution in the form of chemical spills, leaking fuel tanks, pesticides, cleaning fluids, weed killers and fertilisers is merely the tip of the water-contamination iceberg. Below the surface, the iceberg is known to contain fluoride, chlorine and other disinfectants, intended to protect us. The most overlooked sources of water contamination are right under our streets, lawns and floors – and these are the water pipes themselves.

Even in Scotland, safe water becomes contaminated after it leaves the treatment plant. Scales and microbial sediment can build up inside pipe walls and leach into drinking water as it passes along, but no one has yet to perish from water in these parts.

In all I drank:

79 pints of Edinburgh tap water / 4 pints of Aberdeen tap water / 3 pints of Burnmouth tap water / 1½ pints of Marbella tap water [91] / 1 pint of Inverness tap water

---

[90] This is a presumption. Heaven and Earth were created on the first day, meaning that the water was either co-existent with them, or more likely was pre-existent. Technically speaking therefore, God did not in fact create water – just everything *except* water.

[91] As a young British person I was told from an early age not to drink water on the continent. The phrase "on the continent" was brought into being in order to protect the islands of our British Bellies from the commonwealth of Foreign Infection.

Pea-Pea Lover Soup

907g of *Birds Eye* frozen garden peas / a half a cabbage [92] /
1 leek / 2 potatoes / 2 onions / 1 bulb of garlic /
4 pints of stock, made with 5 *Knorr* vegetable stock cubes,
which are *not cubic.*

All of the above were blended until the soup was fit for use. Three plates of this
were eaten, over three nights.

The superiority of this soup is partly owing to its simplicity, although there is
much to recommend the light, fiery pandemonium of a pot of boiling peas.

Eggs Virginia

A recipe from the internet posted by the Stoneridge Bed and Breakfast of
Lexington Virginia. [93]

Includes: 4 eggs / 1 tablespoon of butter / 4 tablespoons of cream /
1 tablespoon of chopped fresh chives / 2 ounces of Gruyere or Swiss cheese,
finely grated

---

[92] *Liberty Cabbage* is a renaming of sauerkraut. The term was used mostly in the US,
particulalry during World War I. Similar euphemisms included *Liberty Measles* for German
Measles, and *Eisenhower Herring* for Bismarck Herring.

[93] I visited the Stoneridge Guest House's website one clouded spring day, internet
grazing and escaping the straitjacket of my desk. Seeing that the Stoneridge's website
offered the above recipe for eggs, I couldn't wait to get home and try it. I ran home with
my tie flapping behind me, moving quickly in order to best utilise the forty minutes that at
the point existed between the office door and my evening meal.

Green Souptember

Contains 2 small onions / 1 bulb of garlic / 2 large potatoes /
10 spring onions / 3 sticks of kale / 1 small cabbage / nearly 2 pints of stock /
50ml *Elmlea* cream [94] / 40 chives

This mixture was blended and I ate 4 bowls. One wonders if the loss of this
recipe would be any matter for regret?

In the culinary calendar, the month of Souptember follows an August *au jus*.

Clapshot

Not my own invention, but something of a (chives = posh) variation on the
Scots favourite.

6 boiled potatoes / 1 boiled turnip / 12 chopped chives / ground black pepper /
1 knob of *Lurpack Spreadable* butter

THE INSTRUCTIONS: Assemble and mash

---

[94] The amount of conjunctive advertising in *The Supper Book* alarms me. While naively
cautioning the reader not to eat the things I ate, I have throughout my eating had no truck
or trouble with those who made them. Hence use Elmlea if you wish, although any other
brand of cream will do.

SAINSBURY'S

Each supermarket has a different name although it is never material to me which one I am visiting. [95] I am not convinced of the differences between the supermarkets which have more in common with each other than they do individual charms. Does loyalty matter? And is it true that everything, after some fashion or another is available in all supermarkets?

There is one final question: who makes all this stuff? The hazards for a lazy cook are many. Supermarkets now employ vast kitchens which manufacture ready-made meals and side dishes on a huge scale. Nobody need even boil a potato if they do not feel so inclined.

9 x *Sainsbury's* Toffee Tiffins, described as *"sultanas, glace cherries and crunchy biscuit in a toffee flavoured base with a smooth toffee flavour topping."* One must thank those producers dedicated to the precise description of their products' makeup. These tiffins were composed thus: A Caramel Base (25%) with Digestive Biscuits (28%), Sultanas (21%) Glace Cherries (6%) and a Toffee Flavoured Coating (20%)".

2 x 250ml *Sainsbury's* [96] organic tropical juice drink

1 *Sainsbury's* Danish pastry whorl with a cherry in the centre

180g of *Sainsbury's* Reserve Gruyere Cheese

150g *Sainsbury's* Italian Mozzarella – *"Milky, slightly sharp, soft cheese when cooked with stringy texture of mozzarella has made it a classic pizza topping"* (sic) / *"Made in the Lombardy region"*

---

[95] I have a loyalty card for Sainsbury's although I am barely loyal to them. I have dated other supermarkets and have had a steady relationship with Tesco while continuing to shop on a casual basis.

[96] The Grocer magazine conferred their 2004 Pay-Off of the Year Award on Sir Peter Davis, who in July of that year left the floundering company with a souvenir cheque for an amazing £2.4 million. SEE NOTE 101 to find out exactly how much shopping that represents.

1 *Sainsbury's* caramel shortcake biscuit

1 *Sainsbury's* vegetable bake

3 x *Sainsbury's* chocolate brownies [97]

3 x fresh chocolate brownies from the *Sainsbury's* in store bakery

1 *Sainsbury's* less-than-5%-fat cupcake

1 litre of *Sainsbury's* no-added-sugar cranberry and raspberry drink

4 x *Sainsbury's* jam donuts

3 x *Sainsbury's Taste the Difference* truly indulgent cookies [98]

50g of *Sainsbury's* "*Fully Prepared*" fresh wild rocket

1 400g *Sainsbury's* fresh cheese salad bowl [99]

---

[97] What's "Soya Lecithin?" Lecithin is found in the cell membranes of all human cells. Each molecule has two faces, like Janus. The fatty-acid in the molecule is attracted to fats – and the phosphoric acid in the molecule is attracted to water. Because of this dual nature, lecithin molecules tend to position themselves at the boundary between immiscible materials, such as oil and water. There they serve many useful functions including Emulsifying, Crystallisation Control, and Anti-spatter (as in margarine). The most concentrated natural and unrefined sources of lecithin are soybeans although the word "lecithin" is derived from the Greek term *lekithos* meaning "egg yolk."

[98] "Gorgeously soft cookies loaded with rich, chunky pieces and bursting with flavour." Of supermarket premium products, I can say only this: it's all the same to Cookie Monster.

[99] This salad cheese bowl was described as follows: "Grated cheddar cheese on pasta and mixed salad with mayonnaise". This is where I realised for the first time that product descriptions are almost recipes! I feel a real ass for buying this, cause in an ideal world I should have these ingredients in my fridge, ready to combine as required.

1 170g tub of *Sainsbury's* hummus

300g *Sainsbury's* noodles and vegetable mix – ready prepared to stir-fry

3 x *Sainsbury's* carrot cakes – "*Moist, lightly spiced carrot cake slices topped with cream cheese icing and a sugar decoration.*" These cakes had over 50 ingredients listed. [100]

1 *Sainsbury's* cherry scone [101]

---

[100] One has intricate eating experiences at the supermarket. Of all the ingredients of these Sainsbury's carrot cakes there were some I could picture and had heard of:

Wheat Flour, Sugar, Sunflower Oil, Rapeseed Oil, Palm Oil, Water, Raisins, Concentrated Apple, Pear and Grape Juice, Rice Starch, Pineapple, Whole Egg Powder, Salt, Carrot, Golden Syrup, Wheat Starch, Desiccated Coconut, Skimmed Milk Powder, Locust Bean Gum, Cellulose, Cinnamon, Mixed Spice, Nutmeg, Caramel Colouring, Modified Potato Starch, Cheese Solids, Lactic Acid, Citric Acid and *Walnuts.*

The ingredients I could neither understand nor picture were:

Vegetable Glycerine, Xantham Gum, Guar Gum, Disodium Dihydrogen Diphosphate, Sodium Hydrogen Carbonate, Titanium Dioxide, Potasssium Sorbate, Polyglycerol Esters of Fatty Acids, Mono and Di-Glycerides of Fatty Acids, Polysorbate 20, Polysorbate 60, Citric Acid Esters of Mono and Di-Glycerides of Fatty Acids, Sodium Dihydrogen Orthophosphate, Agar Gum, Phosphoric Acid and *Beta Carotene*

There were two odds and ends in the ingredients list which seemed inexplicable or incomplete. These were:

Stabiliser (which tells me very little, but reminds me of children's bicycles) and *Flavouring* (which could be any substance on this earth, surely?)

[101] SEE NOTE 95. For Sainsbury's to meet their former director's 2004 pay off, I would have to purchase the items listed in this chapter one hundred and fifty five thousand times. Alternatively, one hundred and fifty five thousand of us could have purchased the above shopping list once from a Sainsbury's supermarket.

HEINZ

Considered honestly, the contribution of Heinz to any diet will always be surprisingly substantial. The characteristic condition of convenience living is a constant stalemate between doing things for yourselves and having *Heinz* do them for you.

Heinz ketchup [102] was introduced in 1876 as a *"Blessed relief for Mother and the other women in the household!"* demonstrating that with humble beginnings, the stretched truths of advertising were here to stay. Henry John Heinz was a marketing master and advertising pioneer. His company had the largest commercial exhibit at the 1893 Chicago World's Fair and in 1900 he erected the first electric sign in New York – a 40-foot pickle. By then Heinz was the largest producer of vinegar in the US, and his ketchup was set to take over the world.

Heinz now sells more than 50% of the ketchup in the US, 48% of the frozen potatoes, 40% of the tuna and over 50% of the diet foods. These are estimate figures which serve to indicate one of this world's greatest love affairs – that between *Man* and *Can*.

Here is where I came on board:

6 x 200g *Weight Watchers from Heinz* baked beans in tomato sauce with sugar and sweetener

5 x 400g tin cans of *Heinz* vegetable soup

5 x 200g *Heinz* baked beans and 4 vegetable sausages [103] (Figure 6)

---

[102] "No fish sauce equal to the following: Ketchup – mustard – cayenne pepper – butter amalgamated on your plate *proprio manu*, each man according to his own proportions. Yetholm ketchup made by gypsies. Mushrooms for ever – damn walnuts!" *Noctes Ambrosianae* with the most obscure of recipe instructions possible.

[103] The vegetarian sausage reflects contemporary taste and feeling. To eat a sausage in virtuous aversion to killing is at last possible to non-vegetarians. WE'RE ALL VEGETARIANS NOW. Meaning that meat-free sausages bring peace to more than just the few Pythagoreans who're interested in such things. Everyone shall benefit!

72

3 x 415g cans of *Heinz* baked beans in tomato sauce

2 x 200g tin cans of *Heinz* baked beans in tomato sauce

2 x 11g (9.2ml) sachets of *Heinz* tomato ketchup [104]

2 slices of toast with approx 80g of *Heinz* baked beans

1 415g *Weight Watchers from Heinz* baked beans in tomato sauce

FIGURE 06 – Heinz baked beans and sausages for those who don't taste meat

180g of *Heinz* low fat mature cheese

1 400g *Heinz* "Special" carrot and ginger soup

1 400g *Heinz* vegetable soup with mixed sprouted beans

---

[104] Heinz tomato ketchup is so ubiquitous that it has created a new human type, for whom place, time and community are global before they are local. You'll see that same ketchup bottle on any table in the world, I'll stake my toms on it.

1 400g *Heinz* cream of tomato [105] soup with three types of sprouted beans

1 395g can of *Heinz* Italian-cheese tortellini [106]

1 400g tinnister of *Heinz* spaghetti hoops in tomato sauce [107]

1 205g tin can of *Heinz* spaghetti hoops in tomato sauce

1 400g tinnister of *Heinz* spaghetti in tomato sauce

1 400g can of *Heinz* macaroni cheese

1 200g tin of *Heinz* macaroni cheese

1 200g *Weight Watchers from Heinz* spaghetti in tomato sauce

2 cups of *Heinz* cream of tomato soup

1 bowl of *Heinz* cream of tomato soup

1 plate of *Heinz* tomato soup with lemon and Worcester sauce and vodka

---

[105] Heinz cream of tomato soup is a food for all time, and states on the label: "This famous soup is adored by families all over the world." It's true! No other tomato soup can touch Heinz, who have perfected their recipe so comprehensively that even fresh tomato soup is a let down. Heinz have been respected ever since their humble beginnings, when they treated their workforce to lunchtime concerts, free manicures and supplied them with a works roof garden. Them was the days all right!

[106] "This can provides 4 weight watchers points."

[107] Buy-one-get-one free. Increased in-store price promotion erodes Burnett's tolerance for Spaghetti Hoops. And his humour. Buy-one-get-one-free used to be known as "BOGOF" – until the joke wore thin.

1 400g can of *Heinz* cream of tomato soup with crème fraiche, sprouted mung beans and Worcester sauce

1 *Ross* [108] "Vegetable Recipes Series" spinach and ricotta cannelloni – described as "*Fresh pasta rolls filled with spinach and ricotta cheese on a bed of tomato sauce, topped with béchamel sauce and sprinkled with vegetarian cheddar cheese and paprika.*"

---

[108] Here's the thing: "Made by H.J. Heinz, Hayes" although Ross is a registered trademark in Ireland. The planet's Food Controllers are not messing about. Financial bunco and double-dooring are common to all enterprise, meaning that we never know who owns what nowadays.

Among others Heinz owns:
Del Monte, HP Foods, Lea & Perrins and Farleys

Among others Unilever owns:
Ben & Jerry's, Bertolli, Colman's, Elmlea, Findus, Flora, Gallo, Lipton's, Marmite, PG Tips, Boursin, Bovril, Blue Band, Brooke Bond, Knorr, JIF, Hellmann's, Pot Noodle, Ragú, Skippy, Slimfast and Scottish Blend

Among others Kraft owns:
Capri Sun, Carte Noire, Côte d'Or, Dairylea, Del Monte (in Canada – see Heinz), Kenco, Maxwell House, Nabisco, Oreo, Oscar Mayer, Ritz, Toblerone

Among others Nestlé owns
Perrier, Nescafé, Carnation, Libby's, Ski, Buitoni, Felix, Aberfoyle Water, Aquarel, Vittel, Milkmaid, Mivvi, Lean Cuisine, Willy Wonka, and a cast of sweeties and chocolates too numerous to mention.

To take an example from the above list, it's easy to see how complicated the straightforward and transparent process of big business really is. Looking for who owns Oreo biscuits, we can see that they are made by Nabisco, owned by Kraft, owned in turn by the world's largest tobacco company, Altria Group (previously named Philip Morris Companies Inc). Proving that it is difficult to lay an Oreo at one single door…

2.2 LITRES OF ALCOHOLIC SPIRIT

A lcohol is a mood-altering depressant drug. It rages in the blood and causes embarrassed gloom and the mounting suspicion that we must have *more*. Alcohol producers have invented a greater amount of drinks than can be properly ordered in one lifetime of drinking, and all of them are capable of driving us into drunkenness, ruin or madness.

It is held that solitary drinking is the preserve of the lonely, escapist, depressed soul. This perhaps is a reasonable enough conclusion, given the despondent motivation behind most mono-imbibers.

However, not every solitary drinker is contemplating suicide, and there are philosophical necessities to be met by drinking alone and if one lives alone it is unavoidable. Deep into the bottle (and consequently, deep into yourself) a weird and wonderful feeling of unity is found. Alcohol is a great social lubricant – and applied on a personal scale, you'll see how solitary drinking can help reach the inner you, the inner joy, the inner madness, and the inner demon we all possess.

This is my list of drinks which contained alcoholic spirit, those known in northern parlance as "Strong Drinks". Over the course of one year, I downed:

15 vodkas with caffeine-free Diet Coke and ice [109]

4 glasses of *Glenmorangie* and tap water [110]

2 *Glenmorangies* with ice and 7-Up[111]

---

[109] Vodka, vodka, by all means, but please don't poison me with caffeine!

[110] After about four drinks the demon will start rumbling and throwing the odd lightning bolt. It is therefore time to allow him to have his say. He'll want to remind you of your triumphs, he'll want to have you reflect upon your failiures and finally he'll challlenge you yet again to stand up for yourself against the world.

[111] This note is intended to divert the attention of those who enjoy Glenmorangie and are angered to see it mixed at all. But where did the name 7-Up come from? There are a handful of theories: 1) There were seven ingredients in the first 7-Up;

1 nut mudslide [112]

1 glass of *Glenfiddich* whisky

1 *Glenfiddich* and ice and water

1 *Glenfiddich* and ice and Diet Coke

5 glasses of *Bell's* whisky and water

5 glasses of *Trenet* premium absinthe and cold tap water [113]

1 50ml bottle of *Johnnie Walker* Black Label old Scotch Whisky [114]

1 275ml bottle of *Glitz* Imperial Lemon Vodka Mixer [115]

350ml of Jack Daniels Old Time Old No.7 Brand Quality Tennessee Sour Mash whiskey in ten measures with Diet Coke and ice.

3 glasses of Morgan's Spiced Rum – *"Righteous True"* / *"Blend of Golden*

---

2) The original 7-Up bottle was seven ounces; 3) The owner saw a cattle brand that looked like "7-Up", and he liked it enough to name his drink after it; 4) The owner named his drink after a popular card game that was also called 7-Up.

[112] A home made cocktail. Vodka, Kalhua, Bailey's and crushed ice – combined with blended nuts instead of cream.

[113] Straplines on a bottle of Absinthe – "Do not drink & drive" / "Spiriteux aux extraits de plantes d'Absinthe" / "Produced and bottled in France" / "60% vol equivalent to 120° US Proof." This drink contained E102 and E133 colours, but also in this mysterious recipe, were wormwood infusion, alcohol, water, natural aroma and sugar. The drink was a parting gift from Eddie Gibbons – who clearly intended that I part with reality for a time.

[114] "Distilled, blended and bottled in Scotland." This was a gift of the distillery, from Marion Macintyre.

[115] Would I drink a bottle of Glitz again? Almost definitely, perhaps not.

Rum, mellow spices and natural flavours" – 1 with pear juice [116] / 1 with water / 1 with Diet Coke

1 250ml *Pimm's and Lemonade*, Nº 1 Ready to Drink, Perfectly Mixed *Pimm's* & Lemonade [117]

3 drams of *Grouse* whisky with tap water

1 50ml gift bottle of Scotch Whisky from *Aberdeen City Council*

4 Pints of *Pimm's* [118] (Figure 07)

FIGURE 07 – Who drinks Pimm's by the pint?

---

[116] RUM & PEAR JUICE. Some initial sickly sweetness that quickly gives way to a perverted peppery nausea and a long lingering sour aftertaste. The drink is decidedly dry on the palate and in a side-by-side comparison with almost any other substance on the planet, there's no question that despite its light body and spritzy citric edge, rum & pear juice is no more than the one-off putrid concoction of a drunk and thus to be avoided.

[117] "1.4 UK Units". This can of ready-mixed Pimm's was a little Christmas present from my love. And so good night, my love, good night.

[118] The PINT OF PIMM'S is a refreshment of my own devising. A tall measure of Pimm's is placed in a pint glass and topped up with lemonade to form a lager-strength fruit cup. Only a Scot could turn Pimm's into lager!

A half pint of *Pimm's*, water and ice

A half glass of *Sambuca* and Diet Coke

1 *Tia Maria* and Diet Coke and ice [119]

1 *Bailey's* "Minis" 70 ml

In this drinks inventory I'm able to offer evidence of the diets of those around me. In the following cases I was merely trying what everyone else was having –

3 glasses of *Remy Martin* brandy

2 *Bombay Sapphire* gins with lemonade and ice

1 *Plymouth* gin and tonic

1 glass of *Balblair* Single Malt

1 *Gordon's* gin and tonic

1 draft of cinnamon brandy [120]

1 *Smirnoff* vodka with Pepsi Max and ice

1 tumbler of vodka and tap water [121]

---

[119] "Only Irish Coffee provides in a single glass all four essential food groups: alcohol, caffeine, sugar and fat." Alex Levine

[120] Liqueur Verino brandy, a present from Greece. The worsted remnants of a drunk's drinks cabinet. "Laughed-at gift liqueurs, reserved for company that never comes." Todd McEwen.

[121] V'n'TW was a favourite late night tipple of Angus Calder and is rather raw; lighter and less rich than the other vodka drinks I have tried.

1 glass of *Macallan* tastes like I don't know how many years old [122]

Half a 700ml bottle of *Isle of Skye* 8 yr old malt [123]

1 triple *Wallace* whisky with tonic water and ice

---

[122] "I let my drinking do the talking." Humphrey Bogart

[123] Here are the traditional Scots instructions for a Christmas cake, involving a bottle of whisky. First, sample the whisky to check quality. Take a large bowl and check the whisky again. To be sure it is of the highest quality, pour one level cup of whisky and drink. Turn on the electric mixer. Beat one cup of butter in a large fluffy bowl. Add one teaspoon of sugar. Make sure the whisky is still OK. Turn off the mixerer. Break 2 leggs and add to the bowl and chuck in the cup of dried fruit. Mix on the turner. Next, sift two cups of salt. Or something. Who cares? Check the whisky. Now sift the lemon juice and strain your nuts. Add one table. Add one spoon of sugar or something. Whatever you can find. Greash the oven. Turn the cake tin round. Throw the bowl through the window. Check the whisky again. Aye and away tae f**uck with you all. All of yous! Ya bas**tards! Sleep.

MOCK MEATS

Over time, textured protein meat substitutes have departed from the early simplicities of vegetarian banger mix and cardboard tasting burgers. Meat eaters may consider this inexpedience of the worst kind, but happily many of us can no longer remember the taste of meat and the bowel sensations thereafter.

No apology need be made. This is in part thanks to a fast expanding market. The variations in today's mock meats are a most encouraging sight. I've been eating these mock meats in the greatest of quantities and thankfully they're now as readily available as commercial pork, industrial beef, and profit chicken.

Mock meats are the stuff of great science. Meat eating is the stuff of great horror. Time will tell who will be the healthier. It may be the animal eaters, digesting the hand reared produce of the organic flocks; or it may be the vegetarians, with their factory science projects. [124]

In one year I ate all of these mock meats:

8 *Linda McCartney* vegetarian sausages with nothing on them

4 *Linda McCartney* sausages and ketchup

2 *Linda McCartney* sausages in a roll with ketchup

2 *Cauldron* succulent vegetarian Lincolnshire sausages

2 vegetarian hot dog sandwiches with mustard

1 vegetarian hot dog sandwich with cheese

---

[124] For his 1957 PhD at MIT, Aaron Brody built a robotic chewing machine that measured the amount of pressure on the teeth generated by chewing a particular food. This provided the first data of its kind and "sparked a new science of food texture," he says – and *chewiness* (as in bread), *crispness* (as in potato chips) and *slickness* (as in ice cream) thereafter became official elements of taste.

FIGURE 08 – Chicken style nuggets complete the vegetarian diet

9 *Safeway* vegetarian chicken style soya pieces (200g) (Figure 08)

2 x 150g each *Tesco* vegetarian creamy pepper escalopes

3 x 114g *Wicken Fen* gourmet meat free quarter pound burgers – *"Made with cereals, herbs, seasoning and vegetable protein"*

2 muffins with vegetarian Lincoln sausage, tomato sauce and mayonnaise

1 *Quorn* ™ pieces in sweet and sour sauce with oriental rice, water chestnuts and bamboo shoots

1 large helping of shepherd's pie made with seared vegetarian burger [125]

1 *Linda McCartney* Country Pie with mashed potato and baked beans

240g of *Safeway* vegetarian chicken – *"Chopped, shaped and lightly seasoned textured vegetable protein in a crispy batter coated with golden breadcrumbs"*

---

[125] This Tesco vegetarian burger was cosmetically treated with "sear" marks to make it look as if it had just been plucked from the slow fire of a barbecue.

AMAZING GRAZE

My pretended ignorance of global food practice is just one reason for the ensuing altercations I have with my conscience. The other reason is my outrage at the suggestion that I should be told what to consume. Surely the end cannot be long delayed? Past experience dictates that the pendulum shall swing when it reaches the furthest point of its arc and when this happens I'll start to eat sensibly with good regard for both myself and the 4 billion others with whom I share the global trough.

1 bowl of mashed turnip

1 dried organic mango slice

1 ½ slices of sultana cake

1 *Tunnocks* caramel wafer [126]

2 x *Rice Crispies* Squares, chewy marshmallow biscuit

1 slice of Gouda cheese

1 slice of Len Wilson's sponge, fruit and icing birthday cake

1 slice of Graham MacQuarrie's chocolate birthday cake

3 slices of Derek Slater's leaving cake [127]

---

[126] As many of you know wafers are subject to a great deal of controversy and debate. But churchgoers be silent. When covered in chocolate wafers can no longer be used for communion and become fun biscuits in their own right. The Tunnock's claim is that "More than 4,000,000 of these biscuits are made and sold each week" – something like 6.6 wafers per second. It's religious.

[127] Food is a mixture of everything: economy, grief, joy, trade, love, policy, celebration and work. There is little in the world that is not represented by way of food.

3 slices of sultana cake and spread

3 x 288ml cartons of *Ribena* "Light", all featuring the *"Win a Donkey"* promotion

40 (= 600g) of *Patersons* bran oatcakes [128]

3 glasses of *Orangina* [129] and ice

2 x 500ml bottles of *Orangina*

1 330 ml can of *Orangina*

200ml of maple syrup of *Medium Rene*, Cossette, Haliburton, Ontario – *"Sirop D'erable Pur"* [130] (Figure 09)

FIGURE 09 – The jar of maple syrup was shaped like a maple leaf

---

[128] Here is a message from Paterson's – "A new pack design has been launched to help convey the oatcake's versatility. The pack design also helps to introduce the product to a younger audience without neglecting our duty to the mixture of ages currently purchasing Paterson's oatcakes." Fast food has broken so many identity-forming connections and made local foods so unimportant that Paterson's now package oatcakes hoping to appeal to a poppy, teenage consumer.

[129] This is what it says: "Shake the bottle! Wake the taste!"

[130] This syrup was a gift from Rabbi Lori Cohen. I am afraid to say that the entire 200ml was drunk from the neck of the bottle, by myself, while waiting for the kettle to boil, shower to heat up, postman to arrive etc. I like maple syrup and as with peanut butter, consider it as a seperate foodstuff to be enjoyed rather than as an accompanier.

1 25cl bottle of *James White* organic apple and crushed ginger drink

1 11g sachet of *Options* Outrageous Orange instant hot chocolate drink

2 pieces of old and cold garlic bread [131]

125g of Organic Vegetarian Banger Mix from *Just Wholefoods* – "*A mixture of organic ingredients for a delicious meat-free Banger, gently seasoned with organic herbs*". I added water to the mix with spring onions and chives, and I made burgers, being unable to fashion the "banger" shape.

1 slice of strawberry cheesecake and single cream

1 cheese, tomato and pepper sandwich with ready salted Hula Hoops on the side brought by Mrs SK at a time of crisis.

1 160g *Co-op* Classic Cheese & Spring Onion sandwich – "*cheddar cheese and red Leicester with Mayonnaise and spring onion on buttered malted bread.*" See note 56 to decide whether a sandwich can be a "classic".

1 200ml carton of *Sunpride* pure apple juice – "*Capture the flavour*" [132]

12 oat & chive biscuits from *House of Bruar* [133]

100g of *Co-op* goat's cheese rolled in black pepper

---

[131] Upon reflection, I think I may have been wrong to eat these. Contamination by exposure must not be underestimated. With each passing hour, the food in the world becomes less edible.

[132] The imperative mood of verb inflection often features in food marketing slogans. Here it is unclear if the instruction is addressed to the manufacturer or consumer.

[133] House of Bruar is one of Scotland's greatest and most remote luxury food outlets. Situated in a curve of the A9 highway at Blair Atholl, Bruar's oaken, battle-hardened face draws traffic from the road and sells the choicest of Scots produce.

100g of *Co-op* garlic and herb soft cheese roule

1 28g *Tunnock's* Caramel Log [134]

2 glasses of iced spring water

1 fresh fruit and nut smoothie [135]

4 x *Bachelor's* tomato and vegetable Cup-a-Soup granules with croutons made up with hot water

1 *Cream o' Galloway* single serving tub of Sticky Toffee Luxury Dairy Ice Cream – *"Simply natural"*

1 taste of hard French cheese described as *plus fort* [136]

1 *O'Brien's* salad with lettuce, tomato, coleslaw and grated cheddar

---

[134] Tunnock's have a new catch phrase: "Crunchie biscuit - Munchie caramel". Meaning what? Munch is a surprisingly old word, with origins in the 14th century *monche*. A munchie however is a craving for food, induced by alcohol or drugs. Caramel (burnt sugar with butter added) is perfect for the quick needs of the addict. Note the difference between this *munchie*, and the descriptor, *munchy*.

[135] And what, people, is a SMOOTHIE? A smoothie is a cold beverage that mixes fruit and juice in a blender and depends on a banana to give it its texture. Originally, the smoothie was created in California where it was used as a healthy, non-dairy alternative to milkshakes, although many recipes for drinks called smoothies are found in Mediterranean and Middle Eastern Cuisine, typically using yoghurt and honey as well as fruit. As a complete aside, a smoothie is also the term used to describe an acomoclitic naturist – *acomoclitic* referring to those who have a preference for hairless genitals.

[136] You must understand that the French take food very seriously and the Michelin rankings are of critical importance to this. People fuss over the details of the silverware in their restaurant in order to move from two stars to three. To gain three stars, a restaurant must not only have truly exceptional food but also must have ambience to match. In fact, a three-star restaurant must be like a total immersion into the mind of the chef, who must be basted continuously in praise.

Half a chocolate pastry – burned to chewy by myself in a microwave oven

1 litre of *Oatly* – "*More than just a drink*" / "*Just oats, water and rapeseed oil*" [137]

1 *Scottish Slimmers* "Positi✓e Eating" cheese crunch on oatmeal bread sandwich [138]

Half an angel cake with pastry cream and jam from the Dunbar Bakery, Dunbar

3 slices of watermelon

7 cloves of garlic [139]

1 and a half litres of *Fuente Liviana* spring water

1 rock bun from Auntie Sheila

12 (= 200g) *Co-op* chocolate chunk & hazelnut cookies

2 slices of hard Spanish goat's cheese

1 sliver of melted goat's cheese

2 knobs of cheddar cheese

---

[137] Oatly is a drink that is milky in texture – although the udder of Oatly is oats.

[138] Luckily the enterprising trolley dude who flogs these things to us workers drops the price to a quid after 3pm.

[139] I chewed on the raw garlic. Brillat-Savarin (the historic authority on taste) notes that taste is the only human sense that requires all other four senses, i.e., the touch on the lips, tongue and palate; the colour and smell; and even the hearing – because the cord of the tympanum contains fibres conveying the sense of taste to the brain. A hail of garlic and I lay down to savour it, my senses dead to the world.

1 chocolate-topped crispie

1 custard slice of the *Masterpiece Bakery* Edinburgh

I had settled into a steady run of epulation, [140] a herbivority that served me well. Even trying to tip the scales with a visit to the *Masterpiece Bakery* did not affect the good results of my deglutition.

---

[140] APHAGIA – The inability to eat or swallow;

COMPOTATION – The act of drinking in company;

DEGLUTITION – The act of swallowing;

EPULATION – The act of feasting;

GLOSSOPHAGINE – One who eats using the tongue;

GUSTATION – The act of tasting or the faculty of taste;

HYPERPHAGIA – Eating too much;

INGURGITATION – The act of swallowing food;

MANDUCATION – The act of chewing;

OMOPHAGY – The eating of raw food;

PANTOPHAGY – The habit or power of eating;

PHYTOPHAGY – The act of feeding on plants;

PICA – Abnormal food craving, often among pregnant women;

POLTOPHAGY – Excessive chewing of food;

PSOMOPHAGY – Swallowing food without thorough chewing;

REGALEMENT – The provision of choice or abundant food and drink.

PROPER MEALS

Here are some of the occasions when I sat at the table and ate a meal, as opposed to making passing grabs at crisps and scones.

4 plates of penne pasta with courgette, pepper and tomato sauce with grated Parmesan

13 sprigs of *La Catalina* brand *"Jet Fresh Imported"* [141] asparagus with melted butter and grated Parmesan

1 slice of plain quiche with herbs, 5 boiled new potatoes and mangetout

1 slice of plain quiche and mashed potato

1 slice of plain quiche with herbs, with 4 boiled new potatoes and leek in cream and white wine sauce

3 helpings of penne pasta with pesto and mustard

3 plates of carrot and celeriac gratin

2 portions of feta, onion and cherry tomato [142] salad with mashed potato and boiled egg

2 plates of penne pasta plus pesto

---

[141] "Jet Fresh" is a most thrilling food descriptor I have read in this age of hysteria. Origin: Sociedad Agricola Drokasa, South Africa.

[142] How do they make those adorable cherry tomatoes? They carry out the following genetic modifications: 1) The plant is modified in order to be resistant to the Monsanto herbicides so that farmers can kill weeds without killing the seedling and 2) The plant is modified to contain in its genetic structure a further pesticide called Bt (Bacillus Thuringiensis). Tasty, and nothing to do with miniaturisation of foods. I am still: does this not raise questions about the use of pesticides in the first instance? Or is it usual to create the cure before the disease?

12 new potatoes and 1 red onion roasted in olive oil and red wine vinegar

1 roasted mini-Camembert with pine nuts and chives

1 portion of spinach and ricotta ravioli with red pepper sauce

1 bowl of pasta with cream and Amethyst Deceiver and Field Blewit mushrooms [143]

3 tortillas with refried beans, lettuce, tomato, grated mature cheddar, natural yoghurt and salsa sauce [144]

4 wraps with refried beans, lettuce, tomato, grated mature cheddar, natural yoghurt and salsa sauce

1 400g *Co-op "Meal Solutions"* [145] series Vegetable Jalfrezi [146]

---

[143] Edible wild mushrooms. The *Deceiver* was an almost luminous violet colour, with a felty cap; while the *Blewit* had a pale beige cap, was much larger, with a contrasting lilac stem. Picked in Roslyn Glen, Lasswade.

[144] Is the idea of ethnic food an insult? As if everyone in Mexico wears sombreros and eats this for dinner? When the Spanish conquistadors arrived in the Aztec capital of Tenochtitlan, they found people eating corn-based dishes of chillies and herbs. Other indigenous foods included beans, squashes, chocolate, avocados, peanut, turkey and vanilla. Over time the Spanish added pork, chicken, beef, wine, garlic and onions to this mix – while trying their best to weed out such *comida prehispanica* (prehispanic food) as iguana, rattlesnake, deer and spider monkey.

[145] Food is so well labelled now. A "Meal Solution" therefore is appropriate when circumstances exile you from the tiny island of *Cooking for Yourself* and onto the vast continent of *Ready-Meals*.

[146] Cockney Rhyming Slang comes with several chicken options, including Chicken Jalfrezi, meaning *crazy*. Other chicken slang includes Chicken and Rice, meaning *nice*; Chicken Curry, meaning *worry*, (as in "Don'cha chicken curry"); Chicken Dinner, meaning *winner*, (as in "Everyone's a chicken dinner, baby"); Chicken Dippers, meaning *slippers*, (as in "Be a doll and warm me chickens by the fire"); and Chicken Oriental, as in *mental*, ("Burnett is pure flaming chicken oriental – ")

2 servings of nut roast with puy lentils and carrots

1 serving of puy lentils with carrots and chilli relish

2 servings of vegetable ravioli in cream of tomato sauce

1 plate of spaghetti, garlic and chilli pepper

2 portions of vegetable lasagne

4 roasted peppers in garlic

1 portion of boiled rice

1 coriander, lettuce & tomato salad

1 bowl of parsnip soup with coriander

1 *Marks & Spencer* vegetable Kiev served with salad

1 portion of pasta bake with cheese

1 plate of pasta, tomato sauce and Parmesan

1 plate of steamed English asparagus and butter

1 plate of raw vegetable soup and 2 sticks of celery

1 pepper and 1 Dutch tomato roasted in olive oil, Parmesan and mascarpone with 3 carrots, served with lettuce

Am I still alive?

*There just seem to be so many items
here of no food value*

A NOTE ON PACKAGING

Packaging is the only deciding factor when a shopper picks a product from the shelf (usually). Sadly, by law anything that is written on packaging about a food must be true. Here are some (therefore) true statements which you will find written on products in *The Supper Book.*

"Solves all your problems" – DR PEPPER

"The UK's best cheddar" – MCLELLAND

"The true taste of the Americas" – DISCOVERY TORTILLAS

"Part of your world" – STORCK

"The heart of a good night out" – SAN MIGUEL

The packaging of food ought to keep the product fresh and safe, provide statutory information, and also entertain. In general, food packaging will include Product Description / Photographic Representation / Weight / Nutritional Data / Ingredients List / Cooking Instructions / The All-Important Product Claims.

Many of the above product claims are listed in *The Supper Book*, as additional notes, eg,

1 litre of *Oatly* – *"More than just a drink"* / *"Just oats, water and rapeseed oil"*

By law, manufacturers must not print any information *on the food itself,* presumably so that the evidence is never eaten. But how would *Oatly* taste if I didn't know that I was drinking *"More than just a drink?"* It would probably taste like a blend of water, oats and rapeseed oil, and I would probably be depressed. I could be drinking *more* than a drink after all.

In total, packaging consists of elements brought together to portray the image decided upon by the food's producing company, while imparting both true and selectively true information. Packaging will incorporate colour, artwork and information, and may allow a glimpse of the food through a packaging window. Some of the most enduring images we have ever seen have been on food and drink packaging. I recall my own favourite, the Kellogg's cornflakes cockerel, slightly bristling with an indefinable air of superiority.

On packaging we also find surreal instructions, which conform to no legal or philosophical norm. The best example of this is found on the packaging of nuts, which tend to carry the warning that the product *contains* nuts. There have been other absurdities over the years, including the following:

Do not turn upside down. (Printed on the bottom of the box.)
TESCO'S TIRAMISU DESSERT

Product will be hot after heating.
MARKS & SPENCER BREAD PUDDING

Why not try tossing over your favourite breakfast cereal?
ON A PACKET OF SUN-MAID RAISINS

ILLUSTRATED BISCUITS

The following biscuits were pretty enough to merit my drawing them. It is likely that these biscuits would have been pushed into my mouth more quickly had they been unattractive, proving that for the purposes of natural selection, the beautiful last longer and are more likely to impress those that wish to consume them.

First there was the tempting tube biscuit with its funny funnel form:

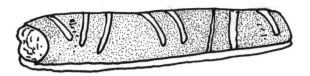

Then there were 2 chocolate wafers, which I dipped in milky coffee:

There were 3 coffee and caramel biscuits, crisp and crumbly:

Then I found 2 white chocolate biscuits with Deli-Choc logo which some folks declare unclean, and look at askant:

Then there were 2 chocolate shortbreads, which reminded me that chocolate and shortbread do not mix:

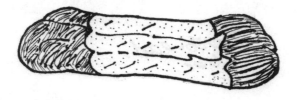

After that there was 1 dark chocolate biscuit with Deli-Choc logo – a straight-dealing biscuit. And lastly, 1 milk chocolate biscuit with Deli-Choc logo – neither of which are illustrated.

This was a group of the most enticing biscuits ever to grace the plate.

HENS' EGGS

B ecause they preceded men in the evolutionary chain, both eggs and birds have been around longer than we have. This means that there is little that can intelligently be said concerning the origins of either.

Cooked eggs feature most often at breakfast, although it is boggling to consider where else eggs are included in the diet. I suspect for example that eggs contributed to my countless ready-made meals. I also suspect that our factories use yolks and egg whites in ways that would baffle the average vegan into submission.

Is there anything that the egg cannot symbolise? According to the teaching of Orphic Cults, God shaped the initial mass of creation in the form of an egg from which all things proceeded. Central European peasants rubbed eggs on their ploughs hoping to improve the crops and newlywed French brides broke eggs on their doorsteps to ensure a large family.

My own family once followed the long-standing model of egg production. Before the 1940's, most eggs were produced by small flocks that scratched their way around the farmyard. My grandmother – as the other farmers' wives – supervised the egg laying operation and the money received from the sale of the eggs was hers alone.

It is a no-wise too florid figure to say that *eggs are everything.*

"A hen is only an egg's way of making another egg."
Samuel Butler

"The vulgar boil, the learned roast, an egg."
Alexander Pope

"I did toy with the idea of doing a cook-book... I think a lot of people who hate literature but love fried eggs would buy it if the price was right."
Groucho Marx

"Probably one of the most private things in the world is an egg until it is broken."
MFK Fisher

97

Favourite egg jokes include:

How can you drop an egg six feet without breaking it?
By dropping it seven feet – it won't break for the first six.

How does a witch make scrambled eggs?
She holds the pan and gets two friends to make the stove shake with fright.

Why did the chicken lay an egg?
Because it would have broken if she'd dropped it.

All of my eggs came from the *Co-op Freedom Food* range. This year I ate:

16 fried eggs

7 boiled eggs (2 with salt)

3 poached eggs

2 fried eggs on toast

1 boiled egg on toast

1 plate of scrambled eggs

1 portion of scrambled eggs on toast

What is the *Co-op Freedom Food* range? The title is suggestive of an easy conscience, or the hope of one. [147] Anybody might call themselves *free*, just as any product may claim that it promotes liberty. Who's to doubt it?

---

[147] The implications are fairly serious – there's food out there that's tainted by unethical production. Either people, or animals, or the natural environment are damaged. The fact that foods are marketed with the descriptor FREEDOM is a sure sign that our guilt is in fact less digestible than imagine.

"I'VE EATEN ALL THE CRISPS"

To think that the crisp is elevated to a food form in its own right is bad enough – but now their variable appearance and taste is such that there will always be a crisp out there for you. If there is not a crisp out there for you, then I imagine it will soon be invented.

We have begun manufacturing on an immense scale foods that are guaranteed not to nourish. Is this a collective suicide or a disease of affluence? The idea of nutrition is dominated by the dichotomy that food that is good, *is not good for you*, and food that is not good, *is good for you*. The gross contradiction is too great.

It's now seen how the odd pack of crisps here and there is readily translated into a multitude of snacks. Regard and you'll see *I've had my bags* –

CRISP	TONNAGE
1 bag of Yoghurt & Green Onion *Kettle Chips*	25g
1 bag of Salt and Vinegar *Monster Munch*	55g
1 bag of Lightly Salted *Kettle Chips*	50g
2 bags of Worcester Sauce flavour *Wheat Crunchies*	68g
1 bag of Crispy Bacon [148] flavour *Wheat Crunchies*	34g

---

[148] "Unless you be a Mahometan you have certainly more than once eaten pig, but in your delight in its flesh, have you ever happened to think through what Odyssey has passed this unfortunate animal before being transformed?" In *Le Cochon* of 1808, Alfred Le Petit described the exact process of porcicide by illustration and text.

1 bag of Crispy Bacon flavoured *Wheat Crunchies* [149]	50g
2 bags of *Golden Wonder* Rib 'n' Sauce Flavour *Nik Naks*	68g
3 bags of *Golden Wonder* Scampi 'n' Lemon flavour *Nik Naks* [150]	102g
1 bag of *Golden Wonder* Barbecue Sauce flavour *Nik Naks*	34g
1 bag of Nice 'n' Spicy flavour *Nik Naks*	34g
1 bag of *Co-op* mini popadoms	55g
4 35g bags of Spicy Tomato flavour *Wheat Crunchies*	140g
1 bag of Prawn Cocktail flavour *Walkers Quavers* [151]	25g
1 bag of Cheese flavour *Walkers Quavers*	25g

---

[149] "Crunchy wheat tubes with sugar and sweetener." No other country produces such a variety of crisps as the UK. With scores of crisps to choose from there will always be some confusion – even a native Briton cannot hope to know them all, and will continually shop for new ones, like it or not.

[150] The comfort supplied by these "Knobbly sticks of corn" may be irrelevant when concidering the health problems of eating too many of them. This points to a deeper dispute about the nature and the destiny of our species – *to fry and die, or to live in greens?*

[151] "The light potato snack" / "Potato snack with sweetener" / "This is a pack from Walkers Multipack and must not be sold separately."

1 bag of Really Cheesy flavour *Walkers Wotsits* corn puffs [152]	34g
1 bag of *Walkers* Spicy Tandoori Masala flavour *Poppadom Bites* [153]	35g
1 bag of *Walkers* Ready Salted crisps *aka* "The Big Eat"	55g
1 bag of Barbecue Beef *Hula Hoops* [154]	27g
1 bag of *Walkers Squares,* Salt and Vinegar Flavour Potato Snack [155]	25g
3 and a half bags of Salt and Vinegar *Discos*	98g
1 bag of *Tesco* plain popadoms "*Authentic Indian Snack*"	60g

---

[152] Nature is a single enterprise. It should therefore be a matter of pride for us all, and perhaps a cause for celebration, that the cheese Wotsits in this bag were sold with the claim that they were the "Best Ever."

[153] "Light and crispy bite size poppadoms in delicious flavours" The poppadom is also known as The South Asian Wafer, and is typically made from lentil or chickpea flour. These are also known as: papadam / pappadom / poppadam / papad / papar and appalum.

[154] Strap lines include – "Get a load of them" and "Beef it up!"

[155] "As square as you like". "Squares" used to have the great novelty name Square Crisps. I think many of us still use this name not knowing that the product has in fact been rebranded. "Squares" are still a marvellous example of public taste being diverted into previously unheard of snack enterprises.

1 bag of Ready Salted "original" *Hula Hoops* [156]	34g
1 bag of *Walkers* Ready Salted crisps [157]	34g
1 handful of Lightly Salted *Kettle Chips*	–
1 bag of *Walkers* Gently Infused Lime and Thai Spices flavour crisps	40g
4 bags of Barbecue Beef flavour *Hula Hoops*	136g
1 bag of unidentified loose Chilli Crackers [158]	70g
3 bag of Salt & Vinegar flavour *Hula Hoops* [159]	102g
2 bag of Bacon & Ketchup flavour *Hula Hoops*	68g
1 bag of *Osem* BBQ flavoured "B'sili" Crisp Hoops	40g

---

[156] Original hoops? It is comforting to observe manufacturers taking direct steps to address the issues that concern crisp eaters.

[157] As far as I can see, crisps will never cease. Kettle Chips have released an ale falvoured crisp and Walkers Monster Munch has been made available in vanilla ice-cream flavour. Both of these crisps have been developed in order that indulgences may be combined. Mintel estimated in 2006 that British people eat a tonne of crisps each three minutes.

[158] "Produce of several countries" – International Co-operation!

[159] Hula Hoop is a trademark, not of these crisps, but of the hip-wiggling ring of plastic.

A handful of ridged crisps   —

42 (loose!) Sour Cream and   —
Chive *Pringles*

1 bag of Cantonese Black Bean   24g
and Spring Onion crackers [160]

1 bag of Thai Sweet Chilli crisps [161]   40g

1 helping of *Walkers* Peking Spare   12g
Rib and Five-Spice crackers

1 bag of *Walkers Sensations* ®   40g
Chargrilled Steak and Peppercorn
Sauce flavoured crisps [162]

1 bag of *Smiths* ® Scampi Fries [163]   27g

---

[160] Black bean and spring onion crackers do not count towards your five portions of fruit and veg a day, for the simple reason that this product contains only tiny quantities of both. Since 2003, the British Department of Health has been mercilessly nagging the population of the United Kingdom to eat 5 portions of fruit and vegetables per day, and have created logos, portion indicators, local initiatives and school schemes to this end. Health ministers stunned the public shortly after this scheme began when they announced that the potato was not a vegetable, an assertion which had to be revised when they opened a dictionary to find out that it was. Potatoes were excluded because spuds provide mainly carbohydrate in the form of starch, and ministers feared that the public would follow their advice by eating five bags of crisps or chips per day.

[161] Opening the packet revealed a weird sour smell, something akin to mild vinegar and stale meat. I almost want to say it was like a freshly douched pork chop. But I won't. Why? Because I ate the crisps just the same.

[162] "All the best of a well-seared succulent steak is perfectly complimented with a creamy and slightly tangy black pepper sauce." One of the most intricate descriptions of a crisp I have come across.

[163] "Cereal snack with a delicious lemon taste." Because crisps are our weakness, we are willing to accept their manufacturers' claims that they are delicious!

1 bag of *Walkers Sensations* ®   34g
Poppadom Bites, Creamy Chicken
Pasanda and Coriander flavour. [164]

1 bag of *McCoys* [165] Thai   50g
Sweet Chicken flavour crisps

FIGURE 10 – The football themed packaging of McCoy's curry potato chips

---

[164] Due to the low moisture content and the puffed structure of the mini poppadom, the crispness factor is high. But a mini-poppadom is strictly speaking NOT A CRISP even though there is a combined relation between the two. These interrelations between crisps and poppadoms add more complexity to the taxonomy of starchy snack systems and one must resort to MELT VISCOSITY in order to properly differentiate the two. The melt viscosity of a mini-poppadom will be higher than that of *any* given crisp.

[165] "If you thought McCoy's thick potato chips couldn't get any better, think again" Many of our nation's thinkers were caught out on this one!

1 bag of *McCoy's* Chinese Sizzling Beef flavour potato chips (Figure 10)	50g
2 bags of *Golden Wonder* Prawn Cocktail crisps	50g
1 *Walkers* Ready Salted crisp	–
1 bag of *Walkers* Salt & Vinegar crisps	25g
8 rosemary snack breads	–
1 bag of *Walkers* Worcester Sauce crisps [166]	34g
1 bag of *Golden Wonder* Sausage and Tomato flavour crisps [167]	34g
3 bags of *Golden Wonder Heinz* Tomato Ketchup flavour crisps	104g
16 *Penn State* Salt and Vinegar pretzels	–
8 Salsa and Mesquite *Kettle Chips*	–

[166] "Our three way protective packaging locks in Walkers freshness." The current three phases in the evolution of crisps are as follows: 1) New flavours are borrowed from popular carry-out meals; 2) Claims are made in relation to standards of preparation, the Holy Grail being the descriptor "Hand-cooked" – with great potential and responsibility being unfairly heaped on to the word "Natural"; 3) Lately, we have been concerned that our crisps have not been fresh enough when we eat them – so now they're fancy foil-wrapped!

[167] This bag of crisps came with the following catchy pack quote, which I reproduce in full – "They [the potatoes] are lightly peeled to help retain their goodness and cooked in sunflower oil to bring you a crisp that's lower (compared to Golden Wonder crisps sold prior to July 2003) in saturated fat."

2 and a quarter tubes of Texas Barbecue Sauce [168] *Pringles*	225g
8 *Shikar* mini popadoms	–
1 Ready Salted crisp [169]	–
4 Ready Salted crisps from a work colleague	–
4 handfuls of Spicy Chilli *Kettle Chips*	–
2 paprika crisps	–
1 Lightly Salted *Kettle Chip*	–
The pickings of Eddie Gibbons' crisps in the Bow Bar	–
1 canister of Sour Cream and Onion *Pringles*	17g
1 bag of *Walkers* Chargrilled Steak flavour crinkle crisps	40g
1 bag of *Walkers* Tomato Sauce flavour crisps	34g

---

[168] Marketeers pay so little attention to what they write. Texas Barbecue Sauce flavoured Pringles come in the "Taste the World" series – as if scores of colourful and delicate national embellishments can be included in something as base as a crisp. Compare also to the following – "Taste the World-Series." What would *that* be like?

[169] The real heroes are the Irish crisp company TAYTO who developed a technology to add seasoning to crisps in the 1950s. After trial and error, TAYTO produced the world's first seasoned crisps, "Cheese and Onion" and "Salt 'n' Vinegar". This world-shatteringly simple innovation, like Oppenheimer's work in nuclear physics, brought about from simple science the potential to destroy the planet.

1 bag of *Golden Wonder* Ready Salted crisps [170]	25g
1 bag of Lightly Salted *Kettle Chips*	150g
2 tubes of Sour Cream and Onion *Pringles*	200g

With allowances made for crumbs, human error, crisps behind teeth, crisps lost to the wind and miscalculated bags, the crisp tonnage for the year was 2.8 kg.

The truth is that the only people who know how many crisps they've eaten are those that don't eat any crisps at all. It's those fortunate people of iron will (or absolute penury) that don't have to worry about eating undue amounts of monosodium glutamate, tartrazine, sodium inosinate or any of the processed cheese powders made from animal rennet.

Walkers are worth singling out, especially since their spokesmen said that in 2001 they sold enough crisps to cover the whole surface area of Holland – an image I'm sure the Dutch cherish. For the Food Commission's Greedy Star award in 2003, parents criticised pop and sports stars who had used their status to promote fatty, sugary and salty foods to children. The band S Club 7 was nominated for their support of *Sunny Delight*, as was Britney Spears for promoting *Pepsi*. The winner however was Gary Lineker's promotion of *Walkers* crisps, whose management company defended his actions with a statement saying that "crisps are a useful source of energy and form part of a balanced diet alongside food such as vegetables and fruit."

It's statements such as these that remind me why I wrote *The Supper Book*. I love the ease with which we can agree with a statement, because we know that nothing in the great world of printed claims is verifiable.

---

[170] The waiter brings you a long skewer. The skewer sways gently from the weight of a bag of crisps impaled on its tip. The tip of the skewer and the crisps are at the level of your mouth, bobbing up and down. The waiter asks you, nicely, to eat the crisps without using your hands. Only then do you realise what an animal crisps have made of you.

KOMBUCHA

Kombucha drink is a symbiotic colony of yeast and bacteria, combined with black tea and sugar and fermented for seven to ten days. The culture has been known for thousands of years and is a rubbery jelly, browny yellow in colour. Kombucha is used as a healthcare supplement and is also known as *Godly Tsche, Grib, Olinka, Tea Mould, Sakwaska, Lingzhi, Japanese Sponge, Russian Jelly, Indian Wine Fungus* and *Fungojapon* – among many other names.

Kombucha tastes of lightly sparkling pear juice. It is also self sufficient with organic acids, low alcoholic content and carbonic acid blocking the development of foreign micro-organisms. [171] The use of this drink spread eastwards after World War One with Russian and German POWs figuring in its dissemination. The fungal disk [172] from which the drink brews, constantly multiplies through germinating and thickens in the tea – like an alien life from – making Kombucha a science fiction food, despite its having ancient origins.

The Kombucha drink is unusual but is not of the spiritual order. Having a physical organism the culture learns to live with you on a friends-only basis. Each disk of Kombucha is a miniature bio-chemical factory, while you are the harvesting god of the kitchen shelf.

Some may know of Kombucha from the biography of the Nobel Prize author Aleksandr Solzhenitsyn, who was diagnosed as having cancer in 1952 and fully recovered at the hospital in Tashkent in 1953. Like other Kombucha advocates, Solzhenitsyn subscribed to the popular belief that drinking Kombucha discourages the formation of cancer, that it prolongs life and heals arthritis, blocked arteries, constipation, joint and back pains – among many other health benefits.

This year I drank 66 glasses of Kombucha

---

[171] Ruth 2:14 – "Come over here and eat some bread and dip your morsel into the vinegar drink." In this passage, Ruth offers a beverage that has been prepared with the micro-organisms of lactic acid.

[172] The fungal disk is a gelatinoid mushroom-web membrane. It is alive and has a frightening tendency to grow skin. I was left alone with a kombucha culture in a turret room for several dark nights. I was sure the fungus was moving about the room in the early hours.

GRAZING THROUGHOUT THE DAY

We think of the four food groups and our three square meals a day, but there is no need for either number. Many of us have taken up a half-now, half-later diet, eating up to six times a day. When it comes to grouping foods and their goodness, the public focus, although often a little skewed, is on macronutrients, as opposed to the traditional categories of dairy / meat / fruit and veg – with foods being split into protein, fat and the current enemy of the people – carbohydrate. There's much to be gained from torching your allegiance to the three square meals a day, and I refer to it as "spreading the nutrient load." As far as health goes there are too many uncontrolled factors to say that any one practice – such as snacking – is bad for you.

250g *Co-op* potato salad

250g *Co-op* coleslaw

1 large apple stewed in cinnamon, sugar, syrup and raisins

3 bran scones with strawberry jam [173]

4 new potatoes in coriander with Dijon mustard

A half litre of bottled water

2 glasses of mango juice

4 wafer biscuits

4 slices of Jarlsberg cheese

---

[173] Fortification with jam can sometimes negatively alter the flavour of a scone. Jam is never best when added at low concentrations. In blander-tasting scones with less sugar and flavourings in their formulas, a coating of jam is helpful in concealing this lack.

A bit of a scone that had fallen on the floor of the office [174]

1 *O'Brien's* chocolate caramel shortbread

4 Rich Tea biscuits

2 toasted teacakes and butter

1 donut with berry jam interior

Half a chocolate farl

1 275ml bottle of *Britvic* J20 apple and mango flavour juice

1 plate of strawberry cheesecake flavour ice cream

7 raw carrots

1 cabbage [175]

3 bruschetta topped with Parmesan cheese

2 pieces (or slices? or servings?) of bruschetta

2 oatcakes with butter and cheddar

1 egg cress and salad sandwich on brown bread

1 *Jordan Valley* chick pea and onion pie

---

[174] "There was no time to sweep the floor till evening, and we slithered about in a compound of soapy water, lettuce-leaves, torn paper and trampled food." *Down and Out in Paris and London* by George Orwell.

[175] For two days I ate steamed cabbage for lunch and dinner. Highly esteemed by both ancient Roman and Greek civilisations, the cabbage is not mentioned in the Bible and so may have been unknown to the Hebrews.

500g of *Cockburn* delicatessen sunflower seeds

1 bowl of wild mushroom soup [176]

1 section of chocolate cake with chocolate fingers

4 oatcakes and Camembert

1 scone with cream and jam

1 cream cheese and chive sandwich

1 cup of vegetable soup

1 portion of cabbage salad

5 cups of hempseed milk [177]

4 oatcakes and Port Salut cheese

A slice of tortilla

1 *Quorndon Muffin Company* chocolate orange muffin

1 slice of plain cheesecake with strawberry and fromage frais [178]

1 portion of avocado and cherry tomato salad

---

[176] So much of this food was prepared by Mr DF, who picked the mushrooms themselves, before souping them in his castle kitchen.

[177] Hemp seeds soaked and blended to make a boosting drink. There is always a suspicion that hemp seeds will suddenly adopt the narcotic powers of their budding flowers and plunge those who eat them beyond the flux of time and the divisions of space, to a state of mind beyond all imagination and thought. It has never happened.

[178] Aberdonian Jokes – "Where's that fromage frais?" Also, "What's that Roquefort?" (TF)

FIGURE 11 – The Gille ginger biscuit. I ate 52 of these during my four-week exposure to them.

52 biscuits of *Gille* of Sweden (Figure 11)

2 slices toasted rye bread with sour cream and chive mix

1 baked potato in skin with butter

1 portion of pineapple and kumquat in fromage frais

3 glasses water and *Belvoir* passion fruit flavoured cordial

3 baked celery hearts [179]

A half an egg and cheese omelette

1 slice of strawberry cheesecake

---

[179] Arrange the celery hearts on a dish in an interesting pattern, dressed with oil and salt. They are good for several hours in this fashion, until you spot a packet of crisps and forget about them.

1 cup of parsnip and carrot soup

Half a raw Chanterelle mushroom, picked by myself in Roslin Glen [180]

10 yoghurt-coated raisins

1 *Onken* raspberry mousse

4 pieces of feta cheese

1 bowl of sprouted mixed brown and green lentils [181]

1 slice of cherry lattice pie with ice cream

2 helpings of couscous with roasted vegetables

1 swig of freshly squeezed orange juice

2 slices of plain quiche

Once more I am eating well again. Of the desires driving me, one governs tyrannously (alcohol, crisps, sweets, chips) while the other is an honest forgetfulness of desire altogether (quiche).

---

[180] Pieces of the woodlands (a pine needle and some moss) were seen on these clean and almost dry to the touch mushrooms. The aroma was fruity, almost like that of an apricot.

[181] The sprout is the transitional state between the seed and the plant. A sprouted bean is a food of quite exceptional vitality, able to provide the incredible growth rates attained by plants in their first days of life.

POSSIBLE DRUG USE

All of the following drugs were ingested and so they must be counted. It has always been the fear of foodies that at some point in the future, food will be replaced by a selection of pills. For evidence of this, see the science fiction films of the 1970s when space travellers popped miniaturised meals and sucked various pastes from nasty plates and containers. [182]

I consumed

14 soluble aspirins and water

12 arnica pillules

4 Nurofen tablets and water

1 aspirin and water

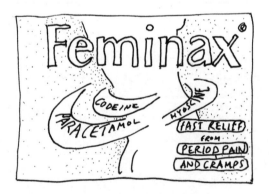

FIGURE 12 – A packet of Feminax

[182] "Food for our space ships! How will it be carried?" asked the 1950 prospectus for MIT. This was from MIT's Department of Food Technology, which was founded in 1944 and dissolved in 1988. Like it or not, SPACE FOOD is here already. In any supermarket one can see products developed to be used "off-planet" – from frozen TV dinners to microwave ovens – from the freeze-dried strawberries in breakfast cereal to Starburst candies and frozen concentrated orange juice. All of these foods benefitted from work carried out as part of America's early space program.

28 Fluoxetine caps and water

2 Tylenol pills and water

8 650mg Tylenol caplets – *"8 hour"* / *"Acetaminophen"* / *"Extended relief"* and water

6 Feminax (Figure 12) and water

Approx 160ml of *Benylin* ® – *"chesty coughs"* Non-Drowsy *"Immediate soothing effect deep penetrating relief"* – made by Pfizer Consumer Healthcare

Cuppa Curry

This was a quickly made curry using:
A 1 lb tin of *EastEnd* brand peeled plum tomatoes / 50g of *Nishaan* minced ginger /
400g of *TRS* brand boiled chick peas in brine / 3 bay leaves / 100g of *KTC*
brand pure creamed coconut in boiled water.

1 bowl of this curry was eaten. The exotic materials of the Middle Eastern
supermarket were here treated to a quick mixing and heating.

Chicken Smartypants

To make Chicken Smartypants gather: 350g Quorn chicken style pieces /
1 red pepper / 3 large onions / 12 cloves of crushed garlic / 3 carrots /
23 sugar snap peas / a little olive oil

Stir frying these add 4 teaspoons of Hot Sauce, named *Ghiottonerie Calabresi.*

Packet Stir Fry Plate

This used a *Blue Dragon* Stir Fry Thai Green Curry Sauce and combined it with
two tomatoes / 100g *Organic* natural soya bean curd tofu [183] /
1 cup of frozen peas.

This was eaten with 1 *Mrs Unis Spicy Food* brand paratha

One and a half bowls of the recipe known as Packet Stir Fry Plate were made and
eaten. It is a partially packet produced preparation.

---

[183] Nae rounds of guid fat beef gin you have tofu? Nae Chunce – and worse – tofu
doesn't taste even remotely nice enough to qualify as SPACE FOOD. Tofu may have
the consistency of something found "off-planet" – but there the story ends. Tofu is like
culinary anti-matter. It's vom enough to inspire the chuck horrors, even in vegetarians.

PUB GUIDE (A-K)

Spread on a single table the map of my drinking would conjure an assault so hard on the liver that I would be forced to quit the campaign before I even began. Spread the drink over a year and it seems less fierce, especially when good company is considered.

There are more then 3,000 pubs and hotel bars on the Atlantic seaboard of Scotland, and just as many on the North Sea shore. Scotland is in fact a coast to coast of pubs, many of them over 100 years old.

Why then are local brewing customs no longer maintained? Most of us have turned from the beers of our predecessors in order to drink mass-produced lager [184] never having tasted porter, amber, western or oat ales. [185]

Times have changed and now we have clean-floored pubs serving lagers that are brewed by the million gallon. We have mirror-plated bogs, police vans, pumping stereo and kebabs. Gone are back-fitments, [186] cut glass, settles and the word *victualling*. Arrived are pub quizzes. Gone are etched or printed advertisement mirrors, wood panels, sconces and snugs – and arrived are crisps and large screen sport. Penny-in-the-slot mechanisms remain but they are now called *bandits*, and "Bubbles" of His Master's Voice fame can still be seen on the odd tin advertising plate.

I still enjoy pub-life and there are many great bars hidden from the brewery-owned monstrosities out there – everything to cater for the bevvy-mad spirit of our age.

---

[184] Mass Beers, Near Beers, Public Ales and Basic Lagers. All otherwise known as Fizzy Keg Beers. They arrive in lorries and are pumped into the pubs. Brew factories produce skunky smelling silos of lager-syrup. The lorries are cavernous beer tankers and they arrive to pish up the towns, refreshing the cellars by the hundred gallon. There are no cellar-men any longer in Scottish pubs – just giant tubes of lager.

[185] I have browsed the excellent *Everyman His Own Brewer*, (London, 1768) by Samuel Child, and I know the great many beers that were once readily available to us.

[186] Now I come to think of it, *back bars* are gone too. The back-fitment is the wooden fitment which stands against the wall; the back bar was the ancillary bar (private or saloon) occasionally provided at the rear of the Scottish pub.

During my annual Pub Guide, I visited:

The Abbotsford Arms, Edinburgh – 2 pints of IPA [187] / 1 pint of Stella Artois / 1 whisky, water and ice

> When Jenners the department store's roof went up in flames on Nov 26, 1892, firemen fought the spectacular blaze from the roof of the Abbotsford. One must visit the Abbotsford for its exquisitely modelled island bar counter and rich Spanish mahogany fittings.

Admiral Nelson, Edinburgh – 2 bottles of Newcastle Brown Ale

> A good thick slice of ale. An exchange student from Atlanta once expressed to me surprise that Newcastle Brown was available in the UK.

All Bar One, Clydesdale Bank Plaza, Edinburgh – 1 pint of Staropramen

> After the cinema one rainy afternoon.

Andrew Edmunds, Soho – 3 glasses of Sancerre 2002

> Good French wine is no rarity. Proof that good eating need not always arise from good cooking.

Applecross Inn, Applecross – 2 pints of McEwans 80/- / 1 pint McEwans Lager

> The just appreciation of lager in the Scottish Highlands is an art – as is the subsequent drink-driving home.

The Argyll, Edinburgh – 1 pint of Belhaven Extra Cold

> With a kipper conscious writer from Orkney and his Californian comrade.

---

[187] IPA is made using Pipkin, Crystal and Wheat malt, along with Fuggles and Goldings hops. At a low alcohol content it's an ideal session ale – you can drink it during an afternoon or evening and still be able to make your way home.

Auld Toll, Edinburgh – 3 pint bottles of Newcastle Brown Ale / 3 pints of IPA / 2 pints of Kronenbourg 1664

If the liquid was not sweet in itself, the Trad Jazz more than compensated.

The Barony, Edinburgh – 1 bottle of Newcastle Brown Ale / 1 Bell's whisky and Tapwater / 3 pints of Becks / 1 pint of Caley 80/-

There are cruel streaks in the Scottish nature which are all forgotten in this gem of a pub.

The Bangalore, Edinburgh – 1 pint of Kingfisher lager

Some people can never seperate curry from lager. [188]

The Belfry, Edinburgh – 2 and half pints of Stella Artois lager / 1 pint of IPA / 1 pint of Budweiser

The gloomy climax to this evening saw me grapple bravely with the pavement and several litter-bins while todlen hame. [189]

Bennets Bar, Edinburgh – 17 and a half pints of Becks / 11 bottles of Newcastle Brown Ale / 2 pints of Carlsberg Export

While living in the vicinity of Bennets, I drank regularly enough (some say) to justify the bar being re-named Burnetts

---

[188] As an accompaniment to food, beer is not ideal. Beer fills you up with gas and dominates the meal, squashing the food to one side. Only the humourously distended stomach can properly cope with beer and curry in any quantity.

[189] "Toddling home"

Bonaparte's, Glasgow – 2 vodka and tonic and ice / 50g of Pringles

Bonaparte's is a railway station bar where many a stiff soul has lain an hour or two in wait.

The Bow Bar, Edinburgh – 20 and a half pints of Landlord bitter / 9 and a half pints of IPA / 3 x 275ml bottles of Becks / 2 pints of Nell's Best / 1 pint of Dark Island ale / 1 pint of Tower Ale / 1 375ml bottle of Peroni Asturo / 6 pints of Tennent's lager / 1 pint of Wylam Bohemia Ale / 3 pints of Gunslinger ale / 2 and a half pints of Deuchars IPA / 1 Balvenie 12 yr old single malt / 1 Laguvulin single malt / 1 Glenmorangie single malt / 1 and half 330ml Highland Spring gaseous water with ice and lemon / 1 Ardbeg whisky / 1 Japanese whisky – "Suntory Hibiki" [190]

I understand that Bow drinkers feel their experience to be near religious. [191]

Berlington Bertie, Edinburgh – 1 vodka and tonic / 3 glasses of red wine

Bertie is only ever visited after dark.

Blind Beggar, Edinburgh – 1 Balvenie and water / 1 pint of Stella Artois lager [192]

A motorcycle bar in the heart of Edinburgh's polite neighbourhood.

---

[190] "You shouldn't have poured all that sake on top of the Suntory. I can't believe Japanese whisky makes a good foundation for anything." James Bond, speaking in Ian Fleming's *You Only Live Twice*.

[191] THE EXEGESIS OF INEBRIATION: Theology does not suggest that alcoholic drink has any spiritual application. Drunkenness however offers the closest physical parallel to what happens to the soul that receives the ineffable happiness of Christ. The idea of the believer being inebriated with Christ appears in Augustine, Gregory, Alcuin and Bede, all of whom suggest that the adept should bevvy hard on Jesus, before going for a Holy Supper and taking a taxi home to heaven. The Trinity of Beer, Wine and Spirit is transubstantiated in the body of the drinker to the Hangover of the Martyr.

[192] Stella has a 5.2% alcohol content – 0.2 to 0.5% more than other lagers. It may not sound like it would make a big difference, but I assure you that it does.

The Blue Blazer, Edinburgh – 1 pint of Flowers Ale

Counselled o'er a gill by Mr McE.

Café Circus, Edinburgh – 1 whisky and soda / 1 hot chocolate

A cheery guid nicht – whisky and chocolate!

Café East, Edinburgh – 4 pints of Kingfisher lager [193] / 3 x 330ml bottles of Carlsberg

The value for money of Café East's £5 meal deal encouraged more drinking.

Café Royal, Downstairs, Edinburgh – 1 pint of Miller lager / 1 whisky and ice plus some of Seán's Diet Coke / 1 bottle of Newcastle Brown Ale

Less couthy perhaps, but certainly more spacious and elegant than its upstairs neighbour, with its tiled frescoes.

Café Royal, Upstairs, Edinburgh – 1 pint of Miller lager / 3 glasses of white wine / 2 pints of Grolsch lager

More couthy perhaps, but certainly less spacious than its downstairs neighbour, with a high flown flourish and majestic vermilion decor.

Cameo Cinema Bar, Edinburgh – 1 500ml bottle of Budvar

Stately blocks of commodious seating, if you can get a seat at all.

Cask & Barrel, Edinburgh – 2 pints of Flowers bitter / 2 pints of Ossian's Ale

Old style hostelries with complex ornamentation are still to be found. This one is full of bikers, Customs and Excise staff and sales reps.

---

[193] I have only once received a drink from another table when dining out. One of these Kingfishers was sent to me from another table by Mr SB who was eating with his wife.

Cell 77, Edinburgh – 2 x 25cl bottles of Stella Artois

The orange ochre of Bohemia was most visible in this self-styled art space.

Cloisters, Edinburgh – 2 pints of Becks / 1 and a half pints of Tennent's lager / 2 pints Deuchars IPA [194]

A Tudor inn meets a Swiss ski lodge and begets a gambling machine and several illuminated keg beer taps.

Corn Exchange, Edinburgh – a half pitcher of vodka and Coke with ice / 1 330ml bottle of Kronenbourg 1664 lager

Famous vegetarian Morrissey played his concert at the Corn Exchange, which was previously an abattoir.

Cumberland Bar, Edinburgh – 4 pints of Kronenbourg 1664

Advocates of functionalism are not welcome in the older bars of Scotland. The Cumberland's pleasant beer garden now lies empty thanks to the gratting and moaning of the pub's fun-killing neighbours, who complained about the noise.

Curlers, Glasgow – 1 pint of Tetley bitter

An efficacious pick-me-up on Byres Road. No dance / trance shit on the sound systems, but instead Eminem, proving to me that appearances can be deceptive.

---

[194] I have never known who was responsible for this brilliant Scottish Limerick:
At an air show at RAF Leuchars,
A pilot shocked all the onlookers,
When he landed his Harrier,
Jumped over the barrier,
And murdered a cool pint o' Deuchars

The Dome, Edinburgh – 1 glass of house white wine

A palace of a pub. The bar was so smart that as usual I wondered if the management really meant to allow me entrance.

The Doric Tavern, Edinburgh – 3 and a half pints of Tennent's IPA

It would be difficult to describe the attracting cadence in the barman's speech as he offered me the final half.

Favorit, Tollcross, Edinburgh – 1 pint of Grolsch lager

Beauty and utility, ideal for the floating drinker. I had neither the fashion sense nor the correct facial hair to stay in Favorit for too long however.

Festival Hall, London – 1 bottle ay Stella / 1 bottle ay Coors Lite

A pop concert, culminating in a memorable riot.

The Golden Rule, Edinburgh – 5 pints of Staropramen lager / 2 pints of Bitter and Twisted ale / 1 pint of IPA / 1 pint of Golden Honey ale / 2 pints of Atlas Latitude ale

A cosy up-to-date public bar with two pleasant sitting rooms. The bridge between the upper and lower bars is narrow.

The Grill, Aberdeen – 1 pint of Tennent's lager

The Grill has two doors on two streets. Between these doors is a bar counter and back fitment which stretch the full length of the premises. There are upholstered bench seats both opposite the bar and in recesses at either end, behind arches of elliptical form. The symmetry is stunning although for many years it was upset by the lack of ladies' toilet facilities.

The Grosvenor, Edinburgh – 2 x 275ml bottles of Becks [195]

Since perfection is becoming increasingly rare there is little point in getting carried away.

The Guildford, Edinburgh – 3 pints of Pilsner Urqunell lager

The utopian timbre of Edinburgh is accentuated when The Guildford is empty and all your own.

Guru Balti, Edinburgh – half of a 33ml complementary Tennent's lager

A non-alcoholic drink would better serve those driving home their carry-out meals, but this lager saved a palate that had just gone stiff.

Harry's Bar, Edinburgh – 1 330ml bottle of Becks

The full blown late 20th century pub with its intriguing blend of functional round tables, office workers, lager, and deep fried fish and chips.

Hillhead Library, Glasgow [196] – 3 glasses of white wine

The launch of one of my own books in Glasgow.

K Jackson's, Edinburgh – 3 pints of Budvar Budweiser / a half pint of Carlsberg lager

For surreptitious tippling at the West Port.

Kushi's Edinburgh – 2 x 330ml bottles of Becks

And many good results.

---

[195] Have a look in any off-sales or pub and you'll always find bottles of Becks. Becks is Germany's leading export beer, and is sold in around 120 countries.

[196] The shelves freely mingled on this occasion with wine. Is Hillhead Scotland's only licensed library?

GRAZING & BROWSING

Heartbeat is better than horsepower – a lesson I refuse to learn. I eat to get me through the next few hours instead of as part of an ongoing life-programme. I would rather sugar myself up 'til dinnertime than sustain myself with a controlling diet, which might offer some overarching nutritional value. Snack options lurk at every corner and contribute to poor nationwide food preparation skills, which in my case led to the following:

1 portion of reheated saag, mushroom and paneer curry in rice

1 340g glass jar of *Co-op* crunchy peanut butter – *"When you crave a crunch!"*

1 454g jar of *SunPat* "Crunchy" peanut butter

1 bowl of stewed Hawthornden plums and *Tesco* Finest vanilla ice cream

2 slices of plain quiche

12 x *Anna's* chocolate vanilla thins – *"Traditional Swedish biscuits with chocolate and vanilla"*

1 portion of red cabbage and apple cooked in cloves and cinnamon

1 110g pot of *Mars Mousse* – with E501, E500, E472b, E442, and E162

3 hunks of brown bread and *Tartex* yeast paté with herbs and garlic – Tartex: *"no meat, no animal fat, no artificial colours or preservatives … just delicious"*

1 500ml bottle of *Findlays* spring water – *"Naturally pure from Scotland"*

1 *Bumbles* cheddar cheese & coleslaw seeded clamshell roll

1 110g pot of *Bounty Mousse* – with E 442, [197] E472b, and locust bean gum[198]

1 *Dalgetty's* Scotch Black Bun [199] "*Naturally rich*" – "*Rich in fruit and topped with a fine crust of short pastry*" [200]

18 small glasses of orange juice [201]

---

[197] We are getting e-mails from our Muslim brothers and sisters inquiring about the Halal (permissible) status of E-Numbers. Halal status is given to food ingredients that are obtained from 100% Halal raw materials without the use of alcohol. Haraam (forbidden) are those obtained from a porcine source or from the use of alcohol. All non-zabiha (the accepted method of slaughter) Halal animal by-products are considered as Haraam because we don't know if Allah's name was announced at the time of slaughtering the animal. Mushbooh (uncertain) status is given to those E-Numbers where the source of raw material is not known, as it could be from a Haraam plant or animal source or may use alcohol-based ingredients. This is a human matter – please note that there is not a single particle of matter in the universe which does not locate its eternal being in the One, and which is not known in the unitive vision of the One. All is god or god is not at all. But God still asks you to eschew the following Haraam: pork or pig based products; blood; animals slaughtered in the name of anyone but God; carrion; any animal found dead; fanged beasts of prey (usually simplified to all carnivorous animals); and all intoxicants. Most agree that frogs are haraam and all agree that fish with scales are halal.

[198] Since ancient times the locust bean has been used for its thickening properties. The Egyptians used locust bean to glue the bandages around their mummies and this same gum is used today as a thickener in salad dressings, cosmetics, sauces, as an agent in ice cream to prevent crystals from forming. Locust bean also turns up as a fat substitute and in pastry fillings it prevents the "weeping" of any water, keeping the pastry crust crisp.

[199] Black Bun: "A black substance inimical to life." Robert Louis Stevenson

[200] What makes pastry short? The word *short* has maintained the 19th century usage, of "crumbly in texture". The butter, which is the sole shortening agent, should thus be squeezed free of all water.

[201] In certain traditions, the orange and not the apple is the fruit responsible for original sin. I believe that oranges have tracked the origins of at least two of the great world religions. First, in the East, oranges crossed India like Buddhism heading for China and arriving about the same time in 2200BC; secondly, in the West, oranges appeared in the second century A.D. and like the Christian faith, were imported to Rome from Palestine.

1 glass of *White's* Premium lemonade with pineapple syrup and ice

1 175g *Müller* Sticky Toffee Custard and Sponge (15% sponge) with E500, E475, E471 [202], E450, E341

1 bag of *Munchy Seeds* chilli mix – *"Sunflower and pumpkin seeds with crushed chillies dry roasted in a savoury sauce"*

1 Jarlsberg cheese, peanut butter, lettuce, tomato and mayonnaise sandwich on a seedy bap

3 *Green and Black* organic dark chocolate coated butter biscuits with ginger

1 *Benedicts* mixed cheese and onion white bread sandwich – *"The natural choice"*

22 stewed apples from 22 Leys Drive, Inverness (Figure 13)

FIGURE 13 – Home grown apples are the first peers of the city garden

This year I ate 21 Birds Eye potato waffles (a total of 1191.75g of potato waffles) – *"Low in saturated fat"* / *"They go well with everything"*. These are apparently made with 115g of potato per 100g of product.

---

[202] 471 is reportedly the most commonly used emulsifier in the food industry. It operates when the foaming power of egg protein needs to be retained in the presence of fat, and in baked goods as an 'anti-staling' agent where it prevents the loss of water. Vegetarians beware – 471 may occasionally be of animal origin.

1 Danish pastry [203] with pecan and maple

1 Danish Pastry

1 75g carton of *Sunita* organic halva – *"Sesame snack with honey"*

1 cup of parsnip soup

1 plate of papaya and redcurrants with lemon juice

Stewed kumquats and pear compote with crème fraiche

1 slice of jam paste and ice cream. Apples from J West in Inverness / paste made by K Burnett of Aberdeen

200g (= 7) *Stockan & Gardens* Original Thick Orkney oatcakes

Dad's cabbage – steamed by me in three servings (see Figure 54)

2 ginger beers and ice

1 (300g) *Cosmo* brand pizza Margherita [204]

2 glasses of mango juice

One and a half slices of *Henderson's* chocolate cake

1 brown bread and Emmenthal sandwich, prepared with *Flora* spread [205]

---

[203] Danish Pastry is known as Vienna Bread in Denmark. Lest war should cause the two to re-name the morsel!

[204] MARGHERITA? Like the drink? Legend names this dish after Queen Margherita of Savoie who tasted this variety of pizza during a visit to Naples in 1889 and declared it to be her favourite. This is a contradictory rumour.

[205] Made by the lifesaving "Mary-Lee"

2 pots of Canada No. 1 maple syrup

0.505kg aduki beans, *Realfoods*, organic produce of Argentina

3 servings of sprouted pinto beans

2 helpings of sprouted mung beans

2 glasses of sparkling spring water

4 baby tomatoes in balsamic vinegar

2 slices of challa

1 carrot cake from the Keemac Bakery

1 *Scott's of Edinburgh* Rocky Road biscuit

1 bowl of sprouted mung beans (Figure 14)

2 x *Santanglio* deli Rocky Road bars

1 *Santanglio* deli caramel shortcake biscuit

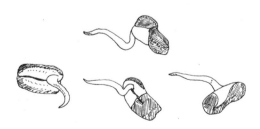

FIGURE 14 – Sprouted mung beans have edged their way into the Burnett diet

1 *Santanglio* deli Malteser cake biscuit

5 *Hovis* wheat biscuits and Port Salut cheese

6 glasses of *Tapuzina* grapefruit drink – "*with fruit pulp*"

5 Carmit wafers

I veer between the ridiculously healthy (sprouts) and the famously unhealthy (cakes and cake bars). Is every personality split by food?   I am comfortable at the crossroads of nutrition – and with Scylla and Charybdis so far apart, there's more then enough room for navigation.

My exact involvement with all of the above food is difficult to determine, due to the pain of ingurgitation.

That is to say, it's hard to eat and think simultaneously!

THE DICTIONARY OF PORRIDGE

During one year in Scotland, I ate 12 plates of rolled oats porridge, sprinkled with pinhead oatmeal and served with skimmed milk.

There are many ways to eat porridge and experience has shown me that each family has developed their own. The following are several words which indicate our fondness for this meal.

blanter – food made from oats, e.g. bread, porridge

brat – the skin on porridge

brose – a dish of oatmeal mixed with boiling water or milk, with salt and butter added

cauld steerie – oatmeal stirred in cold water

crackins – a dish of fried oatmeal

creeshie mealie – oatmeal fried in fat

crowdie – oatmeal and water mixed and eaten raw

drammlicks – the small pieces of oatmeal dough which stick to the basin when making oatcakes

girsle – a fragment of crisp or caked porridge

garnel – a storage chest for meal

luggie – a wooden bowl with one or two handles formed from projecting staves, often used for serving milk with porridge

meal an thrammel – meal stirred up with water or ale, taken as a snack in the North-East

131

neep brose – brose made with the liquid in which the turnips have been boiled

nettle brose – brose made with the juice of boiled young nettle-tops

skink – a thin, oatmeal-and-water gruel

skirlie – a dish of oatmeal and onions fried in a pan

snap & rattle – toasted oatcakes crumbled in milk

spurtle – a tapered stick for stirring porridge

COCA-COLA'S CALEDONIA

We have this drink in Scotland called Coca-Cola. It is made from water and caramel and the populace will grab at a can of it with their hands and give the impression of St Vitus dance in trying to open it. I have tried this drink on many occasions and aside from the burning and acid sensations in the midriff when I have drunk too much, I have found it teeming with bubbles and flavours, which have tickled me.

I am not sure of the origins of Coca-Cola but it may not be naturally Scottish, despite being available in every single shop, pub, club and café in the country. However. Let but two Scots-people foregather at any time and place and who chances to hear them order their national drink, may well overhear the name of Coca-Cola. The Scots have never lacked wind to blow their own trumpets and so they should be proud of this national favourite. Of Coca-Cola I drank:

9 x 330ml cans [206] of caffeine-free *Diet Coke* and ice

6 x 330ml cans of *Diet Coke* and ice

4 x 330ml cans of *Diet Coke*

2 x 1 litre bottles of caffeine-free *Diet Coke*

4 sips of caffeine-free *Diet Coke*

---

[206] There's a new security threat on America's military bases – and it looks like a can of Coke. As part of the Unexpected Summer promotion special cans of Coke contained cell phones and global positioning chips. Military leaders in America were worried the cans could be used to eavesdrop, while Coca-Cola said that no one would mistake one of the winning cans for a regular Coke. The winning cans have a recessed panel on the outside and a red button – and winners activate the can by pushing the button which will call Coke's prize centre. Even though data from the Global Positioning System in the can can only be receievd by Coke's prize centre, military bases, including the U.S. Army Armor Center at Fort Knox asked soldiers to examine their Coke cans before bringing them in to classified meetings. "We're asking people to open the cans and not bring them in if there's a GPS in it," said Master Sgt. Jerry Meredith, a Fort Knox spokesman. The Marine Corps said all personnel had been advised of the cans and instructed to keep them away from secure areas.

2 x 330ml cans of *Diet Coke* [207]

1 330ml can of *Coca-Cola* featuring Luis Figo and the "*1 million footballs to be won INSTANTLY*" promotion

1 330ml can of *Coca-Cola*

1 500ml vanilla flavour *Coca-Cola* [208]

1 310 ml plastic bottle of cherry *Coca-Cola*

1 glass of *Diet Coke*

12 scoofs [209] of *Diet Coke*

---

[207] In a bank vault in Atlanta Georgia there is a paper with 18 ingredients on it. This secret of all secrets is known to 3 or 4 company executives at the same time and in the right proportions it is mixed and poured into the mouths of several billion people at once. Included on the slip of paper are: nutmeg oil, cassia oil, alcohol and coca leaves from which the cocaine has been removed (and shipped to Washington, presumably).

[208] The strap line on this can was "supporting the Olympic dream since 1928" – reminding me that the ability to take pride in the hard work of others is essential to a properly successful marketing campaign.

[209] *Scoof* is a Glaswegian word meaning to steal, or take charge of something that seems to lack an obvious owner. Such as in "These flats wi the boarded-up windies have aw been scoofed long since." Elsewhere in Scotland, the use is exclusively linked to a shot of someone else's drink. Hence: "Gi us a scoof."

MEALS OF A TYPE

We are always on the go and can't find the time to prepare our meals from scratch. With average cooking times of 45 minutes, most traditional cookery is beyond the under 35s, who must spend a certain amount of time working late, listening to music or watching reality television. The following items either contributed to proper "sit down" meals, or entirely constituted them.

1 300g *Cosmo* pizza [210] *Margherita* [211] with one sliced onion and 10 pineapple chunks placed on it by myself

A large helping of vegetable lasagne with avocado salad in Balsamic vinegar

1 portion of ravioli stuffed with pepper and ricotta, taken with avocado and mozzarella, and dressed in mushroom sauce and four varieties of sprouted beans

4 portions of *McCain* "Micro Chips Crinkles". These chips arrive in a box that one *"Must not place in a conventional grill or oven"* [212] (Figure 15)

1 portion of red onion, parsnip and carrot roasted in ground coriander

1 portion of saag aloo with natural yoghurt

1 serving of vegetable goulash with rice and yoghurt

---

[210] Cheese accounts for about 40% of the cost of a traditional pizza.

[211] 11th June 1889. The Margherita pizza is dedicated to Queen Margaret. The famous Italian pizzaiolo Raffaele Esposito was invited to her court in France – where he suggested three pizzas – the Margherita reflecting the colours of the Italian Sabauda flag – the Marinara – and a white cheese pizza. Garlic, considered improper for the delicate palate of a Queen, was avoided and so the Margherita was born. This is a contradictory rumour.

[212] Clearly Micro Chips are SPACE FOOD, given these "off-planet" directives.

FIGURE 15 – Micro Chips "Crinkles" come in this nifty cardboard box

1 plate of avocado, tomato, mixed sprouted beans and alfalfa [213]

2 bowls of potato and leek soup with fresh parsley

3 x 225g servings of *Macsween* vegetarian haggis [214]

2 plates of *Macsween* vegetarian haggis

2 slight portions of *Macsween* vegetarian haggis

1 plate of unidentified vegetarian haggis with parsnip and carrot

---

[213] Alfalfa is supposedly the oldest known plant used for livestock feed, with records of its use as early as 1000 BCE in the Middle East.

[214] Vegetarian haggis is *par excellence*, the greatest Scots dish. Strangers coming to the country are at first scared by it but then they're exposed to haggis *con carne* and the curious rite of animal slaughter. All enjoy vegetarian haggis, most famously made by Macsween of Edinburgh. For the opening of the Scottish Poetry Library in 1984, Angus Calder and Tessa Ransford spoke to master butcher and businessman John Macsween and suggested a vegetarian haggis be created for the occasion. Although initially cool about the idea, Macsween bagged and served a mixture and with the help of Calder's daughter Rachel and Tessa Ransford's daughter Meg Stiven, they made enough for 30 people, with the help of people at Edinburgh's SEEDS co-operative. Macsween subsequently put the haggis on the market, and his firm continues to sell the product to this day.

NIKKI'S LUNCH BAR

A m I hungry? It's been a long time since breakfast and I need to eat. Food is scarce in the office and is usually kept in locked drawers. You need to ask to borrow food if you want some.

Nikki's is a breakfast and lunch joint in the West End of Edinburgh, built to cope with the dietary demands of the nearby office population.

Like other such hard working joints, Nikki's sells scones and bacon rolls in the morning, sandwiches at lunchtime, and homemade cake and biscuits all round the clock.

Here is everything that I ate from Nikki's during a period when the morning scone became an essential in my day-to-day. Please note that butter was not offered by Nikki's, with only a buttery substance known as *spread* being made available.

11 bran scones with spread and jam

6 cheese and coleslaw [215] sandwiches on granary subs

2 bran scones and spread

2 marmalade scones with spread and strawberry jam [216]

2 cherry scones with spread and strawberry jam

2 white chocolate caramel squares

---

[215] I was playing around with Google and checking out various coleslaw recipes, and found all kinds of cool shit, including Salvadorian Cabbage and Savoy Slaw with Buttermilk. In my mind I always picture coleslaw coming in a thick and basic form, like Potato Salad or rhyming 70s horror, Green Bean Almondine. This is not the case. Slaw is a huge multi-purpose compound. Furthermore, if I were to start making food "family trees" slaw would be placed along the same branch as American *chow chow*, Korean *kimchi*, German *sauerkraut*, and Chinese *suan chi*.

[216] Silly me! A marmalade scone covered with jam was too much!

137

2 crispy chocolate-topped syrup bars

1 dark cherry scone with spread and strawberry jam

1 fruit scone with spread and strawberry jam

1 plain scone with spread and strawberry jam

1 lemon scone with spread and blackberry jam

1 blackcurrant and almond scone with spread and raspberry jam

1 strawberry scone with spread and strawberry jam

1 apple & blackcurrant scone with spread and strawberry jam

1 honey [217] & banana scone with spread and strawberry jam

1 apple and cinnamon scone with spread and raspberry jam

1 banana scone with spread and strawberry jam

1 banana scone with spread

1 fried egg roll

1 chocolate log bar

Half a piece of chocolate biscuit cake

---

[217] "'Bee vomit,' my brother said once, 'that's all honey is,' so that I could not put my tongue to its jellied flame without tasting regurgitated blossoms." Rita Dove *In the Old Neighborhood*

Food & Drink Away from Home (F to N)

Restaurants / Cafes / Bars / Stands / Hotels
Pubs / Functions

Some say there's a subconscious link between the palette of design and the palate of taste. Soothing hues of ocean blue on a restaurant wall can betoken dishes of seafood, for example. The zinc bars and blood-red leather banquettes of city restaurants are suggestive of an opulence that can best express itself in the various rich sides of meat available. [218] Just as typical are the more down to earth restaurants, starkly wooden for the vegetarians, or others with their bars moulded from some dark, elasticised material from hell's own design studios.

Close your eyes for a moment and imagine a pleasant restaurant. The wall is hung with art-as-comfort oils, the diners sit in sharp relief against the staff who walk between them. Nobody is paying attention to anything but their own conversation. It is time to eat again and you realise that this is broadly the same experience as you usually have in *real* restaurants.

Favorit, [219] **Tollcross, Edinburgh** (16 visits) – 12 nachos with salsa, guacamole and sour cream swiped from the plates of two friends / 1 plate of nachos with salsa, guacamole and sour cream shared three ways / 1 plate of nachos with salsa, guacamole and sour cream all to myself this time / 1 mozzarella and sun dried tomato panini with side salad / 1 chilli cheese and roast peppers panini / 1 café biscotti / 1 cup of black tea / 1 glass of milk / 2 fizzbomb ice cream sundaes with chocolate and nuts / 2 hot chocolates / 1 tea with milk / 1 small white coffee / 2 bottles of *San Pellegrino* spring water / 2 glasses of tap water and ice / 2 glasses of soda water and ice / 1 black coffee / 2 glasses of fresh orange juice and ice / 2 decaffeinated coffees and milk

---

[218] "And yet somehow the most matter-of-fact person could not help thinking of the hogs; they were so innocent, they came so very trustingly; and they were so very human in their protests – and so perfectly within their rights!" Upton Sinclair, *The Jungle*, (1905)

[219] Favorit, an Edina diner that is both fun and functional. What our forebears used to call a "cat and bagpipes" hostelry.

Favorit, Forest Road, Edinburgh – 1 mozzarella, basil and tomato wrap / 1 nachos with salsa, guacamole & sour cream / 3 Diet Cokes and ice /1 slice of apple & caramel pie and cream / 1 black coffee / 1 Earl Grey tea / 5 hot chocolates

Foo-Foo Supermarket, Bethlehem – 2 pitta bread with hummus

Filmhouse Bar, Edinburgh – 1 hot chocolate / 1 scone and butter with blackcurrant preserve / 1 foaming latte with 2 sachets of white sugar

The Flower Tunnel, Applecross – 1 cheese salad baguette [220] / a half spinach and brie toasted baguette / 3 black coffees with white sugar

Fountain Bar, Edinburgh – 1 Diet Coke

The Four Seasons, East Jerusalem – A half portion of chocolate cake

Frankfurt Airport – 1 black coffee

Fruitmarket Gallery, Edinburgh – 1 and half cups of black coffee

General Services Committee at Dheisheh Camp, Bethlehem – 1 cup of orange drink

Get Genki, Edinburgh – 3 potatoes cooked in salt, pepper and olive oil / 2 carrot and mayo sandwiches / 2 brie and chutney sandwiches / 1 serving of hummus and one of guacamole / 3 and a half slices of chocolate biscuit cake / 1 brie and pickle sandwich / 1 cheese salad sandwich / 1 mozzarella basil and tomato sandwich

---

[220] *Baguette magique* is French for *wand*,
Baguette de fée is also French for *magic wand*,
Baguettes chinoises is French for *chopsticks*,
Baguette de chef d'orchestra is another expression for a conductor's baton,
Baguette de tambour is French for *drumstick*,
Baguette de fusil is French for *ramrod*,
Une baguette de protection latérale is French for *side trim* (on a car).

Ginger Express, Edinburgh – 1 spring roll

GNER Transport, Train Trolley – 2 x *PG Tips* tea with 2 x *Millac Maid* half fat milk capsules with the brilliant sales lines – *"Tastes Like Fresh Milk"* and *"Long Life Skimmed Milk with Non-Milk Fat"* [221] / 3 Lily O' Brien's double chocolate chip cookies (*"Passionate about chocolate"*) / 1 *Carte Noir* coffee (*"un café nommé désir"*)

Great Grog, Edinburgh – 1 mozzarella and sun dried tomato sandwich / 1 black coffee

Guru Balti Edinburgh (2 visits) – Dahi raita / balti sabzi kofta / saag paneer / 1 and a half peshwari nan / 1 and half papad / a little salad / half a portion of pilau rice / 1 chana sweet curry / 1 medium strength chana curry / 1 portion of saag aloo / 1 portion of red onions

Hard Rock Café, Edinburgh – Nachos with cheese, soured cream, spring onions, guacamole and ranch dressing / 2 Diet Cokes and ice / 1 portion of French Fries / 1 vegetable and Swiss cheese sandwich [222] / a shared portion of nachos with cheese and soured cream (= 11 nachos) / 6 potato skins with chives and soured cream

---

[221] The serving of SPACE FOOD is at least appropriate at high speed, as on this train. One cannot generally complain about such conveniences but there always comes a time when they become a bore. During the Mercury and Gemini space missions there were no complaints concerning the food, possibly because the project was so new. The crews of Apollo 7 however complained about the food and even though it was essentially the same as the Gemini food, a minor mutiny saw them not eating at all on some occasions. Astronauts Borman, Lovell and Anders said that even though they had flown for 14 days in Gemini and didn't mind the food, they *did* mind it in Apollo. Apollo 8 crew were therefore given so-called *wetpack* food, which they liked except for the potatoes. Similar reactions occurred in Apollo 9, when the water gun (used to hydrate their food) produced about 60% gas and 40% water which meant that the crew filled their food bags with gas. The crew reportedly swung their food bags around in order to try to eliminate some bubbles, but this method resulted in them being left with large gas bubbles in place of small ones.

[222] In truth, I would have had to dislocate my jaw to do this sandwich justice. Sometimes, this is too much. What starts out as an impressively constructed sandwich, ends up as a mountain of food that just happens to include two slices of bread.

Harry's Bar, Edinburgh – 1 veggie-burger, [223] chips and onion rings with salad, ketchup and mayonnaise / 2 Diet Cokes with ice and lemon

Halo, Edinburgh – 1 bowl of wild mushroom soup / 1 glass of sparkling spring water / 3 slices of bread and butter

Hello, Edinburgh – 1 black coffee

Herbies, Edinburgh – 2 chocolate crispies / 1 watermelon, strawberry and apple juice / 1 black coffee / 2 felafel sandwiches / 4 glasses of fresh orange / 1 slice of toast / 2 felafel, harrisa and salad sandwiches

Hipercor, Marbella – 1 apple and custard tart with crème fraiche

Hogshead, Edinburgh – 1 vegetarian chilli with chips and tomato sauce

The Hub, Edinburgh – 1 spring water / 1 Diet Coke

Hula, Glasgow – 1 white coffee

The Human BeIn, Edinburgh – 1 courgette and celery soup / 1 eggs Benedict [224] with mushrooms / 2 slices of bread and butter / 8 morsels of bread in pesto oil / 3 morsels of bread in Rose Marie sauce / 1 hot chocolate with cream

---

[223] All types of vegetarian eat veggie-burger. But what are the different types of vegetarian? *True Vegetarians* will eat nothing from an animal cooked or processed. *Lacto Vegetarians* will eat dairy products but no meat. *Ovo Vegetarians* will allow themselves just the eggs, while *Semi-Pesco Vegetarians* will eat no red meat or chicken but will eat fish, eggs and dairy produce. *Pseudo Vegetarians* will eat chicken and don't give a shit while *Sancto Pesco Vegetarians* draw the line at red meat. Finally, *Presbo Vegetarians* preach about the abuse of animals to excess, while *Prickers* stab at the consciences of the bloodthirsty and yet would kick at them with leather shoes...

[224] There is now available, and rather predictably, an Eggs Benedict XVI, created to honour the German background of the most recently elected pope. The eggs come with *Sauerbraten* or sausage and rye bread accompaniments in an attempt to offer a Teutonic slant.

IKEA, Edinburgh – 1 plate of chips

Indigo Yard, Edinburgh – 3 slices of French toast and maple syrup / 2 veggie sausages / 1 black coffee / 1 glass of iced water

Insomnia, Glasgow – 2 black coffees / 1 hot chocolate

Italian Connection, Edinburgh – 9" pizza with onion

Jirada Spice, Edinburgh – 1 Pad Kee Mao Park "*Very spicy stir fry vegetables with chilli, garlic, lemon grass and Thai sweet basil*" / 2 spring rolls / 1 portion of egg rice with peas / 1 Gaeng Ped Pak "*Thai style mixed vegetable red curry with coconut and herbs*" / 1 chunk of bean curd [225]

Jolly Judge, Edinburgh – 2 colas

Kasbah, Edinburgh – 1 saag paneer / 1 portion of pilau rice / 1 papad with raita and chutney / 1 peshwari nan

Kushi's Edinburgh – 1 vegetable pakora / 1 battered aubergine / 1 portion of raita and chilli sauce / 2 papad and lime chutney / 1 hot chick pea curry with rice / 1 nan with sesame and herb / five-eighths of a Peshwari nan / a go at the biryani sauce dips / 1 piece of paneer in saag

Kynnaird House, Fraserburgh – 1 cup of instant coffee with milk

The Leith Walk Café, Edinburgh – 1 white coffee / 1 golden crispie

Lochcarron Petrol Station – 1 cheese and tomato sandwich

---

[225] This is the closest carry-out food joint to my home. But can we really eat locally? In September 2005, a restaurant chain in Palo Alto, California, challenged the chefs who run its 190 restaurants to provide diners with at least one meal that is 100% locally grown. One chef based in Oregon decided to track down a local source for salt. Finding no salt locally, he took the drastic step of boiling down seawater and making his own salt. It's a sign of the times that for the purposes of this challenge, "locally grown" meant grown within a radius of 150 miles from the restaurants in question.

Luca's Mobile Ice Cream, currently "mobile" in North Berwick – 1 "Oyster" of vanilla ice cream [226]

Luca's, Mussleburgh – 1 small vanilla 99 ice cream cone [227] with butterscotch sauce

Mcdonald's, Barnton, Edinburgh – 1 large fries / 1 caramel sundae [228]

McLays Hotel, Glasgow – 1 plate of scrambled eggs / 2 slices of toast with *Coronet* Butter and *Coronet* strawberry jam / 1 filter coffee

McTavish's Kitchen, Oban – 1 white coffee / two slices of toast and *Duerr's* raspberry jam – *"est 1881"*

Made in Italy, Edinburgh – 3 slices of cheese and tomato pizza / 1 espresso coffee and milk / half a red berry tart / 2 large black coffees

Málaga Airport – 1 espresso coffee

Maxi's, Edinburgh – 1 Swiss cheese baguette with salad and mayo

---

[226] The Dietary Guidelines of the British government suggest you intake 30 % or less of calories from fat and less than 10% of calories from saturated fat. Conclusion: the recommended upper limit on grams of fat and saturated fat in your diet depends on which political party you vote for.

[227] What is it with this nonsense? The story of the invention of the ice cream cone tells of a seller at the 1904 St. Louis World Fair who, on running out of ice-cream dishes, rolled up a waffle from a nearby stall and filled this with ice cream. Consider the likeness of this to the origin myths of the sandwich, liquorice allsorts etc. All are fortuitous accidents, spiffing aetiologies of necessity and invention with the food being in the right place at the right time.

[228] McDonald's has a US TV commercial featuring ex-employees who tell you McDonald's was the first step on their dazzling careers. I am calculating that the demographic of population versus employment at McDonald's is such that before long they'll reach the point where everyone has worked there at some time. (Did they ask me to be in their commercial? Did they heck.)

The Meadow (or Moo) Bar, Edinburgh – 4 and a half pints of Diet Coke / 2 pints of iced water / 14 black coffees / 1 sip of black coffee and Sambuca / 1 milk coffee with a sachet of white sugar

Me 'n' U, Edinburgh – 1 seeded bagel and cream cheese

Methodist Hall, Edinburgh – 1 apple drink

Monster Mash, Edinburgh – 1 veggie-burger, chips, ketchup & Diet Coke [229]

Montpelliers, Edinburgh – 1 orange juice and ice / 1 plate of spaghetti [230] with wild mushroom and cream / 1 black coffee

Mosque Kitchen, Edinburgh – 1 rice dish with pepper and seeds / 2 portions of dhal / 1 plate of spinach and curried vegetables / 1 portion of vinegar [231] sauce with fine onions / 1 rice and spinach, spiced with cinnamon / 1 *Mecca* Cola (Figure 16) – the straplines for *Mecca* Cola include *"Please do not mix with alcohol"* and *"10% to go to Enfance Childhood Palestine"*

Mundo, Bethlehem – 1 vegetarian pizza plate / 1 330ml tin of *Spring* brand Mango Nectar

The Mussel Inn, Edinburgh – 1 plate of potato and leek soup with 3 slices of baguette and butter

---

[229] There are those who dedicate their lives to dieting but temperance is not the same thing as dieting. Temperance is a way of keeping the body at a distance, and dieting is a way of living with the body on intimate and obsessive terms. Dieting is in fact, a kind of negative greed.

[230] 1995: Minutes before his execution in Oklahoma, convicted murderer Thomas Grasso sent this message from his cell: "I did not get my Spaghetti Os. I got spaghetti. I want the press to know this." Such mistakes are terrible but at least the damage is short lived.

[231] Vinegar, oddly, was Jesus' real last meal. If you remember, He was offered it on a sponge from a vindictive Roman, who had nothing better to do than toy with the dying and pervert their final wishes. See above, re: Spaghetti Os

FIGURE 16 – Mecca Cola, an intriguingly tendentious fizzy drink

The New Club, Edinburgh – 1 and a half croissants / 1 orange juice /
1 black coffee

Newton Dee Village, Bieldside – 1 plain bun [232]

Ndebele, Edinburgh – 1 felafel, mayonnaise and salad sandwich on
a brown "sub"

---

[232] GIRL: Nothing on that bun?
 ME: I think just the bun.
 GIRL: It comes with butter and jam.
 ME: Ah. Those two symbols of self-defeating material progress! Today,
  I wish to taste only the bun.
 GIRL: Whatever.

Paneer, Pea and Chick Pea Coconut Delight

The self-explanatory ingredients were: 6 squares of paneer / 1 cup of chick peas, soaked and boiled / 1 cup of boiled coconut [233] / 1 cup of frozen peas / A little olive oil with which to fry.

Stirred like crazy, this mixture can actually achieve the consistency of food.

Paneer an' Onion Curry

The art of embellishing and presenting food reveals the incredible distinction between those who can cook and those who make Paneer an' Onion Curry.

It takes: 2 onions / 100g of paneer / butter / oil / turmeric / 1 tablespoon of chopped coriander / 1 teaspoonful of Nepal hand mixed spice [234] / 100g of coconut cream and water.

This made two helpings in two bowls. The secret agent that tarted up this minor domestic travesty was coriander. I was quite happy with the result but I have barely mastered the curried arts. Into every corner of the earth there percolates the idea of India and her food.

---

[233] Coconuts are associated with warm idylls and carefree hedonism. If you really are looking for "Da taste of da tropics", some experimentation with coconut, pineapple and rum will enliven the dark winter months. Just avoid idiotic songs and *never* serve a drink in a coconut shell – not even in jest.

[234] This curry powder was mixed for me by Mr TF who has travelled in Nepal. He told me that the word *curry* was from 16th century Tamil, *kari*, meaning sauce or relish. Curry powder is largely composed of turmeric, but almost every spice and herb in the mix is known to improve mental functioning. If curry powder is sprinkled on every meal (including breakfast) for just a few days, a new clarity of mind will be noticed, subtle but undeniable. The price you must pay for this is dear – Curry Coco Pops, Curry Coffee and Curry Cream Cake are just the start.

Pasta Cado

In this one desperate instance penne pasta was boiled and combined with parsley and lemon juice.

This was served with 2 Dutch vine tomatoes and 1 red pepper, roasted in olive oil and mascarpone with Parmesan shavings.

PB's Sugar Snap Meal

You don't need to count the sugar snap peas to make this meal – but I did. In this meal I used 22 sugar snaps / 2 carrots / 2 spoons of butter / 1 onion / 4 cloves of garlic / 2 tablespoons of crunchy peanut butter / 2 teaspoons of hot sauce / 2 squares of noodles

The hot paste was named *Ghiottonerie Calabresi* and was a gift from Seán Bradley.

These ingredients made one large bowl of Sugar Snap Meal. It is a dangerous dish which for guests I would eschew. It combines both peanut butter and chilli, a combination which will accentuate the bile of most.

SCRAPES

Remove the bowl from the mixer and using a rubber spatula, empty the contents on to a baking tray. Then, when Mummy has her back turned, scrape down the bowl with your finger and lick. [235]

This is not merely an illicit way to taste the base components of a cake in their rawest form, but it is both practical and convenient. Every kitchen waste bin reminds me of the value previous generations managed to extract from their foodstuffs. I would like to treat of our immense plastic, organic and liquid wasteage elsewhere.

I swiped the following scrapes:

The bowl scrapings from fudge making

I licked a bowl of chocolate icing

When nobody was looking, and did not even know that I was in the kitchen, I ran a teaspoon in some cake icing and ate that

I scraped the packet of my friend's carrot cake

I ate some of the mixture while making the tea bread to Delia Smith's recipe

---

[235] All life on Earth is pre-engineered to scavenge. Think of one creature that does not search for anything usable among discarded material during its daily period. Scavengers are useful to the eco-system although it is unclear why etymologists insist that the word originates from the Middle English skawager, meaning "customs collector". Any food that is scheduled to be euthanised is in fact fair game, although some leftover recipes are simply too garse to eat. Spaghetti Pie, Potato Fudge Cake and Casseroled Pasta have all been known in the author's time. All were scavenged, leftover recipes – and all were desperately awful.

GRAZING THROUGHOUT THE DAY

Food speaks loudly at all times of the day – it seems to have little effect on us when we eat it and yet it creates everything.

How many eating events are experienced daily? Is there decent ethnographic research being carried out on *snacking*? Will snacks eaten away from home always be higher in fat and sugar – and what is the overall effect of snacking on mood and cognition?

Eating patterns related to snacking are largely unexamined, particularly in connection with certain social occasions such as watching football and going to the cinema. These events might even fall into the category of non-hunger related "emotional" eating, the kind of eating we are most likely to deny. Sometimes snacks can be foods of integrity and offer true flavour. On other occasions they are merely sweets and biscuits which are certain to inflame the blood.

2 peacock shaped biscuits [236]

1 snowman biscuit

1 owl shaped biscuit

1 Christmas tree shaped biscuit

1 elf shaped biscuit [237]

4 oatcakes and butter

1 cheese and mustard straw

---

[236] I should add that itemising your diet for 12 months encourages self-loathing. If you were to ask me to eat these two peacock shaped biscuits again, I swear, I could not do it.

[237] In this western country trying to eat healthily at Christmas is like trying to push water up a hill with a sieve. It's like trying to make a passenger jet fly by blowing air at the wings. It's like trying to eat a packet of biscuits through a straw. It's like all of these things and more.

0.260 kg of sprouted mung beans [238]

0.250kg of sprouted flageolet beans

1 honey biscuit from the *Marks & Spencer* Christmas biscuit box

FIGURE 17 – The preparation of The Supper Book

---

[238] If past seafarers had known about sprouts scurvy would have been all but eliminated. Sprouts contain all the necessary nutrients including Vitamin C and can be grown simply and in a matter of days, so long as fresh water is available for rinsing.

6 vegetarian Aberdeen butteries [239] with butter and syrup

1 slice of raspberry, strawberry, redcurrant and whitecurrent flan with whipped cream [240]

1 slice of red fruits German shortbread paste with single cream

16 x *LU* brand *Belin Monaco Crackers* with the charming motto: "*Découvrez la recette unique de Monaco*"

1 *Heathershaw* Sticky Toffee Cake, from The Heathershaw Bakery, Crookham, Corhill on Tweed

1 500ml bottle of *Snapple* ® Fruit Drink Fruit Punch – "*Contains 12% fruit Juice*" / "*Made from the best stuff on earth*" [241]

12 (= 150g) Border Crofter's Crunch [242] "*Handbaked Scottish Biscuits*"

9 Farmhouse Crunch biscuits

---

[239] Buttery rowies need to be vegetarian given that 6 ounces of lard are used for every pound of flour in the manufacture of the non-vegetarian variety. A Forres baker described buttery rowies as follows: "The buttery is really one of the mysteries of medieval days. It is the by-product of the old, overnight sponge method."

[240] The raspberry, strawberry and redcurrant were grown by William Burnett.

[241] Why is there a "Circle K" as well as the familiar "Circle R" on the Snapple label? The "Circle K" indicates that the beverage is kosher-certified. The Organized Kashruth Laboratories in New York oversees these beverages, satisfying the delicate intelligence of religious observation.

[242] PRODUCT NAMING – In the case of both Border Crofter's Crunch and Farmhouse Crunch a tasty biscuit has been given a rural association. After all – they could have been named Castlemilk Compensation Claims Clerk Crunch and would still be the same biscuit. The primary charge is therefore evocation. Thus, in the sturdy pride of his unspoiled home county stands the Borders Crofter, a man fearfully and wonderfully made. The Crofter views a meadow over which the sunshine glides and the pale young leaves rustle as he crunches his biscuit. Crumbs roll from his tweed and fall on the grassy floor. Another day's work is rewarded with the perfect, rural custom of the biscuit.

1 chocolate-topped golden crispie square

1 175g *Safeway* "The Best" range Timperley Rhubarb yoghurt – *"Made from Somerset Wholemilk carefully blended with cream and a sumptuous compote of Timperley Rhubarb"* [243]

1 175g *Safeway* "The Best" range Woodland Strawberry yoghurt – *"Made from Somerset Wholemilk carefully blended with cream and a delicious compote of woodland strawberries"* [244]

7 *Casado* Magdalenas Clásicas Con Heuros Frescos (classic Madeleines with Fresh Eggs) – a Spanish gift from the parents.

6 sticks of carrot dipped in cream cheese and chive dip

7 tortilla chips dipped in cream cheese and chive dip

2 glasses of *Asda* non-alcoholic red grape spritzer

---

[243] Nearly half of the 1,600 new food products launched in Britain in 2004 were PREMIUM. It doesn't make sense to have half of all new products designated as premium as the term will soon lose its meaning that way. The process of preparing and marketing a food might often involve the careful devaluation of certain terms, most commonly words like *fresh*, *natural*, *new*, *best*, *original* and *whole*.

[244] Any effort will do. Here the strawberries were sold in a pot of luxury yoghurt an marketed with the qualifier "woodland". For the excitement of gastronomes, who are so urbanised as to have forgotten what the woodlands used to taste like, these are ideal.

DELIA SMITH

Delia Smith has created recipes and I have tried several of them. Enforced by the bitter experience of failed attempts at cookery, I was happy to shake away the shackles of my own invention and try something professionally devised. I even bought a cookery book called *Delia's Vegetarian Collection*, which although infrequently used, came off the shelf once or twice and amused me during several hours of instructive bakery.

I cooked four of Delia Smith's simpler creations and cannot exaggerate upon the improvements in my eating conditions.

3 portions of Delia's fragrant and spicy nut rice

1 portion of Delia's carrots and parsnips, roast in ground coriander seeds

2 slices of tea bread to Delia's recipe

1 Delia recipe carrot soup with sprouted mung beans, crème fraiche, Worcester sauce and coriander

THE MAGIC OF MILK

You are best not to drink milk. Milk is by far the most difficult substance to count when you are writing a *Supper Book* because it is added to breakfast cereals and hot drinks with such abandon that one may feel inclined to give up almost immediately. How do you estimate how much milk you have drunk in a year without playing the traitor to your enumeration?

In spite of its liquidity, milk should be regarded as a *food* and not a drink. If drunk in any quantity greater than several sips, milk will form an indigestible clot in the stomach and digestive juices may have problems. So milk may be white but it is not pure, despite its high standing in our diets. [245]

Today technology has superseded the myths of our forefathers and invention has fulfilled our milk-dreams. Some years back genetic engineers programmed bacteria to churn out the hormone that is normally found in the pituitary glands of cows, allowing these beasts (once injected) to churn out up to 15% more milk. Irish myth speaks of the abundant cow, the *glas ghaibhleann*, which didn't even have to birth a calf to produce milk, and technological science has fulfilled its duty and created this animal. Celtic witches were believed to be able to steal milk from a cow just by passing a needle near it – but now milk can appear by the manipulation of cattle through the use of that very tool.

In the Hebrew Bible, Abraham gave butter, milk and dressed calf to the three angels who came to visit him in Gen. 18. This is a challenging meal because it flouts the kosher laws as meat, butter and milk are served simultaneously. [246] Periodically also, idols in Hindu temples are seen to be drinking milk with the family of Shiva (Parvati, Ganesha and Kartikeya) apparently the thirstiest. Although rationalists are sceptical about the phenomenon of idols drinking milk, nobody can deny that it is great for milk sales, which during September 1995's world-wide miracle, jumped in New Dehli and in certain areas of England, by over 30%.

---

[245] Genesis 1: 26 - 28. In which God gives man dominion over earth, fowl and beast on the basis of man being created in the divine image. And the ecological crisis will worsen until such time as we reject the attitude that nature is there only to serve ourselves!

[246] SB Kelly suggests that Abraham and the angels may have enjoyed a lasagne given these ingredients.

The laws of milk are very peculiar. Milk is the gravy of the gods and one of the more helpful of life's gifts. We are such abusers of life's gifts however, that it is not even strange to think of our babies drinking cows' milk while we squirt this same bovine fluid into our coffee at each opportunity. The fact is that most people do not digest milk very well and the whole thing is a tremendous con-job.

My primary milk supplier was the *Robert Wiseman Dairies*. I tended to purchase their 500ml pasteurised semi-skimmed milk carton. In America semi-skimmed is nearly always sold with alliterative titles like *Lite 'n' Lively* and *Brisk 'n' Bouncy*. Every dairy does this for some reason but here we must put up with the more pedestrian *Fresh 'n' Low* (see below). *Robert Wiseman Dairies* semi-skimmed milk was used by myself at home, and was also made available at my workplace.

Also popular, was the 500ml container of *Fresh 'n' Low* ® [247]

1 litre of milk came from *Yester Dairies* East Lothian

There were also 3 x 50ml *Provamel* from *Alpro Soya* organic, unsweetened soymilks. Soymilks do the job of milk after a fashion. They are perfect for the ethically concerned, although largely unacceptable as milk.

I enjoyed 4 "Rich and Creamy" *Coronet* UHT individual milks

And I also purchased 500g of *Suma* fairly traded organic soya beans ("*these beans have been grown in Brazil*") and soaked and blended these into soymilk. This was a rough and costly exercise and created too much kitchen debris to be useful.

I would like to estimate that I consumed 45.7 pints of milk.

---

[247] All of this reminds us that the cult of dieting now occupies religious territory and is competing for our attention with older spiritual traditions based on the acceptance of decay and death. Properly consumed milk can never be bad for you – and is actually *supposed* to make you fatter.

EATING IN WITH FRIENDS

The range of connotation in the phrase "eating in" defies quick description but could loosely be said to describe food and drink that someone else prepared for me and was not paid for. Instead, this food was offered on the basis of courtesy, friendship, and dare I say it, love.

I implored my friends to provide for me so feelingly that all obliged. What sort of monument should be given? Why, my own good health. Looking at the list today, I feel giddy. The pleasantries of my friends and family delight me. Their meals delight me, as do their teas and coffees.

Chance put into my hands so many different meals. When it comes to food people are generous in ways they cannot be in other matters. Likewise we all possess a faculty for reviving ourselves in a shared meal, while disaster besets us, personal and social.

Soon I shall go before new meals, but as I pass through *The Supper Book*, I still wish to think of those who kept me going.

These were:

Amal Danjani, who served me – 1 burma snack treat / 1 bachara snack treat / 1 apple juice / 1 tea with rosemary / 6 fresh dates / 8 black grapes

Archie, who served me – 2 servings of spinach, tomato, artichoke, cheese, sweetcorn and pepper pie

Betty, who served me – 1 cup of lentil and vegetable soup with cheese

Halla Shlabi, who served me – 11 snack herb biscuits / 5 *Twiglets* / 2 fresh dates / 1 mint tea / 1 grapefruit juice / 1 corn on the cob segment

Ian and Pauline, who served me – 1 glass of Ribena and 4 portions of Greek feta salad

Imogen, who served me up – 2 milky coffees / 1 bowl of Hula Hoops

Lean, who served me – A bowl of carrot, parsnip, broccoli and leek soup / 1 veggie-burger on muffin with tomato ketchup, mayonnaise, cheese and beef tomato / 1 bowl of so-called *"Green Soup"* (containing broccoli, courgette, kale and celery) / 1 bowl of so-named *"Orange Soup"* (containing carrot, sweet potato and parsnip) / 3 brown bread rolls and cheddar cheese / 320ml of Diet 7-up / 1 veggie-burger with sliced cheese and tomato / 1 jam doughnut from Dott / 1 bowl of tomato and parsnip soup / 1 black filter coffee / 2 bowls of parsnip and sweet potato soup / 2 slices of bread / 1 bowl of *"Green Soup"* with 3 slices of brown bread, butter and sliced Jarlsberg / 1 taste of Cambazola cheese just to try it / 2 felafel and salad and fresh yoghurt in pitta / 1 bowl of that well-known *"Green Soup"* with 2 pitta breads on the side / 1 veggie-burger in muffin with cheese and mayo / 2 bowls of vegetable soup with ciabatta, butter, gruyère and pepper / 1 felafel sandwich using *Just Wholefoods*[248] brand organic "World Mixes" range wheat-free felafel / 1 felafel with tomatoes and sprouted alfalfa [249] in pitta / 1 brown ciabatta roll and cheese / 1 tomato sandwich / 1 bowl of vegetable soup / 3 bowls of summer vegetable soup with focaccia bread and butter / 1 egg muffin with mayo, ketchup and cheese / 1 boiled egg / 2 slices of toast and butter / 1 rosemary bread, cheese coleslaw and salad sandwich

Lisa, who served me – 1 plate of leek, potato and carrot soup / 2 slices of rye bread and butter

Max Hague, who served me – 2 poached eggs on toast with pepper [250]

---

[248] WHOLEFOOD is food that has been refined or processed as little as possible – as in the case of this company? It is idiocy to deconstruct the names of food companies and their produce. For example "The World Mixes" range connotes globalisation, music, cookery and multi-culturalism.

[249] According to Victoras Kulvinskas in *Survival in the 21st Century*, if we had to live in an underground shelter and could only take one type of food with us, our first choice would have to be alfalfa seed and fresh water – for the preparation of alfalfa sprouts.

[250] It was one of my happiest breakfast tables. There are many details I enjoyed, ranging from the impressive knowledge of my host to the superb setting on the Southern Scottish coast.

Michael and Anat Hoffmann, who served me – 1 segment of challa / 1 glass of Kaddish wine [251] / 1 glass of peach flavour diet ice tea / 1 bowl of pumpkin and mango soup / 1 serving of pumpkin and lime / 1 serving of potato pumpkin carrot in sweet gravy / 1 serving of pumpkin and raisin [252] / 1 serving of amaretto and tangerine / 1 glass of Laguevelin / 2 slices of mango / 4 segments of mandarin / 2 fresh figs

Mohammed Ferras served me – 1 glass of orange juice and a wafer biscuit

Mum and Dad served me – 2 slices of onion tortilla / 2 bowls of home-grown new potatoes, butter, pepper and milk [253] / 1 rock cake (Figure 18) / 3 porridge biscuits / 1 slice of Mum's ginger cake and butter / 2 bowls of Mum's potato and pasta soup

Pat and Sheila, who served me – 2 plates of potato and fish pie with puff pastry, 2 portions of peas, 2 portions of carrots / 2 slices of focaccia bread, 1 spread with Flora / bananas cooked in cranberry and sugar with single cream / 1 glass of *Don Simon* orange / 4 cheese and tomato toasted sandwiches / 2 helpings of corn, lettuce and tomato salad / 1 white wine / 1 orange juice / 2 quarters of plain tortilla and one quarter of tortilla with peppers

Shirley, who served me up – 2 teas with milk / 3 sweet biscuits

---

[251] No animal products may be allowed to taint the wine. Non-kosher winemakers often use egg whites or gelatine to clarify the wine, but kosher winemakers use a clay material called bentonite to drag suspended particles to the bottom of the barrel. They never use animal bladders for filters. Physical cleanliness, in addition to religious purity, is mandated. Tanks, crushers, presses and all equipment must be cleaned three times by modern steam cleaning, scalding hot water and when needed, blowtorches. No barrels used for non-kosher wines may be used in kosher winemaking. No pigs are allowed to carry the barrels, even if goats and men are not available.

[252] The Hoffmann family had grown the greatest pumpkin I have ever seen.

[253] Food is meaning – not only nourishment – ritual – not only consumption – ceremony – and not only act – familial relationship – and not just individual ingestion. Potatoes, butter, pepper and milk is our family's most meaningful meal, expressing: 1. Our thrift 2. Our rural roots 3. Our ability as farmers 4. Our eccentricity (as opposed to the eccentricity of other families). New potatoes, butter, pepper and milk is the most recognisable and cross-generational of Burnett meals.

FIGURE 18 – Mum's own rock cake

Simone and Michael, who served me – 1 black tea / 2 Tropicana orange juices / 2 slices of wholemeal baguette / 5 slices of white baguette [254] / 1 slice of brie / 1 slice of Etorki cheese / 2 helpings of red onion, feta and cherry tomato pie (pronounced "paah") / 1 bowl of strawberries with fromage frais

Seán and Janet served me – 1 plate of 3 spiced rice / 3 bowls of chick pea in rich yellow sauce / 3 okra in hot red sauce / 3 plates of soft vegetables in very hot brown sauce / 1 small glass of Newcastle Brown Ale / 1 and a half popadoms / 6 cups espresso coffee / 3 slices of toasted brioche and butter / 1 black filter coffee and slice of Janet's bakewell tart / 2 teaspoons of Seán's hummus / 4 and a half pints of Edinburgh tap water / 8 roast potatoes / 2 enchiladas and bean and cheese / 1 serving of guacamole / a sample of part-burned puff pastry / 2 puff pastry squares / 2 helpings of vegetable in white sauce / 5 asparagus tips / 6 potatoes in oatmeal / 2 glasses of *Barberino* [255] wine / 1 portion of Eve's pudding and custard / 1 plate of *Beanfeast* and bean mix / 17 chocolate raisins / 1 feta salad made by Bridget Bradley / 3 servings of vegetable curry and rice with sun dried tomato bread / 1 pint bottle of Newcastle

---

[254] BAGUETTES: They came to the UK from France in the late 1970s and people were so confused that they first used them as draught excluders. I recall the first baguette ever to be baked in the Scottish town of Aberdeen. This baguette was so famous that it was displayed in the local museum for a week.

[255] This red wine cost £2.22 a bottle and was the lowest priced wine that that Seán could find – "It really is too low," he said.

Brown Ale / 1 small glass of *Lidl* bitter / 3 florets of broccoli / 4 small boiled potatoes / 3 carrot sticks / 1 plate of *Quorn* pie of Mrs Jan Stewart / 1 plate of ribbon pasta with light tomato pesto and vegetables / 1 plate of noodles and *Quorn* chicken made by Hannah Bradley / 3 x 330ml bottles of *Becks* / 1 glass of house red wine / 1 plate of *Quorn* stir fry with pepper and mangetout in spicy sweet sauce / 1 black filter coffee / 1 plate of noodles with soy and sweet chilli sauce / 3 courgettes in batter / 1 slice of spinach and cheese flan / 2 glasses of *Multivit* juice / some crusts discarded by the family / 1 potato in oatmeal / 1 spinach and potato calzone / 1 quarter pizza with a pineapple ring / 1 slice of cheese and tomato pizza / 1 slice of vegetable and olive pizza [256] / 1 slice of vegetable and sweetcorn pizza / 6 baked baby potatoes / 4 small glasses of orange juice / 1 plate of vegetable curry with saffron rice, papad and nan bread / 1 tomato pakora and one vegetable pakora / 1 roll with Jan Stewart's marmalade / 2 plates (servings I would call them) of Shepherdless Pie / 1 portion of broccoli / 1 portion of carrots / 2 slices of garlic ciabatta / 1 sage and sweet and sour vegetable ball

Steve and Rachael served me up – 1 winter vegetable casserole with cauliflower cheese, plus peas in a portion / 1 slice of apple pie and ice cream / 1 cup of filter coffee with frothy milk

Stuart served me – 1 quarter of a Spanish tortilla / 1 black coffee / 1 plate of pasta with mushroom and mozzarella / 1 saucer of dhal and rice / Macaroni Multi Coloro served with cheese and tomato and toasted, buttered brown bread and peas

Stuart and Sam served me – 3 slices of toast with butter and marmalade / 1 black coffee / 1 spoonful of peanut butter – I wonder if my hosts knew that I took this. Did I ask for it, or was it offered? / 2 slices of focaccia and butter / 1 plate of pasta in tomato sauce / 3 glasses of Rosé wine "*Origin*" / 1 glass of house white wine / 1 chick pea and pepper curry / 1 half of a Peshwari nan / 1 portion of pilau saffron rice / 1 kail and lemon risotto / 1 portion of tomato salad / 3 slices of bread dipped in tomato salad / 2 bread morsels eaten late /

---

[256] Becoming a vegetarian is not merely a symbolic gesture. In fact every time a person becomes a vegetarian, meat sales fall with immediate effect.

1 plate of homemade Kurry [257] / A handsome homemade pizza with coleslaw / 2 glasses of house red wine / 1 peppermint tea / 3 portions of SBK peanut butter noodle / 1 plate of curried crunchy vegetables

Susan and Ian served me – 2 cherry tomatoes / 1 polo mint / 1 sun-dried tomato quiche with *Branston* pickle, potato salad, rocket and lettuce salad and cheddar cheese / 3 and half slices of bread and butter / 1 glass of white wine / 1 bowl of vegetable stew and 3 dumplings / half a bag – approx 15g – of Pickled Onion flavoured *Monster Munch* / 1 vegetable Kiev [258] / 1 slice of Bakewell tart and cream / 4 slices of bread and "spreadable" butter / 1 portion of salad / lotsa paprika kettle chips / 2 glasses of heavily diluted fruit and barley drink / 1 slice of cheese and onion quiche / 1 slice of tomato and onion quiche with cherry tomato salad / 1 slice of raspberry filled German paste and single cream / 1 plate of Risotto de Vegetableys / 1 plate of new potatoes with sautéd leeks and basil / 1 omelette with courgette, mushroom [259] and Edam, with parsley and new potatoes / 1 lettuce and hummus sandwich on a soft white roll with salad / 2 cheese and pickle rolls / 1 plate of *Quorn* Bolognaise with spaghetti / 1 green salad with French dressing and pasta / 1 portion of pasta conches with tomato sauce and 4 *Quorn* meatballs / 1 glass of Diet Coke with 50g *Walkers* "Sensations" Tangy Malaysian Chutney flavoured Crackers

---

[257] I asked my host for the recipe for this curry, but all I was offered was a list. This is the classical approach to cookery, invoking the *Apicius*, a collection of Roman recipes thought to have been compiled in the fourth or fifth century CE. In the *Apicius*, the contents are out of order, some recipes are in the wrong chapters and many of the recipes are truncated to merely being lists of ingredients. The list in this case was as follows: chick peas / peppers / onions / garlic / 2 x tin tomatoes / root ginger (grated) / cumin / coriander / fresh coriander / chilli / cinnamon / fennel seeds. Note that the only instruction included in this recipe was to GRATE the ginger!

[258] Some foodies are so industrious. Frenchman Nicholas Appert, brewer, pickler, confectioner, and chef who discovered the principles of canning foods, also created the KIEV form in the late 18th century, when wealthy Russian households liked to hire French chefs as peacock-like status symbols.

[259] The fact that mushrooms thrive in dark and humid places casts a sinister shadow on their ill reputation. Lucrezia Borgia was fond of serving them to further her wicked purposes, and Roman Emperor Claudius was thought to have been fed them by his wife Agrippina, with fatal results. POISON is so little discussed, but is the most deep-seated of all food's dark secrets.

Tadg and Margaret served me – 1 saffron rice / 2 plates of matar paneer / 1 spicy chick pea curry [260] / 1 fine serving of dhal / 2 croissants with butter and strawberry jam / 1 glass of *Volvic* spring water / 1 basmati rice / 1 aloo fuul gobi / 1 chana bhuna / 2 bowls of potato and leek soup / 4 slices of seeded brown bread with butter / 2 cups of black filter coffee / 1 bowl of vegetable soup

Todd and Lucy served me – 3 cups of milk tea and one butter biscuit / 4 glasses of water

---

[260] HOW DO YOU MEASURE THE STRENGTH OF A CURRY? The strength of the earth's magnetic field can be measured on the ground using instruments such as magnetometers, which can be adapted to quantify the strengths of curry. When used on foodstuffs, magnetometers create a grid system known as the Curry Grid, which is a useful tool in assessing meals both below Korma level and above Vindaloo.

The basic strengths on the Curry Grid are as follows:

MILD – The blue eyes of my angelic girl.

MEDIUM – Easy, although some people will still complain!

MEDIUM HOT – Middle aged folly.

HOT – The Burning Palace. Palsied limbs. Will not however peel the enamel of teeth.

VERY HOT – Eyes water. Nose runs. Place toilet roll in the fridge.

VERY HOT PLUS – High tension hallucinogenic. Mind altering. Mouth jammed and begemmed. Temporary blindness. Bowel tart and moistened. Tooth enamel stripped.

Pasta Repasta

In which I used a 400g tin of *Napolina* [261] chopped tomatoes including juice /
135g tube of tomato puree / 3 onions / 17 cloves of garlic / mixed herbs
and a little olive oil.

This sauce was served over three nights, with whole-wheat spaghetti each time.

Pasta con Scratcha

To make *Pasta con Scratcha* sauce use
4 beef tomatoes / 1 glass of white wine /
4 cloves of garlic / one small onion / 1 135g tube of tomato puree /
olive oil / mixed herbs / and 1 green pepper.

This sauce was served over two nights, with whole-wheat spaghetti both times.

Pasta Smacker

Native dishes have a habit of deteriorating on alien soil,
but not so the classic *Pasta Smacker*.

For this popular teatime pasta meal you will need to find: 2 onions / 9 cloves of
garlic, all cut large / one splash of olive oil / 1 splash of groundnut oil / 1 tin of
peeled plum tomatoes (400g) / 340g of sun dried tomatoes / some basil /
1 glass of red wine / 142g of tomato puree

This sauce was served over two nights, with whole-wheat spaghetti both times.

---

[261] It all depends. It might be best if I just ignore brand names altogether. I would hate
for anyone to think that it *had to be* Napolina.

THE WATER COOLER

A t work the water is filtered and served through a machine known as the *Aquator*. The word *Aquator* is such a great wordplay that it is used by several companies at once, to sell several different items. Thus an *Aquator* is not just an attractive point-of-use water dispenser, (*"able to function within two metres of any mains power and water supply"*), but it is also a water resource modelling system, a weather protection fabric system, and a sewage treatment product. [262]

Even in our cold climes these water dispensers are invaluable. There is never a queue for the water dispenser, because in the office people become thirsty at different times. Water dispensers such as the *Aquator* are great for staff with hangovers, because the clean water offers something vital that cannot be provided by a tap. In the same way that a cellophane wrapped sandwich with a logo is more befitting our uncontaminated workspaces than a homemade sandwich, so the water filter system pursues a violent dismissal of the difficult past when services were not performed at the touch of a switch.

In all, **97 pints** of water were pumped to me through the *Aquator* in the course of one year.

---

[262] I don't know what these other Aquators do but the internet has convinced me that they are available. I am confined to a box of time and space in which I am taught to peck at buttons for an answer. Hence I enjoy the water dispenser. I don't have to turn any taps – I just press a button. It's like everything else around here. I just need to press a button.

94 LITRES OF BEER

B eer is famous in our time. Everyone seems to want it and yet nobody can hold down more than half a dozen pints of the stuff. Due to this challenge, beer is widely abused even though many of our matings are its result.

The following is the list of bottled and canned beers which I drank at home and during drinking sessions in the homes of others. Appropriately enough, this is a golden age of bottled and canned beer. Storage of beer in domestic casks, butts and hogsheads would be absurd and impractical today, because it would involve an effort on the part of the consumer. To ease this burden, beer is therefore filtered and charged with carbonic acid gas before being and squashed into handy bottles and cans. The product is inferior to properly matured and naturally conditioned beer, but nonetheless serves a cheap and potent public service.

Aside from my pub-totals, listed elsewhere, I drank 94 litres of beer in one year. As a result, when I arrived at work some days, my heart was touched by sweet sadness as I smarted from the small wounds inflicted the night before. Beers of the year were:

7 x 275ml bottles of *Becks* [263]

6 x 330ml bottles of *Becks*

4 x 275ml bottles of *Becks*

1 500ml can of *Becks*

3 small glasses of *Becks*

1 500ml can of *Skol* lager

Several sips of *Skol* lager

---

[263] Becks has been brewed in Germany since 1874 in accordance with the *Reinheitsgebot*, the German Purity Law of 1516, which requires beer to be made only from barley malt, hops and water. These days this recipe also includes yeast, but only because yeast's existence wasn't known in the 16th century.

9 x 25ml bottles of *Grolsch* [264] (Figure 19)

7 x 440ml cans of *Grolsch*

4 x 300ml bottles of *Grolsch*

1 500ml can of *Grolsch*

1 330ml bottle of *Grolsch*

13 x 440ml cans of *Budweiser*

3 x 330ml bottles of *Budweiser*

FIGURE 19 – A stubby 25ml bottle of Grolsch

---

[264] Grolsch is not a type of beer. What I am mistakenly referring to here is the flagship pilsner beer of the *Grolsche Bierbrouwerij*, a product that is labelled "Grolsch Premium Lager". Even in a can, this Grolsch is a bright beer with a huge crown of thick foam that leaves bountiful loops of chunky Belgian lace down the glass.

1 500ml can of *Budweiser*

1 1 litre bottle of *Budweiser* [265]

15 x 330ml bottles of *Kronenbourg 1664*

6 x 440ml cans of *Kronenbourg 1664*

1 750ml bottle of *Kronenbourg 1664*

One flat 330ml bottle of *Kronenbourg 1664* [266]

2 x half 440ml cans of *Miller* lager

19 x 440ml cans of *Stella Artois* lager [267]

FIGURE 20 – A 33cl bottle ay Stella

---

[265] It's a bottle of beer bigger than a bottle of wine!

[266] There was approximately 300ml left in this bottle – remaindered from the night before which in this case was Hogmanay.

[267] Stella is too common a beer.

14 x 500ml canisters of *Stella Artois* [268]

9 x 33cl bottles of *Stella* [269] (See Figure 20)

3 miniature glasses of *Stella* – *"drink up lad!"*

1 440ml can of stashed *Stella* [270]

6 x 500ml cans of *Fosters* (Figure 21)

2 x 33cl bottles of *Fosters*

FIGURE 21 – *Fosters tinned Lager*

---

[268] STELLA is brewed by the Belgian super-brewing conglomerate INTERBREW, which also owns the Labatt brand in Canada, Rolling Rock brand in America, Bohemia and Dos Equis brands in Mexico, Tennent's brand in Scotland, Bass and Boddington's brands in England, Staropramen in the Czech Republic, and Oranjeboom in Holland. To name a few.

[269] I know that Stella is not the only beer, but it has a little extra kick to it and it does at least guarantee a gloriously hardcore pished-up romp.

[270] This can was opened and then stashed in a bush at 11.17pm one September night. It was collected and finished later at 1.50am on the road home.

4 x 330ml bottles of *San Miguel* lager [271]

2 x 500ml canisters of *San Miguel* lager

1 and a half 500ml bottles of *Budweiser Budvar*

1 500ml can of *McEwan's* lager

2 x 1 litre bottles *San Miguel* International Premium Lager

4 x 500ml cans of *Red Stripe* lager

2 x 484ml cans of *Red Stripe* lager

2 x 500ml cans of *Sweetheart Stout* (Figure 22)

FIGURE 22 – Sweetheart Stout – it makes your lips puff up

---

[271] "From Seville to Barcelona, the uniquely refreshing taste of San Miguel is at the heart of a great night out." A distance of only 600km – and a modest catchment area in these days of global marketing. At Marbella I passed the factory where this beer is brewed, with its large and sticky stained silver towers, smoke stacks and chain-link fences.

5 x 440ml cans of *Guinness* [272]

1 275ml bottle of *Corona* beer

4 x 440ml cans of *Carlsberg*

3 x 660ml bottles of *Carlsberg* premium lager

1 and a half 640ml bottles of *Tiger* Gold Medal lager

7 x 25cl bottles of *Safeway* Belgian beer

3 x 25cl bottles of *Co-op* French lager [273]

8 x 25cl bottles of *Tesco* Biere Spéciale [274]

5 x 550ml bottles of *Newcastle Brown Ale*

1 swig [275] of Tadg's *Kronenbourg* lager

---

[272] For fun (in Ireland), there is the practice of ordering a whiskey to sip while the stout is being poured. The trick is to order another stout before you're too close to the bottom of the present one so that you don't go thirsty during the transition. If you forget, then you might have to order another whiskey while they pour the stout. After a few whiskies, the stout tastes like mother's milk and the brand of either isn't terribly important, although it just so happened that I witnessed this alcoholic caper committed with Bushmills whiskey and Guinness.

[273] Anagrams of lager are: *argle, glare, large* and *regal* (also its palindromic form). If footnotes were permitted footnotes I would offer a defintion of *argle*.

[274] This Tesco lager was an almost translucent, yellow colour, with a good amount of carbonation and a short-lived, white head. The immediate aroma was of floral hops with some grassy tones, followed by a little graininess and some faint malt in the background. Shortly after that I was flinging CDs across the room at my colleague who was trying to play the trombone.

[275] A SWIG? "He looked up, however, at my coming, knocked the neck off the bottle like a man who had done the same thing often, and took a good swig, with his favourite toast of, Here's luck." Robert Louis Stevenson, *Treasure Island*.

1 500ml bottle of *Morland* brewery *Old Speckled Hen*

1 500ml bottle of *Freeminer* brewery *Gold Miner Ale*

1 440ml cannister of *Tennent's* lager

2 x 500ml cans of *Deuchars IPA*

2 x 1 litre bottles of 1925 *Alhambra* premium lager [276]

1 500ml bottle of *Caledonian* [277] IPA

1 255ml bottle of *Moosehead* lager – *"Since 1867"*

1 440ml can of *Caledonian 80/-*

3 x 33cl bottles of *Leffe* – Bière Belge – Leffe Anno 1240 [278]

1 33cl bottle of *Orval* Biere Trappiste [279]

---

[276] In terms of stomach pressure, two litres of beer are like one large meal. This sudden and vast influx of gaseous liquid was however, according to the label, "Carefully brewed in Grenada, Southern Spain with pure crystal water from the Sierra Nevada mountains", so I felt much more comfortable.

[277] The Caledonian Brewery in Edinburgh is known locally as The Caley. Their beers were until recently produced using water from what is known as Edinburgh's Charmed Circle of Brewery Wells. Now the breweries are dismantled and the Brewery Wells are built over with tightly constructed silver and glass apartments for wine drinkers!

[278] Full marks to Leffe Blonde ("abbaye de Abdij Van Leffe"), "The Authentic Belgian Abbey Beer". The two functions of the mouth – being to ingest the physical and to express the mental – were perfectly united in my three bottles.

[279] Trappist drinking? This was best described by Li Po (701 - 762 CE), who centuries ago wrote a reflective verse on single-handed swigging, called Drinking Alone by Moonlight
A cup of wine, under the flowering trees;
I drink alone, for no friend is near.
Raising my cup I beckon the bright moon,
For he, with my shadow, will make three men.

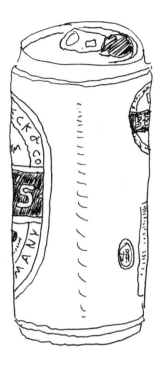

FIGURE 23 – A can of lager gifted at the railway station,
expressly for consumption on the train

1 440ml can of *Becks* that Seán Bradley gave me for the train
(Figure 23)

2 x 33cl bottles of *Bavaria* Holland beer

1 550ml bottle of *Samuel Smith's Nut Brown Ale*

2 x 13.5% Extra Free 500ml-for-the-price-of-440ml tins of
Kronenbourg 1664 Premium Lager – *"Brewed with a unique hop blend*
including aromatic hops from Alsace"

2 x 25cl bottles of unidentified lager

173

2 bottles of unbranded Czech Prague premium lager

1 500ml bottle of *Young's* Acclaim Champion beer

1 500ml bottle of *Skye* Black Isles organic stout

1 660ml bottle of Isle of Skye brewery "*Misty Isle*" bottle-conditioned wheat beer

A glass of *Badger* Golden Champion ale – "*Deceptively Drinkable*" [280]

… and cider:

1 500ml bottle of *Westons* strong organic cider

---

[280] I'm amused to find the word *drinkable* used to market a beer – as if a food could be made more tempting through the qualifier *edible*. While young, I was told that the words *eatable* and *edible* were interchangeable and that they both meant the same thing – causing me to spend much of my adult life demonstrating the contrary. As an adjective I've therefore concluded that *eatable* refers to the fact that something is of a quality suitable for eating, expressing a very low degree of enthusiasm concerning the taste and other properties of that foodstuff – whereas *edible* describes something that is fit for human consumption, merely because the food contains nothing that will poison the eater. Both *eatable* and *edible* suffer the same adjectival description in the dictionary – as referring to something as being fit to be eaten – but I believe their definitions only synchronise as nouns. As nouns, both words effectively refer to the same thing i.e., *eatables* or *edibles* being understood as things fit to be eaten.

CHRISTMAS DINNER

Christmas dinner is the primary stuff-up of the consumer year and is a tradition-laden affair. To have a Christmas dinner one must ordinarily have both a family and a family home – so perhaps fewer people take Christmas dinner than we assume. I wonder if Alfred Suzanne's words are still true on the subject: "*On that day no-one in England may go hungry*"? [281]

Starving or stuffed, the anniversary of Christmas is memorable not for the religious meaning but for the wholesale slaughter of turkeys, geese and all kinds of game. Include the shopping, the waste paper, the staff nights-out and the force-feeding of television – and you've created a *bloodbath*.

What these excesses reveal, particularly in the amount of waste generated, is our astonishing ability to make much celebration from very little. Feasting is however a human norm – although in these lands of plenty, one must sometimes make an extraordinary physical effort to achieve it.

This year my Christmas dinner consisted of the following:

1 bowl of cabbage, tomato and pasta soup, with sprouted mung beans, grated Parmesan, and 6 slices melba toast and butter

1 420g packet of *Quorn* sliced roast – "*Quorn sliced roast with sage and onion stuffing in a rich redcurrant port and citrus gravy*" / "*New*") – with 7 roast potatoes / 1 helping of boiled carrots / 1 boiled potato / 6 Brussels sprouts grown by Mr William Burnett / Several spoons of spiced redcurrant jelly, being the recipe of Auntie Ackie [282]

1 helping of Mrs West's recipe Christmas suet pudding, with brandy custard

---

[281] *La Cuisine Anglaise et Americaine*, Alfred Suzanne. No, these words are not true. According to charity *Shelter* in Great Britain 120,000 children woke up homeless on Christmas morning 2004.

[282] Like other families we have learned through simple measures to achieve commemoration of distant members by means of their recipes.

PETER BURNETT

3 homemade meringues with brandy cream

2 glasses of white wine from my father's yardage, *Coteaux Du Layon, Rochefort* 1992 [283]

2 glasses of red wine – unknown

1 glass of Drambuie

---

[283] Mr Burnett, a share-owner in this vineyard, was invited to events there one year. While visiting the vineyard he was as he put it, "totally and irresponsibly pissed." I have an antidote to this! As sizeable vineyards have up to 12,000 shareholders they have in effect a legion of unpaid ambassadors who care about their product. The perks and privileges which shareholders enjoy normally amount to special wine offerings, discount lunch invites, VIP tours and the chance to use winery facilities for their own private parties. I would extend these privileges to an actual three-month stint making the wine. First shareholders would travel to France where they would arrive in time for the harvest and crush. Shareholders would spend several weeks cutting grapes from the vine using a curved picking knife and filling gondolas which they would then carry to the winery. Then the shareholders would run the grapes through the destemmer and the crusher until only crushed grapes remained. After adding the yeast, the shareholders might imagine they had some spare time during fermentation — but they would be wrong. Most of winemaking involves cleaning the equipment, such as barrels, presses, pipes and tanks, all of which need to be scrubbed and sterilised. In terms of the wine itself, during this time the crushed skins and juice would need to be mixed, and this is best done manually. This is called "punching down", and each shareholder would take a long stick with a flat end with which they would punch through the cap of skins on the fermenting wine until these are fully mixed with the juice below. Using pallet-jacks and forklifts the shareholders would learn to handle and stack wine barrels without breaking any, or letting any roll away. As each barrel loses about 2 bottles of wine per month through evaporation into the oak, the barrels would need to be topped up by the shareholders, who'd climb like monkeys over the barrels filling them. Once this part is complete the shareholders would end their three month stretch by grabbing some gloves and shears and heading back to the vineyards to prune away 95% of everything that grew during the previous season. While doing this, they may be called back to the winery to clean up the lees – 2 gallons of which will be removed from each barrel. The waste lees amount to about 300 gallons of dead yeast and protein and looks like a foamy, blueberry jam, and would need to be removed and sloshed away, after which everything will need to be cleaned again. Most boring of all, before they go home, shareholders would work on the mobile bottling line, carrying bottles, cleaning bottles, checking bottles, counting bottles, sweeping up broken bottles, boxing bottles – and seeing bottles in their dreams.

THE GRAZING GAME

The more available food becomes the less likely we are to eat our regular three square meals a day. It's said that in Britain of yore, a plate was a square of wood with a bowl carved out of the centre and that you took this board with you wherever you went in the hope of picking up a square meal – but this is certainly romantic rubbish. Most believe that the expression *a square meal* was originally American with Mark Twain arguing that it was a Californian miners' term, perhaps referring to the rightness of squares – a figurative sense suggesting that something has been properly constructed. All is bunk, however, and the meaning of food lies in the snacker's crumbs and in the cold leftovers of yesterday's tea. In this mess of remains I continue to snack, eating the following as I go:

2 *Bachelors* Cup-a-Soup – cream of asparagus flavour with croutons

1 *Marks & Spencer* Mexican sweet potato and 3-bean wrap

2 slices of Mum's lemon Easter cake

1 50cl plastic bottle of *Vittel* still spring water

500g of strawberry flavour *Pure Milk Twist*

1 *Co-op* cheese and tomato sandwich [284]

This year I ate 4 *pains au chocolat* [285]

1 litre of chocolate soya milk

---

[284] "Cheddar cheese and sliced tomato on buttered soft grain white bread" – these are strange circumstances – for those of us who cannot make a cheese and tomato sandwich and need to buy one – we are given a description of what a cheese and tomato sandwich actually is.

[285] Verser les œufs, les jaunes d'œufs, le sucre et le cacao. À l'aide du fouet à fil, bien mélanger les ingrédients à basse vitesse, et le voila – PAIN AU CHOCOLAT.

1 300g packet of *CostCutter* ginger nut biscuits

1 cheese, chilli and pepper wrap with salad

1 glass of iced water with lemon

2 cinnamon whirls [286]

1 150g packet of *Maryland* double chocolate chip cookies [287]

1 170g tub of *Co-op* hummus

300g of *Co-op* plain chocolate digestives

250g of *President* brand Emmenthal cheese

1 454g tin of *La Preferida* refried beans with spicy chipotle [288]

1 small tub of guacamole from *Lupe Pintos* deli, Edinburgh

1 70g *Walls* Cornetto – Love Potion Number 3 flavour – "*chocolate & vanilla flavour ice creams*"

---

[286] A few of you want to know more about the fine delicacy of the cinnamon whirl and several have asked how many whirls should be eaten at once. Looking through my diaries in search of whirl information I recalled a time when I was left with five cinnamon whirls after a business seminar, at which these buns are most popular. I learned something important about myself that day when I realised that I would rather die of overeating whirls than die of shame in throwing them out. It's known as the "waste-not-want-not" attitude – and as you see, I obviously lived to tell the tale.

[287] I ate all these cookies in one sitting – and that's 15 cookies man! As Mark Twain was fond of saying: "Deep down in his private heart, no man respects himself much."

[288] I didn't know what CHIPOTLES were – but I looked them up on the internet and found out that they are smoked jalapeno chilli peppers. There is actually an online community for fans of chipotles – including the following links: Chipotle Locations / Chipotle History / Chipotle Reviews / Chipotle Deeds of Heroism / Chipotle Erotica / Chipotles In Space / and Chipotle Buffs Share Stories

1 450ml canister of *Baxters "Favourites"* French Onion Soup – eaten with crème fraiche, cut coriander and sprouted soya beans

100g of *Stockan and Gardens* original Orkney Oatcakes *"With no added sugar"*

2 pitta bread with felafel, cherry tomato, red onion, Greek yoghurt and sprouted aduki beans

1 serving of salad, comprising spinach, garlic, onions, with lemon and olive oil dressing

1 mouthful of soup that turned out to contain something animal, probably **PIG** [289]

1 500ml plastic bottle of *Campina Yazoo* – vanilla ice cream flavour milkshake. *"Vanilla ice cream flavour sterilised milk drink made with skimmed and whole milk"*

10ml of *Bach* Balancing Blooms Flower Remedy – *"Grape alcohol with flower essences"*. This concoction contained Star of Bethlehem (for comfort); Cherry Plum (for strength and confidence); Rock Rose (for fearlessness); Impatiens (so that I would become gentle and forgiving – it didn't work); and Clematis (to render me stable and bring me down to earth). *"Dr Bach believed his essences captured the positive spirit of each flower."* 27% by volume alcohol, grape alcohol solution (= *grappa?*)

1 330ml receptacle of *Sunmagic Natural Start* pineapple and orange drink *"Fruit juice drink with milk and cereals"*

---

[289] CUE THE RANT. Although I'd like to say that no animals were harmed in the production of *The Supper Book*, I cannot, especially given the quantity of dairy consumed. Here I was served some pork in error. The suffering of the pig was criminal first because the animals we eat live more by feeling, than by thought as we do – and secondly because I spat the rest out. Complete vegetarianism is probably the only solution to the efficient distribution of the world's food resources and a key step towards the fair treatment of animals. Spitting out your food is not.

6 wholemeal rock cakes and butter

1 slice of Sarah Hughes' lemon tart

1 slice of Marylyn Ridland's chocolate Easter Cake

1 *Kingsway* muffin with *Philadelphia* cheese and cucumber

A half *Kingsway* muffin with butter and cucumber

1 200ml plastic bottle of *Maltesers* drink – "*Made with skimmed milk*"

18 yoghurt-covered raisins

5 half muffins with butter, peanut butter and jam

Half a slice of carrot cake

Another stolen spoonful of crunchy peanut butter

8 (= 320g) x *Discovery* tortillas [290]

1 *Penguin* biscuit

2 slices of toast with vegetable franks and tomato sauce

1 slice of caramel shortbread

2 slices of grilled halumi cheese

---

[290] The pack-quote is: "The true taste of the Americas." Is this claim worth pursuing? And under what grounds could such a claim be verified? Those unconvinced by the fact may be interested in Plato's assertion in *Phaedo* that neither "truth" nor "thought of any kind ever comes from the body." Hoping to show that the body is so distracted with its needs, Plato argues that eating is about satisfaction and satisfaction is about swallowing everything including the claims and the manufacturer's reputation.

1 wedge of carrot cake

1 toasted cheese and tomato sandwich with mayo and ketchup [291]

2 x 330ml cans of 7-Up [292]

1 *Ashers* French cake [293]

1 slice of sponge cake with a custard centre, icing and coconut

1 litre of *Tropicana* "Original" [294] orange juice

1 Danish iced whirl

1 37g *Tracker* bar, strawberry flavour

1 slice of cherry cheesecake

Half a *Speculoos* biscuit

2 spoonfuls of macaroni cheese nicked from Stuart Allardyce's cooking pot

1 chocolate topped crispy biscuit

---

[291] I know that my efforts to make a toasted cheese and tomato sandwich were wasted by the overpowering taste of the ketchup.

[292] With the football pun on the tin: "Never mind the cup, drink straight from the can."

[293] One purchases a cake that is both French and Scots. The Holy Shrine of Ashers in Inverness is the finest of all bakeries, and it serves part of Moray and the lower Highlands with bakes and sweetmeats. The bakery was established in 1877 and is now run by George and Alister Asher. A great deftness is required for the making of perfect cakes.

[294] *Original* is one of the most common descriptors for food and drink and is a term intended to evoke the first and genuine form of something from which others are derived. Nothing can equal the power of an *original* in times of mass-marketing and choice. The reckless extension of food lines into bizarre cul-de-sacs has brought *original* into play, giving the word a strength that few other words possess.

1 slice of bread dipped in tzatziki

2 x *KitKat* "Kubes" biscuits

350g of *Co-op* macaroni cheese [295]

500g of *Bevelini* brand pasta penne

1 litre of *Tropicana* Pure Premium Sanguinello

1 150g *Müller* "Crunch Corner" strawberry crumble dessert

1 175g *Müller* "Fruit Corner" with cherry fruit

17 poppy seed crackers – eaten plain

210g of Swiss Emmenthal cheese

Newspaper articles, television programmes and food magazines have encouraged our neuroses concerning eating. On the whole however, we are happy when we are eating and only neurotic about it when we are not.

---

[295] Boccacio's story of Calandrino in the *Decameron* celebrates the culinary wedlock of cheese and macaroni, a food which makes several whacky appearances in medieval writings. In the third story on the eighth day of the *Decameron*, we read of that fantastic place called Bengodi where there is a mountain consisting entirely of grated cheese where the people do nothing but cook macaroni, which they roll down the slopes all day. Calandrino delights in this rumour and fantasises about this macaroni, wishing to feast his face on it by lying at the bottom of the hill. The macaroni is intended to highlight Calandrino's gullibility and how much he wants to believe that there really is such a place. In another tale is depicted a medieval version of a polygraph test, which applies the common belief at the time that a person who is lying will not be able to swallow bread and cheese when under examination. As in the more up to date version of the same: *I find that all a little hard to swallow.*

PUB GUIDE (L – Z)

To list the full effects that all this drinking had on me would require a volume in itself. I would have to conjure conversations, empty wallets, piped music, the stink of cigarettes and the laughter heard in public houses.

The Scots have always been drinkers and often to their peril. *"Cases are on record,"* writes Victor MacClure, *"of the bearers at a funeral setting off for the graveyard without the most important item of the procession, the coffin, and going for miles without discovering this mistake."* [296]

The days may be gone when the closes of Edinburgh and goose-dubs of Glasgow thronged with the squalor of unsavoury drunks, but drinking patterns are no more pleasant today. The dungy lewdness of 19th and 20th century pubs has been replaced by brash neon-lit bingeing that thanks to new laws can continue for 24 hours a day. [297]

Even drenched in the deep pools of all this excess and facing this shameful list I regret none of it. As it stands, I can no more deny this list than I can explain it – for in this life each glass comes with its own reason and its own justification.

The L to Z of my public drinking was as follows:

Laird and Dog, Lasswade – 2 pints of Ossian's Ale

> I cycled to the Laird with several branches of holly strapped to my handlebars. I waited on pseudo-traditional bar furniture and delivered the holly to my publisher.

Ma Cameron's, Aberdeen – 1 pint of Lia Fal Ale

> The thousand freedoms of expression prompted by drink are cheerily evident in this old rabbit warren of a pub.

---

[296] *Scotland's Inner Man*, Victor MacClure, p175, London, 1935.

[297] Holy Willie was not a hypocrite – he was merely a drunk. There are few more willing to lecture on the evils of drink than a Scottish drunkard.

The Mansfield Traquair, Edinburgh – 1 white wine

The building was once a Catholic Apostolic Church – but now it's a
wedding and seminar venue, known informally as Edinburgh's Sistine
Chapel because of the murals painted there by Phoebe Anna Traquair.

Mathers, Edinburgh – 2 x 330ml bottles of Becks

"The finest landscape in the world is improved by a good inn in the foreground."
Samuel Johnson

Mezz, Edinburgh – 1 pint of Stella Artois

The Mezz is as tidy as a hive of orderly Scots bees.

The Moo, or Meadow Bar, Edinburgh – 3 pints of Fosters lager / 1 Newcastle
Brown Ale / 1 pint of Becks lager

Thirsty Lunch.

Native State, Edinburgh – 2 x 330ml bottles of Tiger Beer, plus 1 sip of white wine

A barn of a bar, functional, and evoking the (lack of) spirit of our age.

Ocean Terminal, Absolute Art, Edinburgh – 2 glasses of house white wine

That damn nagging in my belly. It's born of art mixing with wine.

Oxford Bar, Edinburgh – 1 330ml bottle of 1664 [298] / Two half pints of Best

False certitude concerning divine intentions saw me nearly run down
when danderin oot the door. One must be canny. The responsibilities of
a publican don't normally extend to the pavement and nearby roadway.

---

[298] This 1664 was smuggled into the bar, resting in my pocket – the Oxford Bar would
never sell such a drink.

Palm Court, Aberdeen – 1 pint and a half of McEwan's Export

The Palm Court taunts West Aberdeen with the muddy thunder of its taps.

Pasquale's, Edinburgh [299] – 1 glass of Nastro lager / a half glass of house red wine

Pasquale has gone now and the patrons are as dumb as mudhens without him. One evening, I witnessed Pasquale fling a leg over the head of one of his diners, without that diner even noticing.

P'tite Folie, Edinburgh – 2 mouthfuls of house white wine

These two mouthfuls were pressed on me in flight.

The Queen's Theatre, Edinburgh – 1 330ml bottle of Budweiser

The show was Randy Newman and it was the first time that I'd heard his songs.

Le Rendezvous, Smithfield – 3 glasses of 2002 Sancerre / 1 vodka and tonic with ice

"Give strong drink unto him that is ready to perish, and wine unto those that be of heavy hearts." Proverbs 31:6

Rowan Tree Hotel, Oban – 1 pint of 80/-

Everybody – including the staff and other drinkers – said "Hello" in this gum-tickler of a bar – an oddity to a city boy like me.

---

[299] Pasquale's was a great place to witness the love delirium brought on the general public through the powers of wine. Chronology is always hazy in the theatre of drink, but I think I was at Pasquale's only a month before he closed.

Roslin Glen Hotel, Edinburgh – 1 pint of Best

A handsome hotel in the deep loch of quiet at the end of the Glen.

St Vincent, Edinburgh – 1 pint of Marston's Pedigree / 2 pints of Carling Extra Cold [300] / 1 pint of Carlsberg / 1 Laphroaig whisky

I had either forgotten, or never learned, the effects of a hangover on my happiness.

Sala, Edinburgh – 1 bottle of Becks / 1 pint of Director's Bitter / half a pint of Kronenbourg / 1 whisky and ice / half a glass of water

> *"Alcohol is necessary for a man so that he can have a good opinion of himself, undisturbed by the facts."* Finley Peter Dunne (1867-1936)

Sandy Bells, Edinburgh – 2 pints of 3 Sisters ale

The wettest of Edinburgh's quality bars, luxuriously dressed with the sounds of folk singers and their instruments.

Scottish Poetry Library, Edinburgh – 1 glass of house white wine

There's light at the end of the bottle.

The State, Glasgow – 3 pints of Becks

The State has always struck me as an ironic although appropriate name for a bar.

Talbot Rice Gallery, Edinburgh – 1 glass Chenin Blanc white wine (Figure 24)

I held the glass of wine by the stem.

---

[300] Cf. Martin Grindal, author of *Warm Beer*, (1724), "A Treatise proving that beer so qualify'd is far more wholesome than that which is drank cold."

FIGURE 24 – A harmless glass of wine

Tennents Bar, Glasgow – 3 pints of Grolsch bevvy lager

Greatly liked and drunk in good order.

The Three Sisters, Edinburgh – 1 pint of Carlsberg lager

Watching Liverpool FC on one of several big screens

Thomson's, Edinburgh – 1 and half pints of Tennent's lager

Thomson himself designed the Bay Horse bar in Leith, (1899) the Leith Hospital (1899), the United Presbyterian Church building (1895) and the Edinburgh Synagogue (1898)

Tonic, Edinburgh – 1 pint of Carlsberg lager

Silver fitments and wide mirrors are almost universal in modern bars. See also backless false leather chairs and long, low sofas.

The Traverse Bar, Edinburgh – 1 Diet Coke / 2 pints of Tennent's lager

The nearer the bar, the harder it is to be heard.

The Tron, Edinburgh – 1 pint of Tetley bitter

Ironically, bars are sometimes modernised in an Olde Worlde style.

Variety Bar, Glasgow – 4 pints of Stella Artois

Nothing is more delightful than to see the city after four pints of strong lager.

The Village, Edinburgh – 1 vodka and tonic / 1 bottle of Newcastle Brown Ale

Outside Newcastle, we need to request that bottles of Newcastle Brown Ale be taken from the shelf – known as *room temperature* to the rest o' ye!

Whigham's, Edinburgh – 1 glass of white wine / 2 and a half pints of Budvar lager

The launch of *The One O'Clock Gun*, a scurrilous Edinburgh freesheet.

Yo! Sushi, Edinburgh – 3 pints of Kirin lager

Not lager country.

Zucca, W11, London – 2 glasses of Chateau St. Baillon 2003

All so redolent of middle class prosperity!

WHEAT JUICE

Wheat juice [301] is a healthy concoction that is refreshing and has a sweet, lemony, sometimes beery taste.

To make wheat juice, fresh water is added to a jar of sprouted wheat. To speed up fermentation the jar is left near a radiator. The resulting brew is an excellent tonic. Wheat juice particularly benefits the intestines and the colon, and is rich in natural enzymes. Wheat juice also helps replace the flora of the intestines, which have been lost due to the consumption of antibiotics (such as lager).

Several internet sites credit the discovery of this drink to Ann Wigmore, although it seems curious that such a basic brew should have remained unknown until 1982.

Still – before drifting into the unending sleep that accompanies modernity, I think it is highly likely that people the world over drank this potion, and variations of it.

I drank 15 and a half pints of wheat juice.

All of which helps cleanse my intestinal tract and reduce the amount of sludge on my colon's walls. It was that very sludge that I was scared of, largely due to information received concerning the bad properties of today's food – a very common theme. It's a strange thing, but we're now aware that aside from keeping us alive, food is also destroying and rotting us, frazzling our minds, clogging our arteries, inviting opportunistic yeast infections into our bodies, disrupting our digestive systems, melting our teeth, constipating our colons, ruining our complexions and leading us to hit our heads on kitchen cupboards. We have declared food as a breeding ground for poisonous bacteria and have entered an age of poor dietary habits, which we would not have imagined a generation ago. As a true alternative to production-line living, some ancient arts have been revived in the hope that our immune systems will revive. Like kombucha therefore (p108) wheat juice is an agent of the true food underground: a guerrilla drink in a world of mass-market meals.

---

[301] Sometimes wheat juice is known as rejuvelac, but it appears too varied a substance to suffer the captivity of a proper name.

SWEETIES

It's thought that the magnesium in chocolate is one of the reasons that keep us coming back for more. [302] It's not just the magnesium however, because the chocolate's caffeine and fatty acids (similar to those in marijuana) are also thought to have addictive traits. Don't be excited – in a typical 43-gram chocolate bar there is about as much caffeine as a cup of decaffeinated coffee and, in order to get the same high that you would achieve from marijuana, you would have to eat 160 pounds of chocolate in the time it would normally take you to smoke a regular joint. [303]

The drug connection is not total bunk. Chocolate is already sold as a "*mood food*", so it seems likely that various other functional sweetie bars will be available in the future. [304] Ironically, as well as acting on the brain the same way as endorphin releasing drugs such as morphine, chocolate also increases the taste for sugar. This makes things worse – so much worse in my case as you will see from the following sweetie total. Over one year, I managed to cram in the following amount of sweets:

20 x 20g *Twix* biscuit fingers [305]

3 x 58g *Twix*

2 x 85g *Twix*

---

[302] Chocolate is high in magnesium which is good for the heart because it calms the system – it is true. But leafy green vegetables or a calcium magnesium supplement can be used instead of chocolate.

[303] PLEASE DO NOT TRY THIS. I made this figure up in order to stress the point. There is no scientific basis to this statement. It is my own wild estimate. The chocolate has fogged my senses.

[304] In France you can buy *Carres Memoire*, a chocolate bar with added choline, a compound thought to boost the brain's memory skills, help you concentrate and "stay vigilant."

[305] It is easy to make suggestions to sweet-toothed Britons. Hence the packet of this Twix suggested "… at school … with your lunch … at work". In my case, "… anywhere you chuffing like," could be meaningfully added.

190

11 *Ferrero Rocher*

3 squares of coconut chocolate

2 x 45g packets of peanut *M&Ms*

75g of *Bonds of London* "Jelly Love Hearts"

2 squares of *Bel Arte* sugar-free crisp chocolate

1 *Elvan Wonder* small chocolate

20g *Kinder* Surprise – "*More milk, less cocoa*" [306]

1 small packet of *Mini Smarties* [307]

2 x 62.5g *Mars* bars

2 *Marks & Spencer* rum truffles

---

[306] The surprise toy in this chocolate egg was a plastic crocodile that is now awaiting future archaeologists in a local landfill site.

[307] Mini Smarties? I thought that Smarties were small enough already, but I was wrong. There is a difference!
1:1 scale measurements:

Smarties, diameter 15mm   Mini-Smarties, diameter 9.5mm

In this tiny packet came 10 Mini-Smarties: 4 blue, 2 orange, 2 red, 1 yellow and 1 pink. Vegetarian groups have criticised Smarties for using an ingredient obtained from crushed beetles. Smarties contain a red dye processed from the dried body of the female cochineal insect collected in Central America. The insect produces the colorant cochineal, otherwise known as carmine or E120. In 2002, the Vegetarian Society named Smarties the winner of its Imperfect World Award at a ceremony in London.

2 x 40g *Mars Delight* ™ bars [308]

1 85g *Mars* ® Big One bar [309]

1 *Storck* Milch Knoppers Gaufrette Lait bar [310]

1 "Jersey Potato" [311]

2 squares of *Poulain* dark chocolate

1 *Galaxy* Silk Collection creamy fudge chocolate (Figure 25)

1 *Bassets* Clarnico Mint Cream

FIGURE 25 – A Galaxy Silk Collection Creamy Fudge

---

[308] This was a "Surprisingly Crispy, Deliciously Smooth" sweet treat, described as "Milk Chocolate with a rippled wafer centre surrounded by caramel cream". The paucity of my being is well-illustrated in my impulse to try every new snack-treat at least once.

[309] A big Mars bar - and Mars bars are big business. This bar is the flagship of the Mars company, who also produce the following sweets on my list: Bounty, Galaxy, Maltesers, Milky Way, Minstrels, Revels, Snickers, and Twix.

[310] "Crispy Knusprig" / "Part of your world". Here it is. A chocolate that is PART OF YOUR WORLD. Semantically this claim is to a cautiously positive form of phenomenalism, the doctrine which states that the external world can be analysed in terms of experiences, and that entities, such as chocolate bars, are only mental creations within our own constructed worlds. At least I think that is what they are implying.

[311] In Jersey, white chocolate and milk chocolate are shaped and speckled to look like a potato and sold as a delicacy.

2 segments of *Divine* milk chocolate

1 10ml tube of *Brain Drops* [312]

1 16g *Trolli* "Monster Eye" – "*Jelly gummi candy*" (Figure 26)

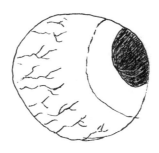

FIGURE 26 – The "Monster Eye", a fine piece of eye candy.

2 x *Lindt & Sprüngli* chocolate squares

6 x *Julian Graves Ltd* Dolly Mixtures = 2 orange and white, 2 pink and white, and 2 yellow

1 30g *Sölen* Darling bar – "*Aerated Milky Plain Chocolate with Peanut Flavour*"

1 *Minuet* Almira – "*Nougat with chocolate flavouring and caramel coating*"

2 x 42g packets of *Galaxy* Minstrels – "*Smooth and creamy GALAXY ® chocolate captured in crispy shells*"

---

[312] Brain Drops were a Christmas present from a family member. No company name was advertised on the package, and the ingredients suggested that the product was made of E numbers and nothing else.

6 chunks of Cyprus Delight [313]

14 pieces of my mother's own tablet

2 and a half (= 25.5g) *Reese's* Cups ® [314]

1 57g *Bounty* Dark – *"Zartherb"*

1 *Lindt* milk chocolate rabbit (Figure 27)

2 *Lindt* milk chocolates shaped as *"Katie the Kitten"* [315]

FIGURE 27 – Lindt milk chocolate rabbit

---

[313] Cyprus Delight is an imitation of Turkish Delight, proving that - "A sweet memory of Cyprus" is possible, with the help of your imagination.

[314] "Now with 3 cups" / "Milk chocolate with peanut butter centre."

[315] According to research, the mammalian sweet receptor is composed of two protein subunits, known as T1 R2 and T1 R3. In a study, reported in the Public Library of Science Genetics, researchers showed a defect in the gene encoding the T1 R2 protein – the taste of sweetness – in domestic cats. The same researchers also detected the same gene defect in tigers and cheetahs, suggesting it is common throughout the cat family. The delicious irony of the chocolate kitten then, is that cats are unable to experience the taste sensation of sweetness.

FIGURE 28 – Two chocolate cats.

1 green fruit pastille

1 red fruit gum

1 180g packet of *Bassett's* Jelly Babies [316]

2 chocolate cats – a gift from HB – with no manufacturer's mark. (Figure 28)

1 500g box of *FAZER 1891 Liquer Fils*, liqueur chocolates in four flavours: rum, punsch, maraschino & cherry brandy (2.8% minimum alcohol content). A duty free gift from Ben Gurion airport.

1 miniature chocolate hazelnut egg

2 handfuls of chocolate raisins

2 segments of white *Toblerone*

2 midget gems

---

[316] Originally Jelly Babies were marketed as Bassett's "Peace Babies" in 1918. Proving popular (the sweet – not the peace) Jelly Babies as they came to be known, have been sold throughout every war up until the present day.

2 polo mints

1 *Cadbury* Flake bar [317]

2 x *Cadbury* Crunchie bars [318]

5 x 60g *Cadbury* Double Decker bars [319]

1 49g *Cadbury* Fuse bar [320]

3 squares of *Cadbury* Dairy Milk Fruit and Nut chocolate

1 miniature *Cadbury* Dairy Milk Caramel bar

1 35g *Cadbury* Raisin Brunch bar

2 x 49g *Cadbury* Dairy Milk Fruit and Nut chocolate bars

1 49g bar of *Cadbury* Dairy Milk Whole Nut chocolate

2 squares of *Cadbury* Dairy Milk Whole Nut chocolate

26 *Xit* peppermint mints

9 *Xit* black tea flavoured mints

2 mint *Tic Tacs*

---

[317] Still advertised as "The crumbliest, flakiest milk chocolate."

[318] Now advertised as "Milk chocolate with Golden Honeycomb centre."

[319] Temptingly billed as "Milk chocolate with smooth chewy nougatine and crisp crunchy cereal filling."

[320] Described imaginatively as "A fusion of Milk Chocolate, Raisins, Peanuts, Crispy Cereal and Fudge Pieces."

Sweetie Case Study: 1 x 230g tub of Revels

This birthday gift (Figure 29) was eaten between July 15th and July 24th The split in this particular tub was as follows:

Toffee Revel	21
Peanut Revel	18
Orange Revel	16
Malteser Revel	15
Chocolate Button Revel	9
Coffee Revel	7

FIGURE 29 – A timely tub of Revels

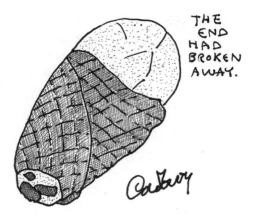

FIGURE 30 – The Cadbury Creme Egg Ice

1 115ml *Cadbury* Creme Egg Ice [321] (Figure 30)

1 *Cadbury* Dairy Milk Cube with caramel [322]

2 x *Cadbury* Fredo Dairy Milk with caramel – *"Dairy Milk chocolate with soft caramel centre"* [323]

1 *Cadbury* Dairy Milk Pigs bar [324]

---

[321] This "Vanilla flavour dairy ice cream cone with a fondant centre dipped in thick Cadbury milk chocolate," was snapped at the base, as I hope my picture demonstrates. Uneasiness regarding the subsequent eating was not however quelled by the melting of the treat into my hand.

[322] How many variations does one chocolate bar need? Sometimes companies go crazy with these variations. Rather than change a product maybe they would like to focus on creating something new? Most of the time the variations are all the same: Give it some caramel / Make it into a square / Shape it like a farmyard animal / Flavour it with mint / Add some biscuit pieces / Make a mini version / Make a mega version / Make an ice-cream version / Add it to a McFlurry / Make it into an Easter Egg / etc.

[323] We believe in the richness of all created things. Why not therefore make a chocolate shaped like a frog? People might buy it and be happy.

[324] We believe in the richness of all created things. Why not therefore make a chocolate shaped like a pig? People might buy it and think it's pork.

1 51g *Fry's* Turkish Delight bar

2 x 53g *Cadbury* Star Bars – *"Milk chocolate with caramel peanut crunch"* / *"Shot through with peanut and caramel"*

150g of *Bramik Foods of Broxburn* yoghurt coated apricots

FIGURE 31 – A Cadbury dairy milk "Crispie"

3 x *Cadbury* Dairy Milk Crispies (Figure 31)

1 *Caffè Bei & Nannini* Lucca chocolate – (Figure 32)

1 50g *Cadbury* Dairy Milk Caramel

1 10g *Cadbury* mini-Time Out

FIGURE 32 – One of those creepy biscuits you get with your coffee – the Bei & Nannini "Lucca" chocolate.

5 *Terry's* Twilight chocolate mints

4 coffee flavoured *Black Magic* chocolates [325]

1 green sugar mouse from *House of Bruar*

1 bite of chocolate fudge from *House of Bruar*

1 bite of vanilla fudge from *House of Bruar*

6 squares of *Green and Black* praline chocolate

6 *Nestlé* mint matchmakers [326]

2 fingers of *Nestlé* Kit Kat [327]

1 37g bag of Maltesers

5 Maltesers

---

[325] Black Magic is a blasphemous travesty of Christian worship. Luckily, industrial food production has ensured that this meaning is now secondary to the popular chocolates I have included here. These four coffee chocolates came with this description: "A coffee flavour cream in dark chocolate dipped in milk and white chocolates."

[326] How can bottle-feeding possibly hurt babies in poorer countries? The water mixed with baby milk powder can be unsafe and it's often impossible in poor conditions to keep bottles and teats sterile. Bottle-feeding under such circumstances can lead to infections causing diarrhoea, the biggest killer of poor children. Baby milk is also expensive meaning that bottle-feeding will contribute to overall family malnutrition. Bottle Baby Disease is the name given to the deadly combination of diarrhoea, dehydration and malnutrition which is the result of unsafe bottle-feeding.

[327] And what's happening now? Most baby food manufacturers continue with dubious promotional activities. They are increasingly investing in health workers and health care systems, spending more money promoting their products than governments in non-developed countries can spend on health education. Advertising in hospitals in poorer countries is unscrupulous as it implies that the product is endorsed by the local health service. Even more effective is the practice of giving free or subsidised supplies of baby milk to hospitals and maternity wards. This encourages artificial infant feeding, which interferes with lactation, and babies are denied the best start in life.

FIGURE 33 – A Pernigotti chocki

1 *Pernigotti* chocolate (Figure 33)

1 chewy toffee sweet with chocolate inside [328]

3 *Bendicks* chocolate coated mints

1 *Bendicks* bitter mint [329]

2 rectangles of *Wawel Krakow* milk chocolate with cream [330]

1 miniature *Lindt* chocolate egg [331]

1 *Lindt* Frohes Fest milk chocolate Christmas tree angel

---

[328] This sweet was unbranded and yet it was supposed to be an éclair. Biting, I quickly realised this little specimen wasn't chewy at all. In fact it was eerily soft – not unlike my own bodily specimens of fat.

[329] Bendicks are the best. Give me what I'm deservin', yo'!

[330] "Superior" – meaning higher in quality, or, I guess, in ranking. Of course it would be plain legal chaos for any producer to state which other products their own were superior to.

[331] Although food is a necessity it's seldom, if ever, treated as such by those who dine on chocolate eggs.

3 *Hershey* Kisses with cookies

2 *Hershey* Kisses with biscuit pieces

1 20g *Hershey* Cookies 'n' Cream bar – *"Chocolate cookie bits in white chocolate"*

1 Beach Ballroom flavour *Aberdeen City Council* complimentary after dinner chocolate

30g of *Tasters* jelly beans. Breakdown: 7 Red, 3 Green, 3 Yellow, 2 Black, 2 Orange, and 2 Pink

1 9g *Café Tasse Thé* bitter chocolate

1 9g *Café Tasse Thé* coffee chocolate

1 9g *Café Tasse Thé* nougat milk chocolate

1 35g *Traidcraft* Geobar – *"Cranberry and raisin fair trade snack bar"* / *"The energy to make a difference"*

1 *Cadbury's* Favourites Bounty (Figure 34)

1 40g *Lyme Regis Organic Foods* dark chocolate covered marzipan bar – *"Gluten free and dairy free"*

FIGURE 34 – Cadbury's Favourites Bounty

FIGURE 35 – Reese's make such sweet delights as the Reesestick.

1 miniature *Ritter Sport* – *"Sauerkirsch-vanille Joghurt flavour Vollmilch Schokolade"*

2 x 42g *Hershey* Reesesticks bars – *"Crispy wafer Peso Neto – Milk Chocolate – Peanut Crème"* (Figure 35)

1 50g *Traidcraft* organic Swiss-made praline chocolate [332]

1 100g *Green and Black's* [333] organic dark chocolate bar with 70% cocoa solids

1 40g *Green and Black's* organic Maya Gold chocolate bar – *"Dark chocolate with orange and spices"*

1 40g *Green and Black's* organic dark chocolate bar – *"Pioneering natural food since 1986"*

4 segments of *Marks & Spencer* Swiss Chocolate Extra Fine Mountain Bar – *"Extra fine milk chocolate with Honey and Almond Nougat"*

---

[332] "The farmers in Bolivia (cocoa), Dominican Republic (cocoa) and Philipines (sugar) are expected to "benefit directly from this purchase."

[333] Green & Black's were one of the first companies to take a risk on organic luxury products. They were also the first company to simultaneously embrace fair trade practices and organic principles throughout their range. In recognition of this, the word *organic* appears on the label of this product no less than 10 tedious times!

FIGURE 36 – I broke off this chunk of chocolate

1 broken chunk of *Green and Black's* organic dark chocolate with 70% cocoa solids (Figure 36)

2 *Thornton's* sweets: Brandy flavour truffle and a Christmas pudding truffle, both decorated with a holly leaf and berry coloured marzipan – 45g the pair

1 *Hershey's Reese's* Nutrageous bar – *"Packed with Crunchy Peanuts, creamy caramel and Peanut Butter"* [334]

5 x *Lily O'Briens* sticky toffee chocolates – billed as *"Sticky toffee caramel smothered in milk and dark chocolate"*

The following *Quality Street* sweets were eaten: 1 strawberry cream; [335] 2 fudge; 3 coconut; 1 orange cream; 1 hazelnut in caramel

---

[334] UPSIDE: The caramel encases the peanut butter filling and the two flavours go nicely together. It's the combination of both in your mouth that you look forward to rather than getting past the chocolate to see what's inside.
DOWNSIDE: Is this snack-combo really necessary? Does a Yankee classic like peanut butter really need to sully itself with a bed of creamy caramel?

[335] I have been working with a therapist who asked me: *Dare you discover your inner centre?* Apparently I am a Strawberry Centre. The therapist went on: "Strawberry Centres like you, Peter, need to be wanted and are generally kind people – just a little misunderstood. Strawberry Centres are also the keepers of the peace, but can actually stand up for themselves

Cadbury Celebrations

"A sparkling selection of the biggest names in chocolate in miniature."

The following miniature sweeties were eaten:

2 Milky Way Celebrations – *"Milk chocolate with a light whipped centre"*

1 Galaxy Celebration – *"Silky smooth GALAXY ® milk chocolate"*

2 Snickers Celebrations – *"Packed with peanuts, caramel and chocolate"*

3 x Mars Celebrations – *"Light fluffy centre with caramel and chocolate"*

1 Topic Celebration – No descriptors issued

---

better than many if pushed."

Establishing the frequency and likelihood of soft versus hard centres in a box of chocolates is one of the more complicated culinary probability problems. But here is how to do it. If each box contains 24 soft centres and 16 hard centres, then the immediate chance of getting a soft centre is 24 over 40 and the probability of a hard centre is 16 over 40. After selecting the first soft centre there are two things that can happen – we can select another soft centre or a hard centre, although the probability of selecting a soft centre is new, given that there's one fewer of them in the box, as well as one less chocolate in total. The next set of probabilities is therefore 23 over 39 for a soft centre, and 16 over 39 for a hard centre.

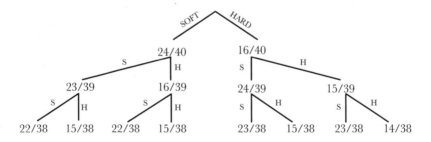

We could therefore ask what the chances are of opening the box and choosing two soft centres in a row. This would be 24 over 40 multiplied by 23 over 39, which equals 552 over 1560, which can be simplified by dividing by 24. Therefore the chances of getting two soft centres in a row in this box will be 23 chances in 65.

Lily O'Brien's finest Irish hand crafted chocolates

Post-Christmas, I took delight in a selection of gift chocolates, three of which I ate. These were:

The Honeycomb Crunch – *"Delicious honeycomb pieces in a crisp chocolate truffle in a milk chocolate shell"* (Figure 37)

FIGURE 37 – The Honeycomb Crunch

The Frappacino – *"An aromatic whipped coffee truffle encased in milk chocolate"* (Figure 38)

FIGURE 38 – The Frappacino

The Chocolate Orange Truffle – *"A bitter sweet dark chocolate truffle infused with a hint of orange covered in dark chocolate"* (Figure 39)

FIGURE 39 – The Chocolate Orange Truffle

GRAZE AWAY

If you don't like eating breakfast, stay open-minded about having a cinnamon pastry as your first meal of the day. Drink at least one bottle of fruit drink or a glass of water. Then repeat your open-mindedness with a snack choice at mid-morning. By early dinnertime, or during your commutetime, you will do yourself a good turn by snacking again, the idea being to spoil some of your appetite for dinner. This is "safe grazing", because we overeat or make poor choices when we're hungry. Commit to it for a year and you'll likely never revert to breakfast-eater status.

2 x *J&J Smith* of Huntly cinnamon pastries [336]

3 x 100g packets of *Bachelor's* Mild Curry flavour Super Noodles [337]

2 x 100g packets of *Bachelor's* Chow Mein flavour Super Noodles

400g tin *Co-op* Healthy Living vegetable broth [338]

16 x 8 inch wheat tortilla pancakes

2 litres of *Co-op* no added sugar lemonade

---

[336] I enjoyed the ingredients list for these cinnamon pastries from Huntly because they included *bun controller*, which is soya, salt and sucrose. There is something in the idea of *bun controller* that is trenchantly opposed to all that we know about food and comedy and the impossibility of their meeting.

[337] Super Noodles and biscuits, Thai Bites and sweets – and my diet challenges the concept of nourishment at every turn!

[338] Under regulations from the UK and European governments our food labels offer an array of barely useful and difficult to understand nutritional information all of which is balanced against lurid marketing colours and unusual symbols and ideograms. More than diet is affected and changes appear in our language. Neuroses are created and if you don't believe me, watch the other shoppers reading product packages.

1 330ml plastic bottle of *Tropicana* original orange drink

11 *Jacobs* oriental spice flavour Thai Bites

1 litre of *Co-op* cloudy apple juice

2 x 500ml cartons of *Just Juice* – 100% pure juice berry fruit flavour

12 x 26.8g each *Bisc&* "*Mars*" biscuits – Simply analysed, these *Bisc&*s were flattened Mars bars lying in a trough of biscuit in which everything was condensed.

1 500ml plastic bottle of *Highland Spring* spring water

10 star thins – they're a kinda biscuit

1 bannock [339] and strawberry jam

Two and a half slices of cake from the Japanese Embassy gifted to my father [340]

6 roast potatoes and garlic

200g pack of *Fox's* Wholemeal Brans

1 330ml can of *Idris* ginger beer

---

[339] The pancake is said to be a reliable reminder of the Auld Alliance, a sometimes tenuous cultural meeting between Scotland and France. Hence Touchwood's *Annals of the Cleikum Club* perfectly sums up the Scots Pancake when it asks: "Is this not omelette *á la Celestine*, or *aux confitures* of our old allies, still lingering in remote places of the country?" Is the *bannock* another invention of Sir Walter Scott?

[340] What is the story of this cake? A delegation from the Japanese embassy presented this cake to my father during their official visit to Aberdeen. Why did my father merit such a cake? Because his colleagues from far away discovered that it was his birthday and wished to thank the Municipality via its nearest representative.

FIGURE 40 – The classic "Classic" biscuit from the Fox's line

16 *Fox's* Classic biscuits – *"Crumbly honeycomb biscuit covered in real milk chocolate"* (Figure 40)

6 *Fox's* Echo biscuits – *"Honeycomb flavour bubbly white chocolate on a crunchy biscuit wrapped in milk chocolate"*

2 *Fox's* Golden Crunch Creams – *"Delicious crunchy biscuits sandwiched with a smooth creamy filling"*

2 x 500ml plastic bottles of Hey Hey Banoffee Pie flavour *Frijj* – *The Simpsons* themed milk drink [341]

2 x 500ml bottles of banana flavour *Frijj* – *"Banana flavour High Temperature Pasteurised Low Fat Milkshake"* [342]

---

[341] This Simpsons Limited Edition "Hey Hey Banoffee Pie" flavour Frijj features the character Krusty the Klown, one of whose catchphrases is ironically enough: "I heartily endorse this event or product!" The disparity between this drink's advertised benefits ("Made with fresh milk", "Less than 1% fat", and "Rich in calcium") and the apparently high sugar content is maybe taking the humour further than is necessary.

[342] Frijj has the creamy consistency of melted ice cream and comes in a plastic bottle similar in size and shape to old fashioned milk bottles – thos that used to be delivered by milkmen.

PETER BURNETT

1 500ml bottle of "D'oh nut" flavour *Frijj* – *The Simpsons* themed milk drink [343]

1 1 litre bottle of banana flavour *Frijj* milk drink [344]

1 500ml bottle of chocolate flavour *Frijj* milk drink – *"Fresh thick chocolate flavoured milkshake"* / *"Gluten free"*

1 74g *Sainsbury's* soft caramel and Belgian chocolate shortbread bar

5 fingers of *Royal Edinburgh* all-butter shortbread [345] – *"Over 50 years of baking excellence"*

6 fingers of shortbread [346]

2 shortbread circles

1 shortbread cookie with chocolate chip [347]

---

[343] "Shake before use." Yes. On opening without shaking, there's definitely a layer of watery liquid on top, so this an instruction best obeyed.

[344] Just about all the Frijj flavours have around 13g of carbohydrate per 100ml. A McDonald's milkshake has 20g per 100ml. These Frijj Simpsons special editions are *gorgeous*, and dare I say it, *flippin' amazing* by the way.

[345] Shortbread – "The triumph of Scottish baking on the old national lines." T.F. Henderson

[346] "The large, round cake of rich, crisp shortbread is in fact the lineal descendant of the ancient Yule Bannock, which is notched around the edge to symbolise the sun's ray." F.M. McNeill

[347] It's bullshit what they did to Cookie Monster. Next thing you know, all those children's TV shows will have to be edited to advocate some crap that lazy-ass parents aren't willing to put into action themselves because they're "too busy working." Less violence in cartoons – plus edited versions of Disney movies because "stupid" is a bad word that denigrates – er – the stupid, I guess.

1 227g jar of *Whole Earth* organic peanut butter with *"Extra nutty taste"* [348]

1 150g *Co-op* Greek style yoghurt – *"Layered yoghurt with honey made with cows milk."* (sic) We all make mistakes though – this yoghurt should be listed on page 56!

6 mini onion bhajis (= 260g) of *Mrs Unis Spicy Foods* with 50g of Chilli Sauce [349]

1 chocolate chip cookie made by Bridget Bradley

5 regular sized pieces of *Let Them Eat Cake* cake [350]

3 very large pieces of *Let Them Eat Cake* cake

A half raspberry biscuit from the French market in Edinburgh

A half almond biscuit from the French market in Edinburgh

A half mini *galette* from the French market, Edinburgh

One portion of pepper, courgette & cheese bake

---

[348] All of this peanut butter was eaten from the jar with a spoon and none of it found its way on to a knife, far less a slice of bread. I didn't notice if it was "Extra Nutty" or not, having no comparator, or nut-taste index to hand.

[349] The largest onion bhaji ever created weighed 131 lb. It was made in November 1999 by three chefs at the Veena Indian Cuisine Restaurant in Cleckheaton. The bhajis I ate were made in Scotland. The question that begs to be asked: Is the success of "ethnic" food a model for reconciliation, a signifier for a shared future, or does it merely gloss over serious problems and concerns? Food is a marker of difference and alterity. Food can also be used to trace one's history. Questions related to cultural differences, history, and memory have been highly contested within modern societies and I am therefore convinced that in future, food will play an increasing role in literary and cultural studies.

[350] The recipe for *Let Them Eat Cake* cake, a vegan thrill, is to be found on Page 432 of the novel *PopCo*, by Scarlet Thomas (4th Estate, 2004).

1 plate of lettuce and feta cheese

4 squares of *Orkney* Cream Fudge

6 sugar snap peas dipped in *Total* brand tzatziki

1 litre of *Bramble Hill* premium orange juice

1 500ml bottle of *Diet Pepsi*

1 500ml bottle of *Oasis* summer fruits flavour drink [351]

1 litre of *Del Monte* Quality [352] cloudy apple and mango juice

1 litre of *Del Monte* Brazilian watermelon juice drink [353]

6 pitta halves and hummus

300g tub of *Co-op* hummus dip

2 x 170g tubs of *Co-op* hummus

170g tub of *Co-op* onion and garlic dip

---

[351] "A blend of fruits in a refreshingly still drink"

[352] "Quality" – that word again!

[353] This juice came from the World Fruits Range - "A refreshing and exotic taste experience of far away lands". Global food producers – who can now move from country to country, acquiring land and selling their products in the global market – pose a unique threat to the environment. These companies did not come about because someone planned them. They arose invisibly from developments in international trade, agriculture and food processing. It is this calm inevitability that seems to obstruct us when thinking about food and realising what we (but always somebody else!) are doing to the planet. It's the same seeming inevitability which keeps food and its production low on our political agendas.

230ml *Galaxy* drinking chocolate drink

1 *Jacob's* custard cream biscuit

1 *Jacob's* Bourbon biscuit

1 and half *Jacob's* digestive biscuits

3 slices of *Leerdammer* cheese

18 cloves of garlic [354]

3 potatoes

4 carrots [355]

1 cherry muffin

140g of *Co-op* Swiss Gruyère

1 slice of lemon tart and crème fraiche

3 x 125g packs of *Carr's* Table Water biscuits

2 x 170g *Waldens* "Meals on Wheels" potato and leek soup [356]

---

[354] These cloves of garlic were eaten raw. Most of them were produced by Victor and Victor, Alicante, Spain

[355] These carrots were was so stunning that on first encounter it was hard for me to imagine that I was looking at garden vegetables rather than alien artefacts created with molecular nanotechnology. Then I realised that vegetables are of course created with molecular nanotechnology, albeit the product of earthly evolution, not extraterrestrial engineering.

[356] While staying with Granny it was a rare opportunity to try her Waldens brand meals-on-wheels. Moreover, Granny used to volunteer for the Meals on Wheels service. Granny rated Waldens' meals tolerably well, but remembered best when the ladies made their own meals each morning before heading off with their hot plates in the van.

PETER BURNETT

1 330ml can of *Cool* brand grapefruit soft drink

1 poppy seed saline cracker

2 salted crackers

1 58ml *Fab* ice-lolly

I have considered the contribution of home baking to my diet and wondered how many of us have any baking experience at all, especially given the demise of Home Economics classes. I also considered the downsides of shop-bought bakeries, which normally contain artificial mixes and can be quite dreary at times.

We may assess home-cooking in terms of its vocabulary and its specific skill set. We should ask ourselves if we really know how to sift or knead, or if we can melt chocolate without ruining the microwave. Those who really go guerrilla in their home baking buy fresh, live yeast, which comes in a sticky block and smells like a warm brewery. These individuals may appear to cookery-illiterates as fanciful timewasters, but at least they're controlling the amount of salt in their diets, unlike the untold millions of people in the grey belts of Britain's towns who are quietly expanding while they wait for the day when they can enter law-suits against the manufacturers who have increased their blood pressure with crazily salty ready-meals.

One needn't attack the supermarkets and large producers at every turn, because they sell what we buy and are responding in a slow way to our demands. The skills that we leave behind are however of interest and one day terms such as *braise, truss, dredge* and *fold* will seem as antiquated as the *yea verilies* of the King James Bible.

TEST CASE: TESCO

Supermarket chains are now the victims of their own popularity. They used to offer convenient, hassle-free shopping. Now they are over-crowded, the shoppers are bad-tempered, and the process of purchase can be time-consuming.

Convenience is a killer, but not of business. Some folks now believe you can visit your local grocer, baker and general-purpose store in less time than it takes to complete a trip to the supermarket. Others have suffered because their local grocer and baker have been exterminated. Local convenience stores can be dirty, over priced, and have no disabled access. Supermarkets, it is clear, believe in marketing over content, and smaller brands have little chance of being represented on their shelves. Convenience stores attract congregations of underage drinkers, and can be poorly stocked. Supermarkets are faceless, which in this day and age is tantamount to being *evil*.

The reason the supermarkets win out is because they represent the spectacle of our lives – for every supermarket is no less than a museum of our modern day. To watch a populace, each on separate quests, is great enough in itself. This however is topped by the appearance of the all-mighty products, which are weird and beautiful, each one in a package that is designed to titillate and excite.

During my year of food itemisation, I paid regular visits to *Tesco* [357] and came away with many treats, as shall be seen below. The theatre of treats is where we all end up, and I'm sure that the treats are the reason we keep returning for more. Our cornershops will never be able to compete – unless they can motivate us to take pride in ourselves again.

1 800g serving of *Tesco* "*Italiano*" spinach and ricotta cannelloni

6 x *Tesco* potato wedges in cheese, onion and sour cream dip

1 *Tesco* cheese and bean wrap

---

[357] On his first day of trading in East London in 1919, 21-year-old Jack Cohen – the founder of Tesco – had a turnover of £4 and a profit of £1. His first ever line was TESCO tea, the brand name containing the initials of company owner T.E. Stockwell, and the first two letters of Jack's own surname.

FIGURE 41 – Everything revolves around donuts

1 *Tesco* pink iced donut [358] with sprinkles (Figure 41)

1 *Tesco* lemon and white chocolate chip muffin

1 *Tesco* chocolate chip muffin

60g of *Tesco* French Brie [359]

1 *Tesco* farmhouse cheese ploughman's sandwich

3 *Tesco* potato croquettes

2 x 200g cans of *Tesco* baked beans with 4 vegetarian mini sausages

1 330ml can of *Tesco* organic slightly sparkling lemonade

---

[358] Incidentally, I prefer to call these donuts *doughrings* as per the North East of Scotland. You would think I was declaring war, however, to witness the sour, scolding, dumpish, faces that correct me in the bakery when I do.

[359] Included in an emergency food bag from Mr SK, when I had no food.

12 *Tesco* jam donut bites [360]

3 slices of brown toast with a 420g tin of *Tesco* baked beans and vegetable sausages

2 x *Tesco* individual sticky toffee puddings with dates

1 glass of *Tesco* 100% orange juice served with ice

1 *Tesco* gingerbread character (Figure 42)

FIGURE 42 – A gingerbread "character" is of unspecifed gender

---

[360] Peter soaks his woes in donuts.

1 250g serving of *Tesco* pilau rice [361]

3 x *Tesco* "*Soft eating*" cranberry and orange cookies [362]

1 400g can of *Tesco* Value baked beans in tomato sauce

---

[361] Pilau, or pilaff; perloo; perlau; plaw; pilav or plov – is a rice dish seasoned in broth. Pilau is known to have been served to Alexander the Great on his capture of Samarkand, and was probably introduced to Spain by Arab people, where it became *paella*. It was perhaps developed in desert regions as a way of cooking rice with no waste of water.

[362] Remember Cookie Monster? A star of the hit children's show *Sesame Street*, Cookie Monster ate lots of cookies in a hilariously exaggerated fashion. He was impatient and wild, and a paragon of unsuppressed lack of self-restraint and over the years, Cookie Monster perfected his art which was all the more impressive for its seeming naturalness. In his own way Cookie Monster rewrote the rules for eating, never being awkward about it. He said the word "cookie!" while he ate and with his loopy appearance, with eyes looking in different directions, and his retina-caressing blue terry-cloth mass, he was a widely enjoyed daytime television star.

Cookie Monster is now fondly remembered by bloggers, upset at the state of our sorry, puritanical world.

Ally, April 20, 2005 12:49 PM "CRAZY!! Why are u changin cookie monster! You people are weirdos!! Seamse street has been on for 30 yrs and now u want to change it around! I remember that cookie monster ate soo much cookies that when i was little i thought that "Hey this muppet eats so much cookies and he is fat, so why should i eat them!" Do u people think that kids today think that cookie monster teaches kids to eat cookies? You know what – that is not true!!!!!!!!!!!!!!!"

Robin, April 20, 2005 12:44 PM "this is crazy!! You cant change my favorite character! what is the point of putting a hairy muppet on a diet? Duh! I think this is the stupidest idea created!! You cant do this to my daughter! She wont sleep now, and now i have to throw out all her tapes, because she is afaid of cookie monster for some reason!"

Josh Jackson, June 4th, 2005 7:11 PM "This is an outrage, the cookie monster has been cut from sesame. as a kid, I was dependant on the cookie monsters antics. Apparently he encourages obesity. this is bullshit. I'm not fat and I watched him every morning. he works it off. help bring him back and sign a petition."

Anthony Small, August 21, 2005 01:49 AM "If you watch cookie monster very cafefully while he is gorging himself on cookies-the cookies don't actually get swallowed. he just breaks them up into little tiny pieces. It should make both camps happy."

BASSETT'S

The company that first made Liquorice Allsorts was the Bassett Company. The story of how Liquorice Allsorts were first created is now quite famous. In 1899, *Bassett's* salesperson Charlie Thompson was discussing an order with a prospective customer when his tray of samples was knocked to the floor. The sweets scattered everywhere and while Thompson was gathering them the buyer took an interest in the resulting jumble and placed an immediate order.

He placed an order for sweets that had been chucked on the floor? It's an odd idea, but ever since the turn of the 20th century, that's been the company line concerning their favourite product.

Immediately after this myth had been widely circulated, Bassett's Liquorice Allsorts went into mass production and today no sweeties are thrown on the floor.

There are now twelve different kinds of *Bassett's* Allsorts [363] all of which were eaten by myself during my annual gorge. Unlike several other sweeties, I would not recommend Allsorts as cooking ingredients, unless you fancy a great mulch of tasteless slop with a slightly sickly edge.

The following 180g packet of *Bassett's* liquorice allsorts was consumed:

5 Liquorice Tube Allsorts

4 Filled Liquorice Tube Allsorts:

---

[363] Meatie Sweeties: (see note 307, for Mini-Smarties)   The second runner-up in the Imperfect World Awards, was Bassett's Liquorice Allsorts, which according to the Vegetarian Society, contain gelatine made from animal bones.

8 Pink Sugary Allsorts: [364]

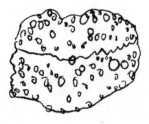

3 Pink Coconut Allsorts: [365]

8 Yellow Coconut Allsorts:

---

[364] This is the only Liquorice Allsort which does not contain any liquorice. In its place is a hard aniseed jelly covered in little balls of sugar. These come in two colours, blue and pink and on average, there are about four to five of these in each bag.

[365] These are maybe the most famous Liquorice Allsort. They are basically tubular pieces of liquorice with coconut paste wrapped around the outside. They come in two different colours, yellow and pink, although in other cheaper brands, orange ones have been reported. Bassett's put on average three to four of each colour in a bag.

4 Orange Liquorice Sandwiches:

3 Pink Liquorice Sandwiches:

3 White Double Liquorice Sandwiches:

2 Brown Liquorice Sandwiches:

1 Pink Chequered Allsort

3 Blue Sugary Allsorts:

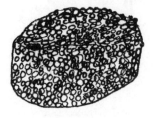

2 White Chequered Allsorts

2 Bertie Aniseed Figures:

Bertie has something of the aspect of a blue sweetie Buddha.

POT NOODLE

What is a Pot Noodle? [366]   As the world turns then all that lives takes nourishment. However, not all foods are able to impart sustenance to those that eat them and some provide barely any more than a fattening boost of energy. Today, Pot Noodles – dried noodles in a dried sauce that require water to make them into a meal – are an essential food for some, adding a technical dimension to our diets that is futuristic, fun, and somehow *anti-health*.

For the purposes of marketing Pot Noodle was once renamed "Not Poodle", presumably because it is not a poodle. Anyone lucky enough to find a small poodle in his or her "Not Poodle" could claim a prize. Other advertising campaigns have included "The Lambshank Redemption", which told the story of a prisoner being punished after smuggling a Pot Noodle into prison. The "King Pot Noodle" sub-brand was launched in 2000 with the character "Big Dave", and in 2002 Pot Noodle commenced the "Natural Noodling" campaign, based on the theme of taking your Pot Noodle outdoors for a game of car park "noodling". Another billboard ad has featured a man being fed a *Bombay Bad Boy* Pot Noodle by a dominatrix, with the tag line "Hurt Me, You Slag!" In 2004, the Pot Noodle brand won a Cannes Gold award in Digital Media for their "Hysterical Girlfriend" adverts.

Just as a macrobiotic diet will guarantee you culinary sainthood, Pot Noodle eaters are heading straight for the dark side. The Pot Noodle is rebellious, smutty and the opposite of health food – an awesome profile for a plastic pot of dehydrated noodles in sauce.

The following list represents my Pot Noodle breakdown for the year. In the course of 1 year I ate 25 Pots.

14 x 89g Chicken & Mushroom flavour *Pot Noodles* [367]

---

[366] After the downfall of the puritan Burnett it was discovered that he had been feasting on Pot Noodles.

[367] "Chicken and mushroom flavoured sauce with texturised soya pieces, dried vegetables and sachet of soy sauce."   SO!   What is the difference between *texturised* and *textured*? The soya pieces are moulded to a rough, almost chicken-like texture – and this is the process of texturisation – which is not, I must add, a term borrowed from textual or literary theory. The state of being textured is the result of texturisation (my guess).

223

FIGURE 43 – The Spicy Curry flavour Pot Noodle.

4 x 118g Chicken & Mushroom flavour *King Pot Noodles*

2 x 89g Spicy Curry flavour *Pot Noodles* (Figure 43)

1 76g *Pot Curry Snack* ® Tikka Masala curried rice snack [368]

---

[368] "Rice in a tikka masala flavour sauce with wheat protein pieces, vegetables and a sachet of spice sauce." Although tikka masala is commonly believed to have originated from the kitchens of Bangladeshi chefs in the UK, the actual original is claimed by many establishments, from London to Glasgow. Others claim tikka masala is a Pakistani dish, while one researcher has sourced it to the Punjab region. Another stream of thought says the first tikka masala was a creative recycling of yesterday's leftovers. That's the oldest story in the recipe book – one of those merry food fantasies we so enjoy – the idea of *necessity meeting with invention*. Perhaps that's the history of cookery in four words.

1 119g Spicy Curry flavour *King Pot Noodle*

1 74g *Posh Noodle* – Spicy Chinese Chicken flavour [369]

1 90g *Posh Noodle* – Mexican Fajita flavour [370]

1 87g *Pot Noodle* Nice 'n' Spicy flavour

POST NOODLE: The Pot Noodle has been advertised with more straplines than it's had flavours. Favourites have included: "*Pot Noodle. The curious cheerleader of all snacks*"; "*Pot Noodle. The lonely housewife of all snacks*," and another, which featured a man and woman with German accents describing it as "*The filthy fraulein of all snacks.*"

Pot Noodle was finally found to be in breach of advertising codes by the Advertising Standards Authority when it appeared on British television in 2002 with the slogan "*The Slag of All Snacks.*" [371] After early complaints this advert was moved to be broadcast only after 9pm, when it still attracted over 300 complaints. The Independent Television Commission eventually requested that the "*The Slag of All Snacks*" advertisement be withdrawn, finding it too offensive to be broadcast at any time of day or night.

---

[369] This spicy chicken flavoured snack was produced in Thailand.

[370] But this Mexican Fajita flavoured snack was produced in the UK. They both cost the same amazing price of 89 pence.

[371] Slags are expected to have loose morals and indulge in casual sex and snogging; although Pot Noodle could have used *slut, floosie, cooze, cock-hound, goer, shagbag* or *scrubber* to acheive the same offence.

AMAZING GRAZE

There are persistent reports from North America of Cookie Monster from Sesame Street coming under attack. Not only nostalgic adults but children are motivated to complain when this heroic character is bullied into singing about carrots and other less exciting snack options. One blogger writes: "*I am very skinny only because my mom fed me the right way!!! Cookie Monster didn't influence me at all!!! If any more changes happen I am going to put this show out of business!! So you better change Cookie Monster back to his old self or I will sue, and I am totally serious on this subject.*" The lessons are plain. Never mess with the classics – especially when it comes to food. Cookies soothe the angry passions, even when they're called biscuits – and we must be left to snack as we please.

3 chocolate chip biscuits

1 415g tin of *Baxter's* lentil and vegetable soup [372]

1 330g plastic bottle of *Mars* milk drink

3 crispy papadoms with green chilli [373]

1 litre of *Princes* tropical juice drink – "*Made with REAL fruit juice*"

4 yoghurt-coated apricot pieces

1 330ml bottle of *Tropicana* Premium multivitamins drink

One and a half *Co-op* Dutch peppers – "*Class 1*"

---

[372] Esau sold his birthright to Jacob for a pottage not unlike this tasty tin from Baxter's. (Genesis 25: 29-34) Why do I mention this? Here in Scotland, Baxter's soup is religiously venerated.

[373] While curry was introduced to Britain by Indian migrants and is at least known as "Indian food", it is not available as such in India in the same form. British curry is therefore a hybrid product born of imagination and adapted to European tastes.

154g of *Orchard Dairy* Grana Italian Padano Parmesan [374]

1 fruit cookie [375]

1 litre of *Copella* apple juice [376]

12 *Rocky* biscuits [377]

FIGURE 44 – Some are slaves to meat while others are servants of Quorn.

---

[374] This cheese was made in Kent where the largest rivers are the Medway and the Stour. If *grano padano* cheese is made from grain (*grano*) from the Po area of Italy (*Padano*), then Grano Italian Padano must mean cheese made from Italian grain in the style of the same Po cheese, regardless of the nearest river. Descriptions can be as deceptive as tastes and appearances.

[375] Instead of trying to brainwash Cookie Monster into telling kids that cookies are bad, they should perhaps dramatise this eternal battle between a healthy diet and junkfood. Perhaps Cookie could meet a skinny, heath-conscious charcacter called Veggie-Monster. This new friend could help Cookie Monster kick the cookie habit. It would work for a few episodes but finally Cookie Monster would come to his senses and BEAT THE SHIT OUT OF HIM.

[376] "Made from hand selected apples." Note the marketing power of the hand as opposed to the fascist promise of the machine.

[377] "Crunchy biscuit covered in thick milk chocolate." I adore these biscuits for their slight taste of coconut, and may well die with one cradled in my lips.

5 *Co-op* Dutch vine tomatoes – *"Class 1"* [378]

2 x 40g *Discovery* soft flour tortillas with nothing on them

1 *Kellogg's* multigrain bar of the strawberry flavour

2 x *Quorn* garlic and herb fillets (Figure 44)

1 400g tin can of *Co-op* vegetable soup

6 potato wedges and Marie Rose dip

2 egg muffins with cheese sauce

200g of popadoms, labelled *"Papads med grøne chili"*

1 *Cadbury* Caramel Muffin – *"NEW"* (Figure 45)

FIGURE 45 – Cadbury's made this muffin and although it was tasty, there seemed little point when there are so many other muffin merchants out there.

---

[378] It's regrettable but a class system does operate in vegetable society. Class I fruit and vegetables must adhere to certain standards of appearance, size, shape, quality and presentation in packaging, allowing for slight defects in colour and slight skin damage. Class II vegetables will retain these essential characteristics, but will have defects in colour and skin injuries, including cracks and rubbing. There is an equivalent to a Class III or "working class" vegetable but nothing is heard of them and often they're immediately junked, or ironically, put to work in hideous factories.

1 plate of strawberries and ice cream

1 slice of coffee cake

1 bowl of strawberry ice cream

1 slice of honeydew melon

2 slices of apple pie and ice cream

1 330ml can of *Sprite*

1 330ml can of *Diet 7-up* [379]

1 500ml bottle of *Yazoo* banana flavour milk drink

1 glass of Ross stream water

5 glasses of Ross rain water [380]

56 slices of *Tine of Oslo* Jarlsberg cheese – 15g each [381]

364g of Swiss Gruyère

---

[379] Aspartame is sold under the brand names NutraSweet or Canderel and is used in products such as diet drinks and yoghurts. It has been linked with more than 90 adverse reactions, including brain tumours and blindness. I drink aspartame in faith and ignore these reports. And so what? I hear that cauliflower is linked to madness and carrots to plague. Toffee squares reportedly lead to bad driving and vodka has made several million people fall over in the snow.

[380] The last happy touch of a primitive sky. This rainwater was collected in a barrel after the old Highland fashion and drunk by myself while living wild in the North.

[381] 56 slices of cheese? Religious melancholy and despair. Unregenerate snacking. Immoderate enjoyment of factory produce. Indicating the advent of remarkable dreams. You can't pass the fridge without opening it to nick a slice.

2 caramelised lotus biscuits

1 170g tub of *Co-op* hummus

1 bite of Margaret's *Magnum* Classic

1 *Asda* cheese savoury sandwich

2 slices of cheese and tomato pizza

1 slice of mascarpone pizza

2 glasses of Ribena Light – "*Low Calorie, No artificial colour*"

1 chocolate and hazelnut croquante [382]

1 pitta bread with hummus and carrot

A half pitta bread soused in lemon and artichoke dip

1 hot cross bun of Inverness [383]

1 truffle from the *West End Bakers*, Edinburgh

1 chocolate & vanilla coconut square

1 *Bachelor's* cauliflower and broccoli cup-a-soup

---

[382] This was my first encounter with the croquante form, which is perhaps a sweet version of the normally savoury croquette. The croquette is fried in breadcrumbs and is an onomatopoeic foodstuff, gaining its title from *croquer*, the 18th century French meaning to crunch. Because of this, the *croque* (as in *Croque Monsieur*) cannot be related to the *croquettte* – but the *croquante* may be.

[383] In 2005, Oaks Primary School in Ipswich asked their bread supplier to remove the crosses from the school's buns on the grounds that the buns might offend some religious minorities. When the complainants discovered that the crosses were Pagan in origin, their protest became an embarrassment.

FIGURE 46 – I had to try Supermalt to see if it lived up to its inherent promise

1 330ml can of *Supermalt* [384] (Figure 46)

3 pints of *Robinson's* Smooth Fruit and Barley cordial, [385] made up with water

One and a half pitta breads with frozen tzatziki and frozen hummus

---

[384] A can of boasts. "The international quality malt drink enjoyed in many countries of the world" – and – "Tasty and highly digestible health drink"

[385] How on earth could *cordial* come to have its two meanings? The adjective, describing warmth of feeling is derivative of the Latin *cor*, meaning heart. The drink uses the same word – but with what heart do we knock back our *cordials*?

2 chocolate chip cookies [386]

1 pint of milk seasoned with strawberry *Crusha*

1 pint of *Gulp* banana milk

1 glass of freshly squeezed orange juice

1 bagel with cheese salad and lettuce

4 pitta bread with melted gruyère

1 100g *Cadbury's* Crunchie milk chocolate dessert (Figure 47)

FIGURE 47 – The detailed lid of the Crunchie dessert creation.

---

[386] But what is eating us? The very same Cookie Monster who sang "C is for Cookie, That's Good Enough For Me", is now advocating healthy eating. Cookie Monster has had his act cleaned up and his attitude to eating politically corrected – and it stinks. There's even a new Cookie Monster song - "A Cookie Is a Sometimes Food," in which Cookie Monster learns that there are "anytime" foods and "sometimes" foods. It is sacrilege, I say, and akin to Oscar the Grouch being tidy and generous.

1 250g serving of *Co-op* tortellini with fresh ricotta cheese and spinach

The only food force-fed that year was a ginger nut soaked in water, (force-fed by AA).

1 slice of cold French toast scavenged like a troglodyte from the kitchen sink, from my friend and flatmate, acknowledged later with apologies and explanations.

1 burned veggie-burger [387] on brown bread with butter, cucumber and ketchup

1 litre of *Wesergold* pear juice

4 *Warburton* pancakes

3 pieces of mild cheddar cheese

75g of *Jordan Valley* baba ganoush in 3 fajita wraps plus 1 pepper and 1 vine tomato – roasted in oil with mascarpone and Parmesan

2 x 165g tin cans of *Green Giant* no added salt or sugar sweet corn – *"naturally sweet – ideal for a low salt diet"*

1 pepper and 2 tomatoes roasted with Parmesan and mascarpone

1 42g Pot of *Vivian's* honey made by George and Margaret Tonkin, Vivien's Honey Farm, Hatherleigh

---

[387] Most of England, Wales and Lowland Scotland is a shore to shore pattern of fields which serve animal production. Everywhere domestic animals compete with forests and wildlife. If only 6.5% of what a cow eats can become in turn eatable by you, then 8,000 kg of plants will yield only 16 hamburgers and even less beef stock cubes! These calculations are untenably broad – but the public still regards animals as raw materials. Therefore the fact that you might be eating up to nine square metres of forest every mealtime is well beyond the mental game.

FIGURE 48 – One of "Tante Agathe's" high concept French Biscuits.

5 x *Tante Agathe biscuits Pour un Jour de Fête* – *"pour retrouver les saveurs de la cuisine heureuse du bon vieux temps"* (Figure 48)

1 200ml bottle of *Capri Sun* strawberry drink *"made with natural juice"* – *"fruit has never been such fun!"*

2 slices of spinach topped pizza

1 *Wall's* Magnum double caramel

Culture implies positive achievements and these value judgments are consequently transferred to the food in question. The double caramel ice-lolly, like the milk chocolate themed dessert, says it all about the economic effrontery of my life.

WE ALL GO TO PRÊT A MANGER

Prêt is the famous sandwich chain which and has an outlet near every office in every major city. Our office was no exception, causing me to judge all other lunch opportunities as primitive, compared to the hi-technology offerings that grew within Prêt's aluminium walls.

Prêt is remarkably modern in tone. There is no smell in Prêt shops, because of a vaguer pungency within their sandwiches which don't suffer the general ferocity of other lunch sandwiches. With necessary steadfastness, Prêt a Manger provides everything for the dynamic luncher. At a time of day when food is considered relative to convenience, Prêt win out in smartness, economy and taste.

Brother and sister mine! Never condemn those who find themselves in such need of fast and healthy food that they pass between the silvered walls of Prêt, because Prêt are as integral to office life as the photocopier and the fax machine, and for all their daft inventions Prêt are your greatest servants, even if you fail to thank them for it.

The enumeration of Prêt items led me to the conclusion that I had eaten the following, over the course of one year:

7 *Prêt* avocado, Parmesan, pine nut, cucumber and black pepper wraps (Figure 49) [388]

7 *Prêt* basil, tomato and brie baguettes

6 *Prêt* hummus wraps

1 *Prêt* "2004 Meal" series Breadless Sandwich

---

[388] The WRAP was the great fashion back then, not only for its neatness, but because bread was considered unhealthy by the enthusiastic lunch-goers of the era. This was because of the CARBS (carbohydrate) content of bread, which many thought was too high. Carbs were in those times, eschewed as unhealthy by people who were as far as I could see, crazy and hungry. That said, weight for weight carbohydrates provide fewer calories than fat or alcohol – although the real problem with weight gain is what people combine with their carbs – i.e. fat and alcohol

235

2 x 65g *Prêt* Power Bars – "*A daily hit full of fruit goodness*"

2 x *Prêt* chocolate brownies [389]

1 *Prêt* carrot cake

1 *Prêt* "*Amazing Breadless Sandwich*"

FIGURE 49 – A Prêt salad wrap, pictured in its gay arraignment.

1 *Prêt* caramel cheesecake

1 milky coffee off of *Prêt*

1 *Prêt* oat and fruit slice [390]

1 *Prêt* toffee waffle

1 *Prêt* banana cake

---

[389] Later I discovered that although Kosher, these brownies may not have been Halal, due to the Vanilla Extract, which is made with 35% alcohol. It should be noted that Kosher does allow some alcohol, whereas Halal does not.

[390] The Prêt oat and fruit slice is stirred with a four-foot oar, according to the packaging. There is a Zen like quality to the sudden awakening this fact inspires. It's not anything to do with the rustic charm of Prêt's oar – but it's the realisation that our lunch is in fact made at all and doesn't just appear as if by magic.

1 40g bag of *Prêt* "*hand cooked*" cheddar & chive crisps

1 40g bag of *Prêt* "*handmade*" lightly salted crisps

1 330ml can of *Prêt* sparkling mixed herbal drink [391]

Prêt's contribution to our diet is best understood in the context of the Office Lunch Break. That said, wherever we are, there is something unexplained and baffling about the rows of precisely wrapped and engineered sandwiches we encounter. Now you'll see all sorts of phrases used in connection with the production of sandwiches, such as "freshly cut", as if to imply there's a special art to making them.

The average UK employee's lunch break totals just under 20 minutes. While Lost Lunch = Lost Productivity, it's obvious that too much lunch will also harm our output. It's more likely these days to see people eating at their desks, not because they're under pressure to work harder, but because grazing really is the most meaningful way to eat at work.

Lunchtime in general does not offer a sufficient amount of time for a worker to relax, refocus, refresh and re-energise – but the great thing about leaving the workplace is that you can visit lunch outlets and meet other lunchers. Better still, the higher up the chain you are, the longer you can take about it. No better fictional description of office lunching may be found than Nicholson Baker's novel *The Mezzanine*.

Lunch from Prêt is contemporary insofar as it satisfies minute concerns, many of which we didn't know we had before we went in there. Although Prêt's lunch is admirably moral (ethically sourced coffee beans, Fairtrade tea, biodegraeable boxes, free range and organic UK ingredients) they somewhat oddly sold McDonald's a third share in their business in 2001.

---

[391] "Yoga Bunny Detox balanced with Ginseng & Echinacea."

HOW TO NAME YOUR FOOD

Sooner or later we're going to have to accept a standardised method for naming our foods. Here is *The Supper Book*'s system for food naming.

1. Start to describe your food with its most basic name. This should be a single noun such as *Curry.*

2. After the basic name add the most general descriptor, such as *Green, Baked, Poor* or *High-Speed.*

3. Continue to add modifiers (separated by commas and spaces), moving from the general to the specific and merging with additional pronouns such as *on* and *'n'.* Examples of subsequent qualifiers could include *chopped, whipped, boiled,* or *Korma.*

4. Add your own name if you like – or the brand name, or the title of the cookbook where you first found the food.

5. Next, try to insert a phrase relating the food's volume to its weight. For example, *Chunky, Kingsize* or *vol au* will all work.

6. Ensure the description suggests that the food will be served on a plate. Reason? It's surprising how much of what we eat comes in bags or plastic containers, which we discard with not a second thought.

Lastly, if you run out of room (the limit for the names of foods is held to be 75 characters), feel free to abbreviate, but try to observe the same conventions each time.

Examples:

Supper Book Poor Chopped Four-Sausage Curry Korma on a Plate 'n' Chips

Or

Gregg's Homebaked Baked Chunk Chicken Bagged Bridie-Bake [392]

Or

Bowled Egg 'n' Cooked Bean Beancake in a Slow Cheese 'n' Egg Sausage Fricassée.

Or

Monkish Monkfish Fillet Fingers on Fresh Cream Crème Fraiche Served Caerphilly with Internet Potato Sauce

---

[392] Note that a chicken bridie is never referred to as a Birdie Bridie.

25 LITRES OF WINE

Ancient cultures considered the drinking of unmixed wine to be barbaric. [393] A Greek or Roman who drank unmixed wine was likely to be a drunkard or a glutton and so at the very least, water was added, usually on a 50 / 50 basis with the wine. In deference to this ancient code, I often mixed my wine, although I usually mixed it with beer – sometimes adding a couple of vodka and cokes as well.

Often, one of my friends participated in this, appearing at my door with a smile – a smile being code for *Let's get drunk*. There was no harm in this and the obvious pleasure, combined with the trivialising of my woes, was repeated several times each week.

Having accorded wine a status above all other manmade liquids – neither beer nor hard liquor carry its religious significance, as they are not made from grapes – drinkers often feel a religious tinge before the first glass of wine, and often again, just after the last. After our last glass of wine we go to bed and we awake the next day, perhaps feeling somewhat seedy, but always sharply aware of the world around us.

Over the course of one year I drank approximately 25 litres of wine, which I calculate is just over half a glass each day.

---

[393] Herodotus writes that Cleomene's madness proceeded from the habit of drinking wine unmixed with water, something that he learnt from the Scyths. Likewise Plato says: "But the Scythians and Thracians, both men and women, drink unmixed wine, which they pour on their garments, and this they think a happy and glorious institution." An exchange between one of the ambassadors and Dicaeopolis in Aristophanes' *Acharnians* also illustrates the barbaric nature of the custom:

A: And when we were entertained, we were compelled to drink unmixed sweet wine from cups of glass and gold.

D: City of Cranaus! Are you aware how these ambassadors mock you?

A variation on this ancient custom is still performed today as part of the Roman Catholic Mass, when the priest pours a few drops of water into the wine and says the *Novus Ordo*:

"By the mystery of this water and wine may we come to share in the divinity of Christ, who humbled himself to share in our humanity."

The itemisation of my 25 litres of wine:

2 x 75cl bottles of *Gato Blanco* Chile 2002 Chardonnay

1 75cl bottle of *Villa Pani* ® 2002 Frascati *"Superiore"*

12 glasses of South African Chenin Blanc (Figure 50)

1 75cl bottle of 2004 Chilean Sauvignon Blanc Chardonnay

1 75cl bottle of South African Chardonnay [394]

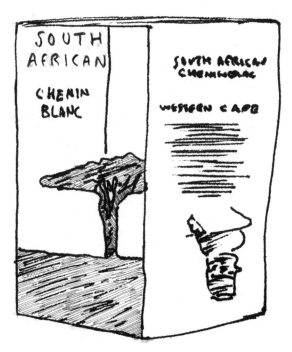

FIGURE 50 – An attachment develops between a drinker and their box of wine

---

[394] As it says on the bottle, "A famous grape" – and more specifically, "A rich buttery white wine from the Western cape of South Africa." The grape is a superior commodity, and was chosen by the Lord to fulfil a great task.

1 75cl bottle of *Les Janelles Réserve Viognier* Vin de Pays d'Oc 2003

1 75cl bottle of 2002 California *Colombard* Chardonnay

1 75cl bottle of Chilean Merlot 2004

4 glasses of *Kumala* Ruby Cabernet Merlot

3 glasses of *Kumala* Reserve Chardonnay 2003

4 glasses *Kendermanns* Pinot Bianco 2002 white wine

4 glasses of *Lawsons'* dry Sauvignon Blanc

3 glasses South African white wine

10 glasses of *Gato Negro* 2002 Merlot (Figure 51)

3 glasses of *Sainsbury's* Chilean Central Valley Sauvignon Blanc

3 glasses of *DUMiSANi* 2002 South African Shiraz

FIGURE 51 – Label from Gato Negro Red Wine

3 glasses of 2003 Western Cape Chardonnay

3 glasses of *Marlborough Villa Maria* Sauvignon Blanc 2001

2 glasses of *Marlborough Villa Maria* Sauvignon Blanc 2003

3 glasses of *Brown Brothers* 2003 *"Estate Bottled"* Chenin Blanc

3 glasses of *Hardy's* "Voyage" unoaked Colombard Verdelho, Chenin Blanc 2003

3 glasses of *George Duboeuf* vin de table rouge

3 glasses of Muscadet et Sèvre et Maine [395]

3 glasses of *Louis Jadot* Pouilly-Fuissé 2002

2 glasses Australian Semillon Chardonnay 2002

2 glasses of *Villa Merria* New Zealand Private Bin Sauvignon Blanc 2003

2 glasses of red wine of unidentified Spanish origin

2 glasses of *Labeye* 2002 Grenache Syrah

2 and a half glasses of Italian Pinot Grigot

1 glass of red wine *Château du sers Lalonde de Pomerol*

3 glasses of *"Two Oceans"* 2003 Semillon Chardonnay

1 glass of *Cuveé Louise* dry white French wine

---

[395] *Boswell: We had wine before the Union.*
Johnson: No, sir; you had some weak stuff, the refuse of France, which would not make you drunk.

FIGURE 52 – A red wine label from the Scottish Co-op.
God prevent me from drinking wine merely because I like the label!

1 75cl bottle of *Co-op Nero d'avola, Frappato* (Figure 52)

1 75cl bottle of *Cles Pioch de la Croix St Roch* Vin de Pays de la Bénouie

1 glass of red wine – *"Primitivo Sangiovese"* [396]

10 glasses of red wine of non-specific nor identified origin

1 glass of Spanish white wine

1 glass of Sauvignon Blanc

2 glasses of Chardonnay white wine

---

[396] "Alcohol consumption in the ancient world was a matter of public endeavour."
Tamra Andrews, *An Encyclopaedia of Food in World Mythology* (2000)

23 glasses of white wine of unknown origin

1 glass of unidentified Spanish white wine

2 glasses of unknown Champagne

1 sip of unidentified sparkling wine

19 glasses of *Freixent* Traditional Method Cava (Figure 53)

2 glasses of *Charles Heidsieck* Heritage Champagne

2 glasses *Charles Heidsieck* Brut Reserve Champagne, mis en cave 1996

2 and a half glasses of *Pol Roger* Champagne

1 glass of *LeComber et Fils* SJP Champagne

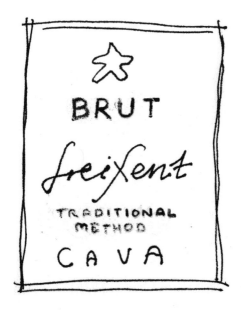

FIGURE 53 – I managed to draw the label although the pronunciation escapes me.

Poor Sausage Korma

To guttle on Poor Sausage Korma you had better be prepared.
It is one of the strangest foods in the Gastrosphere.

You will need one large onion / 1 red pepper / 4 cloves of garlic /
3 *Cauldron* [397] succulent Lincolnshire Veggie sausages
and half jar of *Loyd Grossman* [398] korma sauce. [399]

Two servings were made and eaten with basmati rice.

Fake Chicken Fry

For this *bonne bouche*, collect 1 onion / 6 cloves of garlic / 1 carrot /
1 red pepper / 30 sugar snap peas /
and 1 packet of 175g *Quorn* ® Chicken Style Pieces.

This was eaten in two bowls, with soy sauce.

---

[397] Cauldron again! An inscription on the packet tells us that "Cauldron is about food that's imaginative and easy to prepare." Cookery is a problem which the manufacturers wish to help us solve.

[398] Loyd Grossman Korma curry sauce – "A rich sauce with a blend of coconuts, cream and almonds." Aside from being a Sauce Boss, Loyd Grossman OBE is involved in museums work in the UK, and is among other things, Chairman of the Public Monuments and Sculpture Association. Sauce and sculpture in one man!

[399] Studies such as *The Supper Book* have been instrumental in shedding light on the simple fluctuations in appetite which result in the random purchasing of Loyd Grossman sauce products.

Pea And Cabbage Soup

5 potatoes / 2 leeks / half a cabbage of Bill Burnett (Figure 54) / 1 bulb of garlic / 454g frozen peas / one and a half pints of stock / 125ml of single cream. [400]

This made 3 bowls of pea and cabbage soup

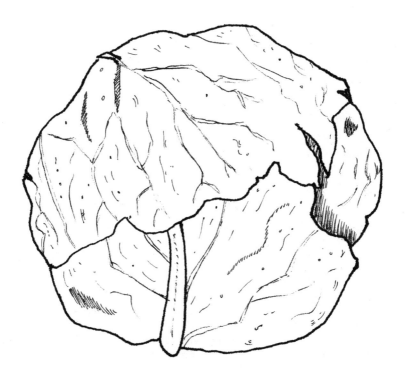

FIGURE 54 – Mr Bill Burnett grew this epic cabbage

---

[400] How to cook this recipe: Take kabbidge and perboyle it tender then take it up and wrynge oute the water cleane and chop it very small and then set it upon the fyre wyth sweet little herbies in a panne of freezed pease and seaosne it and then set it in a platter to coole and then fill your pot and so bake it to soup.

FRUIT BASKET

Fruit has long been a convenient receptacle for the fantasies and projections of the keen dietist. From an early age we are encouraged to believe that along with vegetables, fruit is the key to good living. But when it is possible to obtain vitamins and nutrients chemically, what will the point of fruit be? [401]

Most of the fruit in *The Supper Book* was what we may consider to be of perfect shape, because it was bought in supermarkets which test for this kind of thing. The more we demand a particular size and shape however, the further our fruit has to travel; and remember up to 40% of fruit is thrown away due to damage during transport and harvest. That fruit could make a lot of pies. [402]

I wonder if there is common ground between the processes of grafting and genetic modification? Current GM projects include the development of fruits that ripen slower and apples that don't brown so quickly when cut. The genes responsible for the sweetness and smell of strawberries have already been discovered – and the debate is unresolved as to whether an organic fruit may be better for you than one with boosted nutritional contents.

---

[401] It's quite scary to think how close mankind has come to destruction. Our future lies at the mercy of large-scale production and distribution operations, which have kept us alive only in order to maximise their profits. Last Friday night, in between crisps and beers etc., my neighbour moseyed over and invited me to his very own "Arboretum Orgasmica" for some eats. I got on my flip flops, my old comfy law school sweatshirt and adidas windpants, and I followed the semi-dorky thirty-something up to the end of his garden, where we began to pick apples and pears from his trees. I couldn't believe it at the time, but I was scared of the fruit – as if I were eating from a triffid. It may have been the beer and the crisps but I was genuinely frightened of my neighbour's produce – simply because it hadn't come from a plastic packet, or been picked from a shelf.

[402] Do consumers really demand fruit to be a certain shape? The irony is that the size and shape of fruit is mainly the concern of the big retailers rather than the consumers. An issue that is of concern to consumers is the presence of pesticides – but of course, pesticides are used by growers to meet the supermarkets' cosmetic requirements. Indeed, the preoccupation with appearance is forcing growers to use more pesticides than ever. Despite the fact that British growers see the best possibility of their survival in local marketing initiatives, regrettably, small shops are in decline.

In the fruit basket this year, were the following:

48 bananae [403]	7 dates
42 red grapes	4 slices of melon
37 oranges [404]	3 Williams pears
19 green grapes	3 other pears
18 satsumae	2 tangerines
17 tomatoes	1 clementine
10 Royal Gala apples [405]	1 Forelle pear
11 other apples [406]	1 redcurrant

---

[403] The banana is included in this list, but it is not a fruit! The banana is in fact a giant herb. Bananas is grown from cuttings and each plant only ever produces one hand of fruit before dying. No fertilisation takes place and the flowers are sterile. Of course, a plant cannot be grown from a banana seed – and for this reason, the Buddha chose the banana plant as the symbol of the futility of earthly possessions. He was a wise man that Buddha and knew better than to plant a banana seed on this earth.

[404] 6 of these 37 oranges were South Africa Valencia. The Valencia is a late orange, and has a great many pips under its smooth skin.

[405] "You first parents of the human race ... who ruined yourself for an apple, what might you have done for a truffled turkey?" Jean-Anthelme Brillat-Savarin (1755-1826)

[406] It's astonishing that up to 50 different chemical pesticides are used on apples alone. Of the UK apples tested by Friends Of The Earth in 2004, 70% contained residues of more than one pesticide. Residues included *Prothiofos*, banned in the UK, *Carbendazim*, a suspected hormone disrupter, *Chlorpyrifos* an organophosphate which has been severely restricted in the US, *Folpet*, a carcinogen; and *Dimethoate*, an organophosphate.

GREGGS

A re Greggs the Bakers aware that their logo – :: – is equivalent to the Braille for the Letter "G" ? If not then this may be further proof that serendipity acts when we are too busy with our endeavour.

Greggs is the UK's leading bakery retailer specialising in savouries and other bakery related products, even appealing to the vegetarian palate with their unelaborated cheese pies and bridies. [407]

Is it important that the *bridie* should have its history recorded? I think so, and guess that the word *bridie* is a corruption of the phrase "bride's pie" – although what this says concerning the standard of catering at old-time Scots weddings I hardly like to consider. Greggs is where to go to study that section of baking in which to find the *bridie* and the *pasty* (otherwise known as the *pastie* [408]). With more than 1200 retail outlets in the UK, it means that the study of this subject is available to all of us with generous ease. Below are Greggs' profits for 2004 and their equivalents in pastry products. Profits are itemised post-tax and are based on a turnover figure of £504.2 million for the year.

	2004 £	What's that in bridies?	What's that in macaroni pies?
Profits	32.3 million	43,648,647	48,939,392
Earnings Per Share	282.1 pence	3.8	4.3

Source: "A Slice of our Life; Annual Report and Accounts 2005", by Greggs PLC

---

[407] The messiest question of our time: WHAT IS THE DIFFERENCE BETWEEN A PASTIE AND A BRIDIE? A bridie contains mainly beef and onions, while a Cornish pasty's filling has potato and swede with a little beef. A bridie is like a Bhaji, which was developed in Gujarat for long distance journeys on foot. It is also like a Sussex Churdle, which contains liver, bacon and vegetables with a cheese topping – because all are wrapped in a round pastry base, which is then turned over and folded down to enclose the contents.

[408]	EATEN BY MINERS	POTATOES & SWEDE	SOLID FILLING	COOKED FROM RAW	CRUSTY PASTRY
PASTIE	x	x	optional	x	x
PASTY	✓	✓	✓	✓	✓

William Shakespeare at Greggs

In The Merry Wives of Windsor, Act 1 Scene 1 the Page says "*Wife, bid these gentlemen welcome. Come, we have a hot venison pasty to dinner.*"

In All's Well that Ends Well, Act IV Scene III, Parrolles says: "*I will confess to what I know without constraint: if ye pinch me like a pasty , I can say no more.*"

And in Titus Andronicus, Titus bakes Chiron and Demetrius's bodies into a pasty, and forces their mother to eat them.

I ate:

10 *Greggs* macaroni pies

6 *Greggs* cheese and onion pasties [409]

4 *Greggs* crumpets and spread

3 *Greggs* iced donuts

2 *Greggs* truffles

1 *Greggs* buttered crumpet

---

[409] PASTIE OR PASTY: How to identify a PASTY: The solid ridge of pastry, hand crimped along the top of the Cornish Pasty was so designed that the eater could grasp the food while dining and then throw the crust away. Sometimes, when pasties are being made, each member of the family has their initials marked at one corner. The true Cornish way to eat a pasty is to hold it in your hands and begin to eat it from the top down to the opposite end of the initialled part. That way the pasty's rightful owner could consume any left over portion later. It is said by church historians that early Irish Priests created pasties in order to transport food as they walked about the countryside preaching. I am an orthodox fellow but on this point I will not give the church the credit. The following have been recorded: Apple Pasty; Date Pasty; Herby Pasty; Mackerel Pasty; Parsely Pasty; Rabbity Pasty; Rice Pasty; Stargazy Pasty (Usually a whole herring wrapped in pastry with its head sticking out one end); Windy Pasty (made with lard, suet and jam).

Half a *Greggs* Fly Cemetery [410]

3 *Greggs* Pink Jammies (Figure 55)

1 *Greggs* caramel shortbread

1 *Greggs* macaroni pie with *Branston* pickle

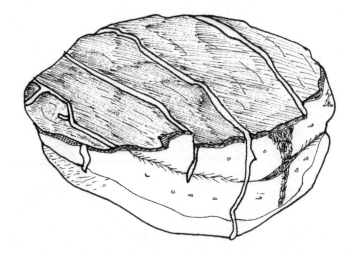

FIGURE 55 – The Pink Jammie is perhaps the most luscious of all Greggs confections

---

[410] The Fly Cemetery is the name of a cake that includes currants, apples and raisins in a flaky pastry topped with sugar. There's something about dried currants in biscuits that evokes squashed flies, whether it be a garibaldi or an Eccles Cake (which very annoyingly is sometimes called an Eccle Cake in Canada.) With currants poking out of the side, these sugar-topped biscuits really do evoke a mass of dead insects, and hence this gruesome name has evolved. Where exactly the name derives from is much in debate and although Scots people are sure that it was their idea the rest of the world thinks differently. In terms of origin, the name fly cemetery features in Scots glossaries from *Leith Patter* to the *Aberdonian Doric* website – but the definition is also found in the *Dublin Slang Dictionary* and the *Mersey-Talk* website, as well in the *Australian Slang Dictionary*, which records that the name derived in Southern Australia.

SKY SUPPERS

The Sky Supper, although much maligned in the past, is today more often surprisingly good than it is inedible. There was once a belief not merely applying to food, which stated that a captive audience could be treated to anything that you cared to offer them on a *like it or lump it* basis.

These days are gone and now aeroplanes serve pocket meals which as much as other foods have benefitted from the enormous advances being made in industrial food production.

So what is the point of in-flight meals? Is their main purpose to kill the boredom of the flight? I think so. Everything comes wrapped up as if for spacemen [411] and is an adventure in microdining. It's all so airtight like the aeroplane itself – a far cry from the good old days of flying, when male passengers wore ties and meals were served on proper crockery and were eaten with metal cutlery.

FIGURE 56 – In flight meals are sealed in a plastified world of their own.

---

[411] The present method of space feeding seems to be satisfactory – but what lies in store for future astronauts? Cooking with an electric stove is impossible in space because of the gaseous environment of the spacecraft, but that may not always be the case. Developments of systems involving food, water, and waste management have not kept pace with the building of boosters and other sophisticated systems. We must demand adequate attention to the space food programme. At present the crew-members don't even want to defecate because they hate to use the hand-held straddle trench. This straddle trench is a bag with a sticky rim on top, and it is difficult to place one's ass correctly. Some think aeroplane toilets are little better.

In 2005 a strike at the catering company *Gate Gourmet* forced the cancellation of all *British Airways'* flights and led many to question the point of providing airline meals at all, especially on shorter flights. Many of the stranded passengers seemed perfectly content with BA's emergency "delibags" and vouchers to spend at the terminal. Amazingly, *Prêt a Manger* did a roaring trade in sandwiches, fruit salads and drinks during the strike.

Getting a meal on board a plane is pricey and there are strict hygiene rules. Vegetables tend to be steamed to maintain some crispness and meat is boiled slowly and then covered in sauce to ensure that it retains a level of moistness when reheated on board. Master over the elements, man must prove that *food can fly*. My own total of Sky Suppers was as follows:

The first *Lufthansa* Food Tray – 1 salad with a mozzarella lump (I didn't eat the olive) / 10g *Lurpak Spreadable* butter / 20g of *Holland* Dutch Edam / 1 bread roll / 1 *Lufthansa* cheese sandwich "Guten Appetit" / 1 *Lufthansa* baba [412] (Figure 57)

FIGURE 57 – The Lufthansa baba in its plastic vessel

---

[412] Was is das, das baba? The baba was originally an innocent *kugelhopf* which was doused in Maderia and set alight one evening by mad King Stanislas Leczinski of Poland. Prepared in this way, and named after the hero of the King's favourite book, *The Thousand and One Nights*, the baba was transferred to Paris when Stanislas moved his court there following an assassination attempt.

The second *Lufthansa* Food Tray – 1 portion of *Alpenhaim* brand Bergspitz Camembert / 1 small roll / 1 baby salad / 1 *Chenbach* brand plain yoghurt / 1 sachet of herb dressing / 1 spiced apple pastry in a bed of custard (This meal is pictured in Figure 56)

1 10g bag of *Roland* original SnackPearls – *"new"* – *"Gratismuster"* (Figure 58)

FIGURE 58 – A SnackPearl

2 airline beers, being 25cl *Warsteiner* premium verum – *"Einesder besten Biere unsever Zeit"*

1 *Lufthansa* rye bread and cheese sandwich, with the motto – *"enjoy"*

1 apple juice

1 *EasyJet* [413] tea and milk

---

[413] Many airlines are following the example of the low-cost carriers who – having cast a tired eye over the ritual of dining in the sky – have banished in-flight meals altogether.

Food & Drink Away from Home (O to Z)

Restaurants / Cafés / Bars / Stands / Hotels
Pubs / Functions

In the swanky centres of our cities a highly committed group of reasonably paid men and women in white hats work to provide people with meals that they have never heard of before. These men and women are never seen by the diners and compete with each other for the daftest fare with the most foreign sounding of names.

Why should it be that we never see the chefs? Does their invisibility increase our need for them to meld common expectation with creativity? If you are a chef, what you create has to pass through the hands of the waiting staff. As part of your creative work as chef, you need to have your menu represented and served the way you like, and this is why we will never see you – because you have waiters and waitresses as your extra limbs.

Just look at my **O to Z.** Nachos – arrabiata – Thai sweet and sour – risotto – guacamole – saag paneer – and Diet Coke. There is never a question of a recipe being considered "stolen" versus "borrowed" or "collected".

Only later, once I had inexplicably lost my sense of taste, did I realise that chefs today are our only acceptable remaining messengers of world peace.

Here is where I ate and what I took:

Oban Backpackers, Oban – 1 white coffee

Old Orleans, Edinburgh – 1 shared popcorn appetiser / 1 plate of nachos / 1 portion of potato skins / 1 mushroom burger with cheese / 1 portion of salad with ranch sauce / 1 frozen margarita [414]

---

[414] Common margarita ratios are:
  The "2:1:1" – 50% Tequila; 25% Triple Sec; 25% Fresh Lime Juice
  The "3:2:1" – 50% Tequila; 33% Triple Sec; 17% Fresh Lime Juice
  The "3:1:1" – 60% Tequila; 20% Triple Sec; 20% Fresh Lime Juice
  The "1:1:1" – 33% Tequila; 33% Triple Sec; 33% Fresh Lime Juice

Outhouse, Edinburgh – 1 hot chocolate

Pasquale's, Edinburgh – 1 and a third bruschetta / 1 plate of penne arabiatta / 1 black tea / 4 chips and salt / a half portion of eggplant and Parmesan / 1 pizza with onion / 1 glass of Diet Coke / 1 glass of liqueur on the house / 2 Amaretto biscuits

Patisseries Suisse, East Jerusalem – 1 *Rombouts* filter coffee

Peckham's, Edinburgh – 1 25cl glass of *Gleneagles* still spring water / 1 25cl glass of *Gleneagles* sparkling spring water / 6 potato skins with sour cream, Thai sweet and sour sauce and salsa / 1 tower of vegetarian haggis, neep and tattie smothered in whisky and herb sauce

Le Petit Paris, Edinburgh – 1 bowl of split green pea soup / 1 bread and butter / 1 glass of tap water

Pinsent Masons Business Breakfast, Edinburgh – 1 almond croissant

Pizza Express, West End, Edinburgh – 1 portion of cheesecake with a scoop of vanilla ice cream and raspberry sauce / 3 grapes / 3 black coffees / 2 plates of baked aubergine in tomato and Parmesan / 1 pizza Margherita / 1 black coffee and *Martin Bucer* Sambuca / 1 Diet Coke and ice / 1 glass of iced water

Prima Pizza, Edinburgh – 1 10" pizza with onion and pineapple / 4 slices of sliced tomato and garlic pizza with *Hellmann's* mayo and a squeeze of ketchup / 2 slices of vegetarian pizza / 3 slices of garlic and tomato pizza / 2 slices of garlic bread

Police Box Coffee Company, Buccleuch, Edinburgh – 1 black coffee / 1 white coffee

Potter Roll, Edinburgh – 1 black coffee with fruit scone and spread

Ramzy Burger, Bethlehem – 1 bowl of caramel and chocolate chip ice cream with sauce and sprinkles

Refresh, Edinburgh – Half a tangy lemon cake bar / 1 white coffee

Le Rendezvous, Smithfield – 1 asparagus risotto with lemon and Parmesan

Rialto, Edinburgh – 1 cup of white coffee and brown sugar / 1 Diet Coke [415]

Roslin Glen Hotel, Edinburgh – 4 roasted vegetable fajitas with guacamole, sour cream and salsa / a half portion fried potato wedges

Royal Ettrick, Edinburgh – 1 Idris "Fiery" Ginger beer with ice and a slice of lime / half a veggie-burger in a bun [416] / a Mediterranean roasted vegetable wrap with feta cheese, fries and ketchup / 1 portion of salad with balsamic dressing

Saddler's, Forfar – 1 cheese and onion pastie [417] and baked beans

Sainsbury's, Berryden, Aberdeen – 1 Interserve [418] cheese roll with the following statements on its packaging – "e.meal grab & go" and "Eat on day of purchase" / 1 Sainsbury's Earl Grey tagged tea bag from the "Teas of the world range"

---

[415] An analysis of studies in America until 1996 found that 92 per cent of independent research papers expressed concern that aspartame may be linked to illnesses such as brain tumours, blindness and seizures. As well as fizzy drinks and chewing gum, aspartame is found in sweets, beer, spring water and vitamins. It is 200 times sweeter than sugar but contains virtually no calories.

[416] So. As Frankfurt bequeathed the world the Frankfurter and Hamburg the Hamburger, so did the German city of Cheeseburg produce the Cheeseburger. Where am I going for my German weekend break? Why – am going to the old country town of Veggieburg.

[417] In the fifth century BCE Zarathustra became a hermit so that he could contemplate philosophy free from distractions. Legend has it that he survived in the wilderness for 20 years on nothing but water and daily slivers cut from one ancient and gigantic cheese. This style of cheese intrigues me. What if such a cheese could provide for a thousand pasties? How many more philosophers would grow wise and happy in this country? And what if such a cheese could be so old as to feed several generations of philosophers? That all great human minds could over time, fodder from one immemorial block? I'd love to see it happen.

[418] Interserve is clearly something from the imagination of William Burroughs. The naming of food is anything but straightforward.

258

La Salarella, Gibraltar – 1 black coffee

Salvo Café Restaurant, Edinburgh – 1 hot chocolate

Sarti's, Glasgow – 2 cups of tea and milk

Shell Oil Petrol Station, Corstorphine – Cheese and Onion *"Classic"* sandwich – *"Cheddar cheese and sliced white onion in a white sub roll"*

Simon's Salad Bar, Edinburgh – 1 hummus and roasted red pepper granary sandwich with complementary Golden Wonder Tomato Sauce Crisps (34.5g bag)

Shamania, Edinburgh – 1 and a half papad with aniseed, onion and chutney / 2 spoons of vegetable curry / 1 plate of saag paneer [419] / 1 portion of dhal / one and half chapati / 2 scoofs of *Fanta* Lite

Shiel Bridge Petrol Station – 1 coleslaw and cheese sandwich

South China Inn, Edinburgh – 1 portion of egg fried rice and sweet and sour sauce

Southern Cross (SX) Café, Edinburgh – 1 hot chocolate

Southside Community Centre Café, Edinburgh – 1 black coffee and toast

St. Andrew's, Jerusalem – 3 slices of toast, butter and apricot jam / 3 slices of toast, butter and strawberry jam / 2 black coffees / 1 banana and apple fruit salad / 1 orange juice / 1 *Bio Yoplait* walnut and apricot yoghurt mixed with bran flakes

St George's West, Edinburgh – 1 *Twinings* cranberry, raspberry and elderflower tea – *"Expert Blenders since 1706"* / one local mince pie

---

[419] The smaller the joint the better the saag paneer. If they don't take credit cards then they don't take nonsense. SP is always in the words of my grandfather, "cheap and good" and hecka-tasty – and I eat it to take care of my soul which people try to beat down and steal from me every day of my freakin' life. In some places you gotta order the SP hot, or else they give you some wussy-whitey version... try it hot... it rocks.

Stromboli, Edinburgh – 1 slice of pizza with tomato / 1 330ml can of Diet Coke

Tesco, Oban – The *Tesco* All Day Vegetarian Megabreakfast = 1 fried egg / 2 hot tomatoes /1 hash brown / 1 cup of tea / baked beans / half a fried potato scone / 1 large folded omelette / 3 vegetarian sausages [420]

The Three Sisters, Edinburgh – 1 Diet Coke

Thirsty Lunch, Edinburgh – 1 cheese and coleslaw sandwich / 1 veggie snack bite

The Traverse Bar, Edinburgh – 1 Diet Coke

Uppercrust, Waverley, Edinburgh – 1 large coffee and milk

Valentino Café, Bethlehem – 1 felafel in pitta / 1 mint tea

The Vancouver Muffin Co., Glasgow – 1 black coffee / 1 and a half Empire Biscuits [421]

Vespa, Glasgow – 1 Diet Coke / 1 black coffee / 1 penne pasta with cherry tomato, ricotta and basil / 1 slice of garlic bread

Victorian House Hotel, Glasgow – 2 hash browns / 1 portion of baked beans / 1 portion of scrambled eggs / 2 glasses of fresh pink grapefruit juice

---

[420] This *Megabreakfast* also included the following items which remained uneaten – another fried egg / the other half of the fried scone / 2 slices of toast / 2 more cups of tea.

[421] "The Russians have caviar, the French fine wine, but beating them all, the Scots have the delicious Empire Biscuit. The biscuit material is soft and crumbly when fresh and even softer should you leave it for a day or two thus establishing its biscuit credentials. The filling is that indistinguishable stuff that has no natural ingredients and no real taste; but it performs its duty of holding the two biscuits together very effectively allowing the eater to work his or her way around the edge leaving the section with the cherry on it as a prize at the end of the session. This biscuit has absolutely no potential for dunking. Indeed even the thought of putting something like this in tea is abhorrent." Phil Parker, *Nice Cup of Tea and A Sit Down*

The Village Eatery, Edinburgh Airport – 2 slices of toast, butter and blackcurrant jam

Mrs J. West Memorial, Leys Drive, Inverness – 2 cups of black coffee and lemon cake / 1 slice of cherry cake / 1 black coffee with soya milk / 1 *Options* Mint Chocolate

West Lothian College, Livingstone – 1 cup of green tea

Whistlebinkies, Edinburgh – 1 Diet Coke

The World Famous Maggie Dickson's Pub, Edinburgh – 1 pint of Diet Coke and ice cream

Ye May Gang Faur and Fare Waur, [422] **Stracathro** – 1 chocolate crispie

YMCA, Beit Sahur – 2 coffees with cardamom

Yo! Sushi, Edinburgh – 2 deep fried battered carrots & soy sauce / 5 fried vegetable pieces & soy sauce

Zucca, W11, London – 1 plate of penne with broccoli, mascarpone and almonds / 1 glass of *Hildon Spring Water* / 1 black coffee / 1 bite of apple & blueberry crumble

---

[422] A translation of this name might be "you may go far and fare worse." We will all go far – and it is likely we will fare much worse. There are in fact three possible scenarios regarding our future food supply:

1. The richest fifth of the world (that's us. Hi.) continues to eat well, consuming animal products and engineered convenience food.

2. The world will go back to subsistence living (ha ha).

3. Through the wonders of science and capitalism, there will be enough food for everyone (corporate fantasy – but still the favoured outcome.)

BREAKFAST CEREALS

To thee O Kellogg I cried, What profit
is there in your cereal!
Thou has loosed my pyjama and
girded me with break.

The ancients discovered gods or goddesses for almost every thing or activity. Vicyua, a robust and healthy goddess, ruled over Eastern gastronomy and saw that foods were pleasing as well as nutritious – a combination found more readily in breakfast cereals than anywhere else.

Evidence of cultivated cereals from the beginning of the post-glacial age has been uncovered in Syria, on the banks of the Euphrates. The long march towards breakfast began in earnest around 10,000 BC, when farmers in the Near East began to favour select mutations in cereal crops. Here therefore is evidence of cereal growth by design and the first evidence of a culture giving some proper thought to what it may wish to eat for breakfast.

12,000 years later and the principles of cereal manufacture remain the same, and many farmers still make breakfast cereal. First, experiments are carried out in nitrogen-fixing the seeds, so that the farmers can buy special fertiliser for their crop. Then the crop is harvested, using a combine harvester with snap rolls that strip the stalk and leaf away from the ear. Finally the farmer fortifies the breakfast cereal with riboflavin and his team of designers dream up a cartoon character to market the result. [423]

---

[423] Characters such as Snap, Crackle and Pop, Tony the Tiger, Cap'n Crunch and Honey Monster. Both advertising and breakfast cereals were developed at same time and place – in late 19th century America – and both took advantage of mass-market production and were pioneered by people who were at best colourful, and at worst completely larcenous. CW Post, a contemporary of Dr Kellogg, established a rival company and concocted medical conditions such as *coffee heart*, *brain fag* and *coffee rheumatism* in order to sell his grain drink; as well as inventing a wide range of ailments to sell his Grape Nuts, a barley based food containing neither grapes nor nuts. The first fictional breakfast cereal characters appeared in the 1930s, with Snap (of Kellogg's Snap, Crackle and Pop fame) being one of the earliest arrivals, first appearing in 1931. Although breakfast cereal characters are fictional, actual-fictional breakfast cereal characters have included *Powdered Toast Man* from The Ren and Stimpy Show; *Archduke Chocula* from Futurama; and *Friedrich Nietzsche*, who

The final stage of cereal manufacture is the lurid box, which will feature the new cartoon character and legends such as: *Same Great Taste! Fortified With Vitamins and Iron*; *No Artificial Colours* and *To Open Slide Finger Under Centre Flap*.

The breakfast cereal is then ready for transportation to your local supermarket, and the farmer can go back to bed, pleased that yet again the soil has yielded its sacrifice for the benefit of our *brek*.

My breakfast cereal total was as follows:

3 x 560g boxes of *Alpen* No Added Sugar

56 *Weetabix* with milk and sugar

1 375g box of *Nestlé* Cinnamon Grahams

1 450g box of *Quaker* Sugar Puffs – "*Nutritious wheat puffs coated in honey and brown sugar*" [424]

1 375g box of *Nestlé* Cookie Crisp

1 375g box of *Nestlé* Honey Nut Cheerios

1 375g box of *Nestlé* Golden Nuggets [425]

1 17g box of *Kellogg's* Cornflakes mixed with 25g box of Frosties Chocolate and hot cows' milk

---

appears on MTV's Nietzsche Pops cereal. The best fictional cereals have included *Spunco Sugar Corn Waste* (Jimmy the Hapless Boy); *Colon Blow* (Saturday Night Live); and *N'yuk-N'yuks* from The Three Stooges.

[424] HOW TO PUFF: 1. In GUN-PUFFING wheat grains are heated under pressure and the moisture in the kernels flashes off as steam. The starch gelatinises and the kernel expands, dries and sets. 2. OVEN-PUFFING is similar but uses regular oven pressure. The resulting product is similar to a gun-puffed product, but with slightly less volume.

[425] A gift from Shirley Campbell. What better gift than sweet nourishment itself?

1 25g boxlet of *Kellogg*'s Honey Nut Loops combined with a 25g boxlet of *Kellogg*'s Frosties and a 20g boxlet of *Kellogg*'s Rice Crispies served with cold cow's milk [426]

2 x 30g box of *Kellogg*'s Coco Pops

1 30g box of *Kellogg*'s Coco Pops Crunchers

1 17g box *Kellogg*'s Cornflakes – "*Toasted flakes of golden corn*" [427]

1 25g box *Kellogg*'s Frosties – "*Sugar frosted flakes of corn*"

1 20g box of *Kellogg*'s Rice Krispies – "*Toasted Rice Cereal*"

1 23g box of *Kellogg's* Rice Crispies Muddles [428]

---

[426] A few of you want to know more about the deadly practice of Cereal-Mixing, as in the case of Coco-Pops *Crunchers*. In past years we have been introduced to many such travesties including *My Little Pony* cereal, *Fruity Pebbles®*, *Urkel-Os*, *Cinnamon Mini Buns*, *Chocolate Cookie Crisp* and *Oreo O's™*. Cereals have appeared looking like mini waffles and banana nut bread, and have tied in with media events – such as *Jurassic Park™ Crunch*. Here are the percentage probabilities of what happens when two or more breakfast cereals are intermingled in the same bowl.
    5% – EXPLOSION! Internal damage possible if eaten
    15% – IMMISCIBLE. The cereals are destroyed as one cancels out another
    50% – MISCIBLE. Cereals taste as per normal, unless their flavours are contradictory, eg, Muesli & Coco Pops / Count Chocula & Quaker Organic Bran / Cocoa Pebbles & Cocoa Puffs
    25% – COMPATIBLE. A result which causes one or more of the cereals to work with 150% taste efficiency
    5% – DISCOVERY! In 5% of mixes, a special formula is created which causes an entirely new breakfast cereal to be created

[427] It is sometimes said that John Harvey Kellogg invented cornflakes to stop masturbation – but I think the argument was a little vaguer than that. Kellogg believed that pure and moderate eating would encourage pure and moderate moral habits whereas rich and fatty foods would excite the passions and encourage moral profligacy. Cornflakes were therefore thought to encourage a wholesome spiritual outlook in life – but I wonder what Kellogg would have made of us tossing over our cereal (see page 94).

[428] "Four tasty multi-grain shapes" / "Helps keep kids healthy from top-to-toe" / "Multi-grain cereal shapes with a natural probiotic"

6 bowls of *Kellogg*'s Special K with milk

3 bowls of *Alpen* No Added Sugar with milk

2 bowls of *Kellogg's* Rice Crispies with cow's milk and sugar

2 bowls of *Kellogg*'s Cornflakes and milk (Figure 59)

1 bowl of muesli and milk

1 bowl of *Safeways* Checkers and milk

0.505g bag of *Alternative Lifestyle Shops* honey and almond crunch –
equivalent to 3 bowls – and milk

1 bowl of *Safeways* cereal rings and milk

Just how much milk was poured in here we cannot see – but cereal always
comes with milk. Allowing me a modest 95ml of milk per bowl of cereal, and
given my above tally of bowls, I calculate that I drank an incidental milk total of
8.93 litres. As such this is equivalent to "friendly fire" in the cereal wars.

FIGURE 59 – The Kellogg's logo as it is rendered in the Arabic

AT THE KETTLE

Today people delight in variety – but consider – only two generations ago there would have been at most two choices at the kettle, being tea and coffee. One generation before that and the choice may have been restricted to merely *tea*.

Tea is no longer a substance found in one form and over the period of a year I appear to have drunk at least 23 different varieties. Further, I tried the juice of lemons in hot water, which is delightful, as is the juice of ginger in hot water. Ginger is hard to juice, but once a small amount is obtained, a few drops in a mug of boiling water are delicious and for sure, great for the digestion.

The Aviemore Problem

At sea level, water boils at 212 degrees Fahrenheit (100 Celsius). For each increase of 500 feet of altitude the Fahrenheit temperature at which water boils goes down by 1 degree. That means that if I live in Aviemore, my water will boil at 203 degrees Fahrenheit (95 Celsius). The water for my tea would be boiling as the tea manufacturers recommend – but it is certainly not the same boiling that occurs at sea level.

Does this mean I will never experience a proper cup of tea if I live in Aviemore?

The following "Hot Water Drinks" are included in my list:

249 cups of tea with milk [429]

161 instant coffees with milk

36 black instant coffees

---

[429] Tetley is the default brand of tea in this home. "Tetley contains LESS caffeine than either a cup of instant or ground roasted coffee – and that's a fact!" Once, I caused a normally calm friend to scream when I put the milk in a cup of tea before I poured the water. Some will sympathise with him. My brother-in-law adds, "Tea then milk – tastes like silk – milk then tea – tastes like wee."

FIGURE 60 – Jasmine Tea, from far away

34 cups of jasmine tea produced by the *Fujian Tea Import and Export Co. Ltd* [430] (Figure 60)

26 Lady Grey teas

20 *Clipper* organic nettle teas [431]

19 *Eleven O'Clock* brand organic Rooibosch Tea [432]

19 cups of juiced ginger in hot water

18 mugs of filter coffee

---

[430] "Sprouting" / "Green Tea & Jasmine Flowers"

[431] "A herbal infusion of young nettle leaves with a clean, fresh flavour." / "Now commonly known as a painful stinging weed, the young leaves of a nettle plant produce a surprisingly refreshing infusion."

[432] "Eco-Cert" / "A soothing naturally caffeine-free pure Redbush tea." Eleven O'Clock tea is described as "The Timeless Taste" – is that supposed to be a joke?

17 Darjeeling teas [433]

17 cups of *Jackson's of Piccadilly* ™ pure green tea [434]

17 cups of peppermint tea

17 cups of *Bioforce* golden grass tea – "*Product of Switzerland*" [435]

15 Earl Grey teas

15 cups of black unmilked tea

14 *Clipper* organic fennel teas

11 cups of raspberry and echinacea tea

9 cups of instant coffee with soya milk

8 filter coffees with milk

---

[433] Superstition No. 1: If bubbles collect on the surface of your tea, money is coming your way (i.e. If bubbles there be, then cash thou shall see.) Superstition No.2: Small pieces of tea that float on the top of the cup mean a visit from strangers (ie. If tea floats in your cup, then your solitude's up.)

SHAPES IN TEA LEAVES: *Triangles* mean good news; *Squares* suggest the need for caution; and *Circles* bode well for great success. (i.e. 3 sided forms and the news will be warm; If the tea leaves are squared, you'd best be prepared; Circles in your brew, mean YIPPEE for you!)

In reading tea-leaves however, most of the clumps will form random shapes, such as a spider, a map of Japan, or the face of Harrison Ford. With a little creative staring, many other shapes may be determined.

[434] "This delicate China Tea has a light, refreshing 'just picked' taste and is naturally rich in anti-oxidants."

[435] This tea contains the following weirdo selection of healthy-herbs: golden rod, birch leaves, knotgrass, horsetail and wild pansy. "Golden grass tea can be found in almost every health food shop in Europe." / "A cup of this tea is often said to be the antidote to the stresses of modern society." Marketing again! Said by whom?

FIGURE 61 – A free sample of decaffeinated instant coffee

10 *Nescafé* [436] brand decaffeinated instant coffees and milk

8 cups of lemon juice in water

6 decaffeinated filter coffees with *Sambuca* [437]

5 *Nescafé* instant decaffeinated coffees

4 free sample packets of decaffeinated *Nescafé* (Figure 61)

4 espresso coffees

4 *Co-op* "99" teabags in a 12.5g free trial pack [438]

4 cups of decaffeinated filter coffee

---

[436] When all soluble materials have been vigorously extracted from an organic product, it has been made into "instant" form. The technology to do this is about 100 years old, but there are still many possibilites to be explored in the future. Is there anything grown from the earth that has not been freeze or spray dried that could be useful in that form? Other beans perhaps? Freeze-dried ice cream was a popular early astronaut food. Why can't we planet-dwellers get that too?

[437] *Sambuca* in filter coffee is a beverage to be studied. There is a wide distribution of motivating factors in my being driven to drink it again and again. These include the richness of the experience and the fact that the combination of flavours created an actual holiday atmosphere in my mouth. The Italians call this *caffè corretto* (corrected coffee).

[438] The Indian monk Bodhidharma fell asleep by meditating. To ensure this would never happen again he cut off his eyelids. A tea bush sprang from the spot where the eyelids landed, producing a drink that would forever banish fatigue. This is a popular myth waiting to become a marketing myth. I can see the advert now....

3 cups of *Ayurvedic* "Rejuvenate" tea [439]

3 manzanilla teas [440]

2 tea and soya milk

2 mint teas made with with mint leaves

1 lemon and elderflower tea

1 Earl Grey tea and milk

1 cup of hot chocolate

1 camomile and lime flower tea

1 cup of black tea with sugar [441]

1 lemon and ginger tea

1 Nepalese tea

---

[439] This tea is a liquid rendering of the ayurvedic practise of restoring balance in the mind/body system, as popularised by Deepak Chopra – "an uplifting infusion of lemon, cardamom, fenugreek and gotu kola believed to rejuvenate in Ayurveda." Does this tea have any effect on those who don't believe in "ayus" or in fact in the any of the revelations of the Indian creator god Lord Brahma?

[440] Manzanilla is known in English as camomile. I planted some of this herb in my Goddess Garden even though my tribemate said that her plant was destroyed by neighbourhood cats rolling in it. She was however wrong, as her German Camomile was an annual and she didn't know that the perennial variety is Roman Camomile and that the cats were innocent! I gave her a cutting from my Roman Camomile, and it thrived along the north fence of her patch – yay!

[441] If there is a national dish that unites the United Kingdom under a common British identity, it is the Cup of Tea that sees them through everything from blitzkrieg to blood-donation. Perhaps the cup of tea testifies to nothing more than the fact that the British diet has depended for two centuries or increasing amounts of imports from India.

4 cups of instant coffee with soymilk [442]

1 fennel tea of *Dr Stuart* 2.0g – *"only natural products"*

1 black filter coffee with "D'oh nut" flavour *Frijj* milk drink

1 mint tea [443]

1 cup of *Horlicks* made of milk

1 200ml can of *Kenco* ® Cappio – *"froth-top system for the perfect iced cappucino"* – *"Coffee Flavour Drink made with Milk, Cream and Instant Coffee"* – *"chill, pour, settle and indulge!"*

1 250g canister of *Cadbury* drinking chocolate – 5 cups made with hot water, and 4 with soymilk

1 cup of this tea – 1 *Tetley* and 1 *Dr Stuart's* botanical camomile tea bag in a half mug of boiled water, the other half of the mug filled with milk

1 11g sachet of Limited Edition *Options* Go Bananas flavour instant hot chocolate drink – *"only 40 calories per drink"*

200g of *Ovaltine* with hot water and milk = 17 drinks

Just how much milk was poured in here is difficult to calculate. Allowing me a modest 50ml of milk per drink, however, and given my above tally of drinks with milk, I reckon that I drank an incidental milk total of 21.6 litres. As such, this is equivalent to "friendly fire" in the kettle wars.

---

[442] Instant coffee and soymilk do not combine well, creating a mild brown lumpy drink, rather than the usual "white" coffee of cow's milk.

[443] Provided by Menta Poleo of Compánia de las Indias.

CHRISTMAS CAKE

Christianity, initially a Mediterranean religion, made the grape a central aspect of its mysteries. This is one of the church's many inheritances from Judaism, which like other Near Eastern religions made much of the three sacramental foods: oil, bread and wine. Because the Christian church was marketed with symbols associated with viticulture, pastors in colder climes began to wonder how they may compete. Even though the Roman legionaries of Julius Agricola had planted vines to grow a Reisling near Nottingham, this was not sufficient to give the Northern Christian psyche the boost that it now feels from Christmas Cake. [444]

Christmas Cake is still made in these parts and by more people than I had imagined. Increasingly I find the idea impossible that there is a connection between food and religion, although tradition is hard to suppress. The underlying rituals of our diets concern us eating the same thing at the same time each year – so our fathers and our mothers – and our children's children – we hope!

This year I ate the following slices of Christmas cake:

6 slices of Jean White's Christmas cake – the last of these slices had the word "*Merry*" written on it in red food dye

4 pieces of Christmas cake made by Susan White

1 piece of Christmas cake made by Tadg Farrington

---

[444] There was a time when folks would eat porridge on Christmas Eve in order to line the stomach after a day's fasting. Gradually, guidwifes and other Dark Age doxies began to put spices, dried fruits and honey in the porridge to make it a special dish for Christmas. Later this was turned into a Christmas Pudding, because it became so firm with fruit that it could be tied in a cloth and boiled for several hours.

INGREDIENTS

The following items were utilised in the cooking process, appearing in my horizontally stacked food presentations as side dishes, snacks or lazy suppers.

1kg of wholewheat spaghetti

200g of *Rachel's* organic crème fraiche

1 250g container of *LAT.3RI* brand mascarpone fresco colle

250g *Co-op* garlic and herb coleslaw

500g *Organics Epicure* brand penne pasta – *"Made with 100% organically grown Durum Wheat Semolina"*

250g of *McLelland* Seriously Strong Cheddar [445]

1 packet of *Invernizzi* Mozary Mozzarella – *"Formaggio fresco Italianodi latte pastorizzato"*

454g *Birds Eye* garden peas – *"Only the smallest and sweetest"* – *"Vitamins in peas guaranteed"* – *"Only the freshest peas picked to frozen in two and half hours"*

200g of cheddar cheese, medium strength

A half-kilo of potatoes

A half lettuce

---

[445] McLelland advertise with the strap line: "The UK's best Cheddar". Curious that no other cheddar producer can question McLelland for making this claim, while if another cheesemaker were to make the same and identically-worded claim, then McLelland would be at liberty to question them.

McVitie's

The biscuit is the perfect food for keeping and carrying. It can be stored over winter to keep against famine and is useful when people come for tea. The Romans produced the *buccellatum*, a twice-baked biscuit or bread – ideal for their soldiers on the road – and this is in fact what the word *biscuit* means – twice baked. The Greek *paximadi* and the German *Zwieback* both mean the same.

In 1650, an officer in Cromwell's army wrote: "*Nothing is more certain than this, that in the late wars, both Scotland and Ireland were conquered by timely provisions of Cheshire cheese and biscuit.*" Cromwell believed in the powers of the *buccellatum* for his soldiers and ordered the old royal palace at Greenwich transformed into a biscuit factory. The biscuit did its worst for Scotland and many of our castles lay in crumbs after Cromwell's motivated men had finished their afternoon tea.

McVitie's are my main biscuit supplier. The McVitie's milk chocolate digestive is a figurehead for the entire chocolate biscuit world, outclassing all contenders. The balance between biscuit and chocolate in this biscuit is appropriate and the taste is faultless. No parlour need ever be ashamed with these in stock.

My *McVitie's* total was:

3 x 500g packets of *McVitie's* digestives [446]

2 x 300g packets of *McVitie's* milk chocolate digestives – "*wheatmeal biscuits covered in milk chocolate*"

1 300g packet of *McVitie's* digestives [447]

1 300g packet of of *McVities's* plain chocolate digestives

---

[446] Does the digestive biscuit help us to digest? Or is the name simply indicative of the fact that the biscuit like other foods, is ultimately *subject* to digestion? Melville's Ishmael in *Moby Dick* frets about those who ask such questions and call themselves philosophers. "So soon as I hear that such or such a man gives himself out for a philosopher," he writes, "I conclude that, like the dyspeptic old woman, he must have broken his digester."

[447] Other pack quotes include: "The sign of a better biscuit" / "The Original Digestive" and "✓source of fibre".

1 200g packet of *McVitie's* digestives

1 330g packet of *McVitie's* Ginger Nuts

3 x 300g packets of *McVitie's* Hob Nobs – *"Full of the goodness of oats"*

1 200g packet of *McVitie's* Krackawheat biscuits

1 200g packet of *McVitie's* white chocolate and raspberry cookies (= 9 biscuits) [448]

1 300g packet of *McVitie's* Caramels

17 other *McVitie's* milk chocolate Caramels, in addition to those

10 chocolate Hobnobs

8 *McVitie's* "Toasting" waffles

7 *McVitie's* digestives

6 *McVitie's* Taxi biscuits – *"Miles more caramel"*

5 *McVitie's* *"My Jaffa Cakes"* bars [449]

2 *McVitie's* chocolate digestives

1 *McVitie's* digestive biscuit [450]

---

[448] Many people find Cookie Monster's (See Figure 62) eating style offensive. He's kinda messy and what irks them most is that it doesn't appear that he eats any of his biscuits, just spreads a lot of crumbs about the place.

[449] These were "Cake bars covered in plain chocolate, with the smashing orangey bit."

[450] This biscuit was stolen from the private stash of the head of the Edinburgh location of St. James's Place Partnership with the assistance of the office manager, who did not like to see me hunger.

FIGURE 62: Cookie Monster from Sesame Street. Once he ate biscuits with abandon every day – now the American Century has got to him and he's been pilloried for being a bad example.

1 slice of *McVitie's* Jamaica Ginger Cake

4 *McVitie's* Boasters

1 *McVitie's* chocolate brownie topped with *M&M* "Minis" [451]

1 150g *Müller* "Corner" with the taste of *McVitie's* Jaffa Cakes

Although biscuits are more likely than other foods to contain genetically modified materials, *McVitie's* have taken a lead in this field and have ensured their entire crop of biscuits is GM free. Following a campaign by *Greenpeace, McVitie's* were also among the first to cease use of fish oils from industrially caught fish in their biscuits.

---

[451] "A delicious chocolate brownie covered in milk chocolate" – confectionary and biscuits combine and mutate yet again.

Risotto à la Malaise

Arborio [452] risotto rice cooked in white wine and the juice of 2 lemons, with
150g of rocket and grated Parmesan cheese. This also included 1 clove of garlic /
1 small onion / 1 tablespoon of olive oil / and 125g butter.
Made three servings, all of which I ate.

Sortie Vegetables

A grab-bag of vegetables can create a thrilling autumnal meal! I had 3 carrots /
2 parsnips / half a fennel stalk / 32 chives / half a red onion

These were chopped and mixed with butter and roasted for 30 mins.

Sortie Vegetables was served with mashed potato, which was mixed with yoghurt,
4 prunes and a handful of sprouted mung beans.

Souped Perthshire Garden Vegetables

7 carrots / 2 leeks / 8 red potatoes / 1 red onion
All these vegetables were from the garden of Alan and Jan Stewart.
Add from the supermarket: 1 bulb of garlic / two sticks of celery and
1 and a quarter litres of vegetable stock.

This soup was blended and I ate 3 bowls. It is good sometimes to taste a
certain area of your country, as in this instance, Perthshire. Rarely are we given
something so pleasant to think about while we eat.

---

[452] In Italy it is said that there is no creature on land, in the sea or in the air that has
not eventually ended up in a risotto. Like polenta, rice shapes a gastronomic dividing line
between northern and southern Italy – with rice placed squarely on the northern side of
the Po, where the water supply in the Padana Valley is ideal for its cultivation.

THE BIG BUY OUT

I was sitting at home, eating my fare and minding my own business. The world continued around me. I was enjoying a *Safeway* chocolate chip muffin and was thinking about nothing more than how I would like to visit once more, the old country of my birth. By the end of that afternoon however, a big-business buy out meant that although what I ate at lunchtime was a *Safeway* chocolate chip muffin, what I digested, was a *Morrison* chocolate chip muffin.

Muffling my surprise, I was amazed to read that 56 stores were to be refurbished at the rate of three a week, erasing the memory of *Safeway* and condemning its history to the ancient confusion of past producers that are never heard of again.

In brief tribute however, I can tell you that over the course of one year, I ate the following products from that fast-changing company:

4 *Safeway* "Smarties" biscuits

1 *Safeway* iced lemon donut with "sprinkles"

1 *Safeway* lemon donut with sprinkles

1 *Safeway* chocolate chip muffin

4 litres of *Safeway* Glencairn still spring water

1 *Safeway* cinnamon Danish pastry

1 *Safeway* white chocolate & lemon muffin

1 *Safeway* chocolate chip muffin

1 *Safeway* iced gingerbread man

1 250ml carton of *Morrison* freshly squeezed pasteurised orange juice

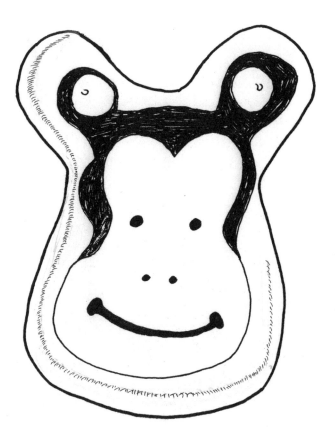

FIGURE 63 – Monkey-faced biscuit

1 *Safeway* orange and chocolate "Monkey" biscuit (Figure 63)

1 55g packet of *Morrison* "*Quality and value*" crispy seaweed [453]

1 *Morrison* pink donut with sprinkles

---

[453] Sea-Wrack (or Rock-Week) is the real Scots article. It is said that as recently as the 1950s, the citizens of Scotland ate seaweed in times of scarcity. Further, the Scots for many years used the young stems of tangle (or sea-lettuce) as salad. This supermarket seaweed was nothing so nutritious or practical, but was 55g of "deep fried shredded cabbage seasoned with a blend of aromatic spices." And sea-free.

NUT FEAST

Nobody knows anything about nuts, including what purpose they serve in nature, other than to accompany our beer and wine. One of the most unexpected discoveries I have made of recent years is that like beer and wine, nuts may be drunk.

And I don't mean inebriated. I mean drunk. Once soaked in water, the enzymes of nuts begin to release from the starch and the softened nuts can be blended into rich milks, which are wonderful for cooking, as well as being a positive boon to health.

It all sounds too good to be true. I totalled the following amount of nuts over the course of one year:

3 x 50g bags of *KP* dry roasted peanuts

3 x 50g bags of *KP* spicy chilli flavour peanuts

3 x 50g bags of *KP* [454] salted roasted peanuts (Figure 64)

3 x 200g bags of *Tesco* roasted salted extra large peanuts

2 x 150g bags of *Sainsbury's* salted cashew nuts

1 35g bag of *KP* salted roasted peanuts

1 200g bag of *Tesco* roasted salted peanuts

1 250g bag of *Spar* roasted and salted large peanuts

1 375g bag of *Hider* salted jumbo peanuts

---

[454] "Nuts about nuts" was the KP slogan at the time of my eating. What amuses me most about this stuff, I realise, is that slogans and strap lines are devised by people who meet in order to decide what they think is most likely to impress me about their products. They second guess us all with simple ideas that annoyingly stick with us.

FIGURE 64 — The KP logo was cleverly designed to look like a half nut

1 100g bag of *Co-op* roasted and salted cashews

1 110g bag of *Wholesnax* cashew nuts

1 150g bag of *Wholesnax* honey roasted peanuts

1 50g bag of *Planters* salted roasted nuts

1 100g bag of *Dormen's* caramelised peanuts

1 50g bag of mixed nuts from *Nuts Shop*

26 pistachio nuts

10 almonds

6 dry roasted peanuts

7 walnuts

15 Brazil nuts [455]

1 cashew nut

1 handful of dry roasted peanuts

12 salted almonds

6 hazelnuts

50g blended almonds

50g blended hemp seeds

50g blended hazelnuts

4 chocolate coated Brazil nuts from *Bramik Foods* of Broxburn

2 handfuls of *KP* Mild Curry peanuts. This is precisely the sort of thing one grabs from another person while out drinking.

Some salted peanuts during a late night nut attack in Glasgow

---

[455] "I have always been very keen on nuts, and as a boy I was a big fan of the Brazil. Tough, strong and incredibly resilient, the Brazil is surely the Chieftain tank of all the nuts. It's a young man's nut, of course. To break it, to penetrate its ironclad body, you need to be equal to it in every way. It's a contest of strength, willpower and sheer nerve." From *Bravenet Blog*

CASE STUDY: 1 cup of nuts brought to my door at Hawthornden Castle, Lasswade. This cup of nuts &c. represented an afternoon treat at the castle.

13 Brazil nuts
9 sultanas
7 peanuts
3 hazelnuts
2 pieces of crystallised ginger
2 raisins
1 walnut
1 almond

CASE STUDY: 200g of mixed nuts and raisins of *Bramik Foods*, Broxburn *"The best – naturally!"* This 200g pack contained:

265 raisins
182 peanuts
8 hazelnuts
6 almonds
5 cashews
5 brazils
2 walnuts

My advice is to always wash your hands before counting mixed nuts and raisins. Count your nuts on plates or in piles on your bed.

YUMMY

Now *The Supper Book* has closed and all within has been consumed. I shall itemise more at another time.

Not one drink nor one bite undescribed
Every thing I ate and each that I imbibed
Or ate, that is swallowed
Whole, mashed or boiled,
With all the drink that followed
All I can say is this –
I'll try that list.

PB

The Hoffmanns' pumpkin has been eaten too.
See page 159